Spelling Strategies and Patterns:

What Kids Need to Know

D1558104

by Sandra Wilde

*first*hand
An imprint of Heinemann
A division of Reed Elsevier Inc.
361 Hanover Street
Portsmouth, NH 03801-3912
www.firsthand.heinemann.com

Offices and agents throughout the world

ISBN 13: 978-0-325-00841-7
ISBN 10: 0-325-00841-8

Library of Congress Cataloging-in-Publication Data

Wilde, Sandra.
    Spelling strategies and patterns : what kids need to know / by Sandra Wilde.
        p. cm.
    Includes bibliographical references and indexes.
    ISBN 978-0-325-00841-7
    1.   English language--Orthography and spelling--Study and teaching (Elementary)
I. Title.

    LB1574.W54 2008
    372.63'2--dc22

                                                            2007036006

Printed in the United States of America on acid-free paper

12 11 10 09 08   BB   1 2 3 4 5 6

DEDICATION

To the children and teachers of P.S. 180, the Hugo Newman Preparatory School, and their inspiring and hard-working principal, Dr. Peter "Dr. Mac" McFarlane.

ACKNOWLEDGEMENTS

My first thank you on the project goes to Lucy Calkins and all the other wonderful people at Columbia Teachers College Reading and Writing Project, who welcomed me as part of their community when I was in New York on sabbatical in 2004. Lucy's intelligence, energy, and leadership have brought tremendous accomplishment and change to literacy in New York City schools and around the country, and she and those who work with her gave me the opportunity to be a part of their "think tank." They also made it possible for me to visit schools and explore the teaching of spelling in classrooms where rich reading and writing were taking place. Among all the staff developers I had the chance to work with, I'd like to make special mention of Tom Marshall and Jane Bean-Folkes, who have continued to be spelling buddies.

In the schools, I owe a large debt of gratitude to Dr. Peter "Dr. Mac" McFarlane, principal of P.S. 180 (Hugo Newman Preparatory School) in Harlem, literacy coach Carolyn Montalto, and teachers Barret Baer, Rachel Nall, Amanda Pagan, Andrea Rankin, Marie Regaudie, Jhimy Rodriguez, Lesley Simmonds, Akosua Walker, and Wanda White. They invited me to carry out weekly spelling lessons with students in grades three through five, which enabled me to try out and refine my ideas about teaching spelling to kids in the upper elementary grades. The quality of teaching at P.S. 180 shone through in the children's writing and their engagement in the ideas we were exploring. These students exemplified my firm conviction that spelling can be as exciting to children as any other topic. It is to Dr. Mac and the teachers and children of P.S. 180 that *Spelling Strategies and Patterns* is dedicated. In New York, I am also grateful to Sharron Hayes, and two second grade teachers as well as two second grade teachers in Washington Heights (whose names I've forgotten but will add in a future printing), all of whom gave me further opportunities to work with children.

In Portland, Oregon, I'm so grateful to principal Molly Chun and three teachers who invited me to videotape lessons and photograph children in their classrooms at Faubion School. Those children's shining faces grace the cover and pages of this book, and they can be seen in all their intelligence and animation in the DVD. Thanks, too, to Gayle Paige and Kathy Provencher at Smyth Road School in Manchester, New Hampshire for allowing us to photograph their students.

At Heinemann, I believe that all the people who worked with me on this project put in at least as much time as I did on it, if not more. As editors, Tina Miller and Amy Gilbert helped form and refine my original manuscript into the form that you see today, and revealed themselves to be part of a rare breed, spelling aficionados. Tina's work on the list of the 500 most frequent words was especially diligent. David Stirling directed the videotaping at Faubion School; both the kids and I lost our nervousness because it went so smoothly. Stephanie Levy has overseen production with competence and patience. Leigh Peake has been a terrific supporter of this project, and special thanks go to Lois Bridges who helped me initiate it.

At Portland State University, I'd like to thank my students - prospective and current literacy teachers, who continue to inspire me and challenge my thinking. All of my colleagues continue to provide me with an important professional community; I'd like to especially thank Swapna Mukhopadhyay and Yer Thao for the stimulating conversations I have with them, and Dean Randy Hitz for providing us with strong, intelligent leadership. I miss former colleagues Sara Davis and Xiaqing Sun-Irminger.

In my larger professional community, I'd especially like to thank Yetta and Ken Goodman for their ongoing support and inspiration for the last 26 years. It was because of the opportunity I had to work with Yetta, while I was a graduate student, on a research project about the writing of Tohono O'odham children, that I first developed my interest in spelling.

Special thanks to secret brownies Valerie and Kara Canfield, and to Sandra Taylor.

I miss my mom, Anita Axelson (1921-2006), and Bill Kruger (1945-2006). Their spirits have been with me.

Table of Contents

 Patterns

✳ INTRODUCTION

When I told a class of second graders in New York City that I had seen a sign in Penn Station for "bananna" smoothies, they were surprised that a word that so many of them knew how to spell had been "messed up" by an adult. They wondered if the sign writer had forgotten to edit, and debated whether they'd buy a smoothie there; if someone doesn't know how to spell *banana*, would they know to include the right ingredients?

Teachers aren't always sure what they should be doing about spelling, and I'd like to suggest, and use this curriculum to show you, that we can help kids learn about our spelling system and how it works by engaging them in conversations and inquiry that draw on their natural interest in written language and build on what they already know. In other words, we're helping them to construct their own knowledge of how this important language system works.

An effective spelling curriculum should include a combination of reading, writing, and teaching. Spelling curriculum doesn't need to be—shouldn't be—long lists of words to memorize, tedious rules that don't work very well anyway, or twenty minutes a day of worksheets. There *is* room for helping kids learn the words they miss a lot in their writing, and for thinking about spelling patterns like why *cake* and *kite* start with different letters, but there's also room for exploring where our words come from and whether the words we see misspelled out in the world are that way by mistake (like "bananna") or on purpose (like *Krispy Kreme*). And one or two lessons or explorations a week is plenty of time to spend on spelling; it is, after all, only a small part of writing.

These spelling explorations work best in a classroom where students are reading and writing regularly, if not voraciously. Most of the words that we know how to spell are acquired through reading, not intentional memorization. (See Krashen, 2004, for a summary of the research supporting this.)

And volume of reading makes a difference. When you see a word in print once, you'll probably be able to spell it better than before you'd seen it (particularly if it's a long or tricky word), and the more times you see it, the more likely you are to be able to spell it correctly. This "reading effect" is why first graders fairly quickly go from spelling the word *of* phonetically (probably UV) to spelling it correctly, which doesn't happen so quickly with less common words. It's why I saw a third grader write LAUHG for *laugh*, when a few years earlier she probably would have produced LAF; you know she'd seen it in print even if she didn't get the order of the letters completely right. Every minute students spend reading books that contain words they don't know how to spell is a minute spent becoming a better speller, and kids should be reading at least half an hour a day.

You also need to write in order to learn how to spell. Writing is how you try out and put into practice your developing knowledge about how words are spelled, whether it's knowing the spelling of particular words or inventing the spellings of those you don't. Teachers and the general public don't always realize how noncontroversial invented spelling is among researchers in the field. Even the report of the National Reading Panel and the book *Preventing Reading Difficulties in Young Children*, both quite traditional on other matters, recommend the use of invented spelling by young children (National Reading Panel, 2000; Snow, Burns, and Griffin, 1998). Young children's spellings primarily represent sounds, then move beyond the merely phonetic by incorporating information about spelling patterns like long vowels and double letters. (More about this later.)

But learning to spell isn't just about being thrown into a room with books, pencils, and paper. Teaching plays a big part, teaching that focuses on getting kids thinking about spelling, helping them to care about it, and developing strategies for getting better at it. Teaching is what's often been missing from the typical spelling curriculum; instead, kids may be put through a program where they're asked to carry out worksheet (or similar) exercises with words, and then memorize them for a test. They're rarely even taught *how* to memorize them.

I'm not sure I've ever met a teacher happy with how her students are spelling, regardless of what program (or absence of program) she uses. I really hope that *Spelling Strategies and Patterns* will help you become, if not fully happy with how every child in your class is spelling, at least happy that you're helping all kids become better spellers and, ideally, having some fun teaching them about it.

SO HOW DO KIDS LEARN HOW TO SPELL?

I just asked this question and now I'm going to reframe it: how do children develop as spellers? Thinking about it this way acknowledges that it's a gradual process that goes on for a number of years. We see parallels with learning to talk, but it's different because, most linguists believe, human brains are hard-wired to learn speech in a way that they aren't for written language (Pinker, 1994). Everybody learns to talk well enough to be accepted by their speech community (with rare exceptions); not so for spelling.

But given the right experiences and support, children can learn how to spell well enough to produce a correctly spelled final draft of a piece of writing by the end of elementary school if not sooner (which I think is an appropriate goal). And the bulk of it happens unconsciously, in a way that feels acquired (picked up on your own) rather than taught (told by someone else). I'll describe the highlights here, with a little more attention spent on typical developmental patterns in grades 3-5, the focus of this curriculum. Understanding how this development happens will set the stage for thinking about the role of the spelling curriculum in supporting the process.

From Scribbling to Spelling

If we define spelling as using letters to attempt to write words (to the best of one's current ability), young children begin to write before they begin to spell. Pencil and crayon get applied to paper (hopefully not to walls!) and scrawls turn into scribbles, in the sense of marks that are starting to take on first the shape (linear) and then the characteristics (letter-like forms) of written language. (See Harste, Woodward, and Burke, 1984, for some great examples of what this looks like.)

How does scribbling turn into spelling? There are two components of the transition to spelling: learning letters and using letters to represent sounds. Typically children learn the letters of the alphabet either before they start school, in kindergarten, or a little of both. They learn both the names of the letters and what they look like, and begin to learn the sounds they represent. With the slightest encouragement, they begin writing with invented spelling by figuring out what letter might represent each sound in a word. Young kids may start by writing just the initial consonant of a word, then include more of the consonants, then the vowels. What matters is not how correct the words are—how can they be correct, since the child hasn't seen many words in print yet?—but the active thinking about how written words are constructed. I've written about this at length in my book *You Kan Red This!* (Wilde, 1992), but a single example will make the point clear. A five-year-old who spelled *caterpillar* as CADRPALR included all the sounds, given that a /t/ between vowels sounds like a /d/, and that vowels before /r/ tend to not be heard as separate sounds. Since phonics is the relationship between sounds and letters, this child has proven himself adept at phonics, and has the foundation for further development, which of course goes well beyond phonetic spelling.

From Phonetic Spelling to Standard Spelling

There are obviously a lot of differences between phonetic spelling and standard spelling, particularly as words get longer. A young speller can get *dog* right pretty easily, since the letters fit the sounds, but the writer of *caterpillar* has to know that it starts with a *c* rather than a *k*, that there are two different vowel letters before the *r*'s even though you can't really hear them, and that it has a double *l*. And this is just one word!

Fortunately, it's easier for our brains to learn how to spell pretty well than it would be to program a computer to do so. (Some researchers tried to program a computer to turn sounds into spellings using rules and didn't do very well; with 203 rules, the computer spelled only 49.9% of 17,009 words correctly; Hanna, Hanna, Hodges, and Rudorf, 1966.) Humans have both the ability to remember the spellings of a lot of individual words and to form intuitions about spelling patterns based on all the words they've seen. Here's what goes into moving toward more correct rather than merely phonetic spelling.

First, many sounds can be spelled in more than one way. This is true for both consonants (coat, koala) and vowels (feat, feet). We get better at using the right letter or letters in two ways: we see them in particular words and remember them, and we develop an awareness of how spelling regularities work. A young child might think that GACIT works just fine as a spelling for *jacket*, but an older child, like an adult, knows that it just doesn't look right unless you use a *j* for the first consonant sound and have a *k* in there somewhere for the second one. There are rules underlying the spellings of both of these sounds, and those rules are included in this curriculum, but the rules are only a formalization of what we've picked up intuitively about the spelling system. If you aren't sure about this, see if you can state the rules for spelling the /j/ and /k/ sounds. You probably can't, but you still knew that GACIT just couldn't be right. Once a child has picked up a sense of these rules, you won't see that spelling from her, even though she may spell the word JAKIT before she gets it right.

Another aspect of spelling that writers need to learn is that there are patterns that go beyond the spelling of individual sounds. When do we double letters (and is there a reason why)? What changes do we have to make in a root word when we're adding a suffix to it? How do I know if a word has a silent letter? Again, much of this knowledge is picked up intuitively, but there's enough pattern and regularity for teaching to also have a role.

Then, to be a good speller, you just have to learn a lot of words! Just taking some longer words from a single section of a primary-grade dictionary, we see *railroad*, *reindeer*, *restaurant*, and *rhinoceros* and realize that their spellings are far from predictable. Since we're familiar with the words, their spellings may seem set in stone, but to a child hearing them without having seen them in print—and perhaps not realizing that *railroad* is a compound and that rhinos aren't related to dinosaurs—RALERODE and RINOSAURUS might seem like perfectly reasonable spellings. There's also the problem of confusing words that sound the same or similar, a difficulty even for adults.

What all of this comes down to is that to be a good speller you have to both know a lot and be very picky. Fortunately, it doesn't all have to be taught formally. There's room for the occasional memorization of word spellings, but we didn't learn most of the words we know how to spell this way; we just picked them up.

A useful framework for thinking about the growth from phonetic spelling to standard spelling is that it's developmental, in the sense that it's a gradual process that occurs largely unconsciously through seeing words as we read. As we read, we pick up and internalize both the words themselves and the spelling patterns they incorporate. Spellings get better (realizing that double letters exist) before they become correct (putting double letters in the right words). But there's still, obviously, a role for teaching, which is what this curriculum is all about. That role is twofold: encouraging kids to explore the patterns that they're already starting to internalize, and supporting them as they develop the strategies that help them fine-tune their spelling as they write.

Spelling's Easier for Some Kids Than Others

Most kids who read a reasonable amount are going to end up being pretty good spellers, particularly if their natural development is supplemented by the kind of teaching I've suggested in this curriculum. But two groups of students need to be mentioned here because their progress is likely to be slower and more frustrating.

Some kids just aren't good at spelling, and this group covers a wide range. In some cases, spelling is pretty well the only issue; these are the students who just have a hard time getting words spelled right, even though their literacy may be perfectly okay in other ways. This is the kid—or adult—who may love to read and be a perfectly competent writer yet is still (often self-described) a "terrible speller." Countless teachers have told me that their husbands are like this (though it's not a gender thing)! The best way to think about these spellers is that they have less natural ability to remember the spellings of words and are less likely to be able to tell from looking at a word if it's spelled correctly. These students will benefit from instruction, and especially from instruction in spelling strategies. It's not their fault, but they can still work at their spelling and, with conscientiousness, spell well enough when they need to.

At the other end of the weak speller continuum are those students whose literacy in general is less advanced than that of their classmates. They may be in Title I or special education, or they may just be the weaker students in the regular classroom. Spelling is just one of our concerns about them. These students, too, will benefit from instruction, but sometimes lessons that are clicking for the rest of the class may go over their heads, requiring one-on-one follow-up.

I've included suggestions for working with less successful spellers, as well as a few lessons particularly for them, throughout this curriculum. I also think it's important to keep two principles in mind in working with them. First, reading is the single most important contributor to their becoming better spellers. These are often students who aren't reading much, and if we're wanting to improve their spelling, getting them to read more should be the highest priority. Second, we shouldn't over-focus on their spelling. It's natural when a student's spelling is so much weaker than that of others the same age to think she should perhaps be memorizing word lists, particularly because spelling is such a visible deficit, but this would be misguided. There's certainly room for memorizing a small number of common words (see Strategy 7 on one-second words), but these students' spelling development needs to come primarily like those of other children does, through reading.

The other group of students we need to mention here is English language learners. It's impossible to generalize much about this group because there are so many variables. Are they native-born or immigrant? How old were they when they began to speak English, and how long ago was that? How similar is their language to English? Does it use the same alphabet as English? Does the teacher speak their language? Are they literate in their home language?

However, there are two generalizations that we *can* make. English language learners' development in spelling is likely to be behind that of the native English speakers in their classroom, and their spellings may reflect influences from their first language. Other than that, their development will be similar, and this group will include naturally stronger and weaker spellers just like everyone else. When a teacher knows the child's first language, she can better understand the specific differences she's likely to see in his spelling. I've included examples from Spanish in many of the pattern lessons, since it's the most common second language in the United States. But helping English language learners improve their spelling goes hand in hand with their continuing knowledge of English, and just as with everyone else, it comes primarily from reading. I remember when I learned French in college, spelling was tricky, and it was useful to learn a bit about the rules and patterns of French spelling, but I learned to spell words mainly through seeing them in print.

ABOUT THIS PROGRAM

At this point, I'd like to tell you about what I've developed here—how this curriculum is arranged and how to use it.

Strategies and Patterns

Spelling Strategies and Patterns is made up of 65 lessons, half of them strategies, half patterns. Let's define how I'm using those two terms. A spelling **strategy** is a lesson that, in most cases, helps students spell words better as they go about the process of writing. Many of the strategies are extended answers to the question, "What should I do when I'm writing and don't know how to spell a word?" This big question includes subquestions, each of them worth multiple lessons, such as "How do I look up a word in the dictionary if I don't know how to spell it?" and "How do I edit my writing for spelling?"

Exploring spelling **patterns** means looking especially at information that will help us know what to do when it's not obvious what letters are in a word. If you haven't seen *kangaroo* in print, how do you know whether to start it with a *c* or *k*? Why is *keep* spelled with two *e*'s rather than *ea*, and how do I know how to spell that long *e* sound in any word that has it? Spelling patterns also include some topics that are for general knowledge and fun, such as learning why the spelling of a word sometimes gives a hint as to what language it came from.

Fitting Spelling into Your Day

How much time should teachers and kids spend on spelling? I'd recommend, at most, one strategy topic and one pattern topic each week, depending on what you think your kids already know and need to learn. The lessons vary somewhat in length; many can be done in fifteen minutes or so, while others may run longer or can be carried out over two days. I've also suggested follow-up ideas, often involving just a brief return to the idea as part of writers' workshop later in the week. I believe that in most classrooms today not much time is spent on spelling, in contrast to classrooms as recently as the 1980s, when traditional spelling textbooks were close to universal. Those programs typically had about 20 minutes of activities a day in a one-week unit, in practice mostly done as seatwork, although they all recommended active teaching as well. Most teachers don't use them anymore, and, in my experience, often don't have much of a spelling curriculum because they aren't sure what to use instead of a textbook. Yet many teachers believe that they should be spending fifteen or twenty minutes a day on spelling and do so through commercial programs (other than traditional textbooks), ideas from books they've found at teacher stores, or ideas of their own devising. What I'm proposing is that yes, we should teach spelling, but in a way that builds on the writing kids are doing and their natural interest in language and in ways that promote active thinking and don't take up tons of time. So let's see what that might look like.

The Lessons

Each of the lessons in this program includes a combination of background information for the teacher and an explanation of how to teach the lesson. The lesson features include:

» Who, When, and Why

This section includes basic information about identifying what developmental level the lesson is most appropriate for, when in the school year the lesson might be taught, and why the topic is important. For example, with patterns, are the kids' invented spellings suggesting emerging knowledge of this pattern? And with strategies, what do they know how to do (for instance, with a dictionary), and for whom is this the best next step?

There are also some ideas in most lessons about differentiating instruction. The lessons are designed for grades 3 through 5, but I've indicated how they might play out differently with older and younger kids, as well as ideas for working with struggling spellers, English-language learning (ELL) students, and so on. In particular, in many of the pattern lessons I've provided information about the sounds and spelling of Spanish, since this is the largest ELL group in the United States, and the English and Spanish languages have many similarities.

» Background Knowledge

Since the English spelling system is complicated, for many of the lessons I've provided background knowledge, often linguistic. For instance, how *do* we know when to double a letter? This will help any teachers who feel that they don't know a lot about spelling rules to get a general sense of how different patterns work, as well as answer questions like "Why don't we have a double *x* in *fix*?" I've sometimes erred on the side of including more rather than less so that you'll have the information, but don't feel obliged to absorb it all.

» The Lesson

The most detailed section comes next: the lesson itself. I've tried to lay out exactly how I would present the idea of the lesson in a way that will get kids to actively think about the topic and figure out, for themselves and with each other, how the pattern works or how they might apply the strategy. Although I often suggest actual language to use in the lesson, it's not meant to be a script, since some of what you'll do will be based on how the students respond. I hope I've written the lessons in such a way that you really *get* what each one is trying to accomplish and can improvise based on where the kids go with it.

» Next Steps

The lessons also include ideas for follow-up and assessment, based on the understanding that the concepts kids have learned about will be strengthened if they get a chance to try them out in their writing and sometimes their reading, then later revisit the topic briefly as a class. For instance, they might talk a day or two after a lesson about their successes and challenges in using guide words in the dictionary. Follow-up may come in either of two forms: what can students do that same day after the lesson is over, and how can you follow up a day or two later?

Not every lesson needs to be evaluated, but sometimes assessment can be an outcome of activities you're doing for their own sake, or you can go about it more formally, as well as getting a sense of how well the lesson worked for the class as a whole. For most lessons, I've suggested an idea for a free-write—if you like, students could keep a spelling journal to enter these reflections on what they've learned; this not only helps them crystallize their thinking but serves as an evaluation tool for the teacher. (See page xv for more information about spelling journals.)

The **Lesson at a Glance** chart includes the main points of the lesson in an easy-to-access format, and is intended for you to refer to as you teach.

Lesson at a Glance: HOW TO SPELL THE /S/ SOUND

What to Do	What to Say	What Kids Need to Know
INTRODUCE		
• Write the words **sad, send, cent, sit, city, sock,** and **sun** on the board or on chart paper. • Discuss as a class what sound the words start with. • Have students work in pairs to create a list of words that start with the /s/ sound.	"Let's read these words together. What do you notice about what sound they start with? What do you notice about what letter they start with?" "Work with a partner and see how many words you can write that start with the /s/ sound. Write them in your spelling journals in two groups, depending on which letter they start with. If you aren't sure, make your best guess."	Lots of words start with the /s/ sound, but sometimes they start with an **s** and sometimes they start with a **c**.
EXPLORE		
• Ask students to share their word lists. • Say the words **sit** and **city** aloud. Discuss how to know whether the words start with **c** or **s.** Repeat with **celery** and **secretary.** • Write the words **sit, city, celery,** and **secretary** on the board or on chart paper. • Ask students to think about how to spell those words. Have them discuss with a partner whether there is a way to tell if the words start with an **s** or a **c.**	"Let's share the words you've written. Now, close your eyes and listen to me say these two words: **sit, city.** Is there any way that you can tell just from listening to them which one starts with **c** and which one starts with **s**? If you do know which one starts with each letter, how do you know? Let's try it with another two words. Close your eyes and listen again: **celery, secretary.** Can you tell what letter they start with?" "Here's something to think about with a partner: when you listen to the words **sit, city, celery,** and **secretary,** you can't tell whether they start with an **s** or a **c.** So then how do you know which letter to use when you write them?"	Just from listening to a word with the /s/ sound, you can't tell whether it starts with an **s** or a **c.**
DISCOVER		
• As a class, share what partners discussed. • Distribute copies of page 272. • Review initial word lists and, as a class, sort them under the headings **sa, ca, se,** and **ce.** • Have students work with a partner to fill in /s/ words that start with the remaining patterns. (See Sample Words for examples.)	"Let's share what you came up with. Is there any way—besides just knowing the word—to tell whether to use **s** or **c**? Let's try something. Look back at the lists you did with your partner, and let's list all the /s/ words that start with **sa.** Okay, now let's list all the /s/ words that start with **ca.** Let's try another pattern. What are your **se** words? What are your **ce** words?" "Try working with your partner and see where	Some /s/ words start with **sa,** but not **ca** (unless students have mistakenly included some words that start with the /k/ sound). There are words that start with both **se** and **ce.** The only patterns that have words in the **c** column are **ce, ci,** and **cy.**

At the beginning of every lesson, you'll find the **main idea** of the lesson—the most essential spelling understanding that the lesson covers.

The **Who, When, and Why** section helps you decide when to teach the lesson by pointing out what developmental levels it is appropriate for.

The **Materials** box tells you what you'll need to have on hand.

The **Background Knowledge** section offers helpful linguistic information and any background knowledge that might be helpful for you to know.

The **chalkboard** points out words you'll want to write for children to see.

132

Pattern 1 SIMPLE PATTERNS

HOW TO SPELL THE /S/ SOUND

✳ The most common way to spell the /s/ sound is, of course, with the letter **s,** but sometimes it's spelled with **c** before **e, i,** and **y.**

Who, When, and Why

Materials
▸ spelling journals
▸ copies of page 272

Since there are so many words using the letter **s,** and since you can hear the sound in the name of the letter *(ess),* children make the connection very early in their spelling. But the letter **c** can also represent the /s/ sound, and you can also hear the sound in its letter name *(cee),* even though **c** can represent the /k/ sound too. Therefore, particularly as children become familiar with words like **cent** and **city,** you'll see them sometimes using **c** to spell the /s/ sound. When kids have this awareness—that there's more than one way to spell /s/—they're ready to do some exploration of it. Younger students might not be able to grasp and apply the rule very well; in their case, the lesson is more about developing some awareness of the pattern than applying it consistently.

Background Knowledge

The /s/ sound is usually spelled with **s,** and sometimes with **c.** The **c** spelling occurs only before **e, i,** or **y,** and the **s** spelling is more common. Beyond that, it's a matter of knowing the specific word. For Spanish speakers, the same rule applies in Spanish. Other English spellings of /s/, as in **scissors** and **psalm,** are rare.

The Lesson

sad, send, cent, sit, city, sock, sun

1. To get kids thinking about different spellings for the /s/ sound, write **sad, send, cent, sit, city, sock,** and **sun** on the board or on chart paper.

   Let's read these words together. What do you notice about what sound they start with? What do you notice about what letter they start with?

   🔖 Work with a partner and see how many words you can write that start with the /s/ sound. Write them in your spelling journal in two groups, depending on which letter they start with. If you aren't sure, make your best guess.

2. After they've done this:

   Let's share the words you've written.

Spelling Strategies and Patterns

Helpful icons let you know when kids will work in pairs, or in their spelling journals.

A **reduced version of the handout** gives you a quick look at what resources go along with the lesson.

Practical tips and important points are called out in the sidebar.

Next Steps can include follow-up tips, assessment ideas, and ways to extend the spelling lesson.

When applicable, easy, medium, and harder **sample words** are provided for you to use in case students don't come up with enough examples to explore.

Then:

Close your eyes and listen to me say these two words: **sit, city.** Is there any way that you can tell just from listening to them which one starts with **c** and which one starts with **s**? If you *do* know which one starts with each letter, how do you know? *(Probably just from knowing that specific word.)* Let's try it with another two words. Close your eyes and listen again: **celery, secretary.** Can you tell from listening what letter they start with?

3. Write the words **sit, city, celery,** and **secretary** on the board or on chart paper.

Here's something to think about with a partner: when you listen to the words **sit, city, celery,** and **secretary,** you can't tell whether they start with an **s** or a **c.** So then how do you know which letter to use when you write them?

4. After they've finished their discussion:

Let's share what you came up with. Is there any way—besides just knowing the word—to tell whether to use **s** or **c**? Let's try something. Look back at the lists you did with your partner, and let's list all the /s/ words that start with **sa.** *(Record the **sa** words they offer in the correct section of the chart.)* Okay, now let's list all the /s/ words that start with **ca.** *(There won't be any, unless they've mistakenly included some words that start with the /k/ sound.)* Let's try another pattern. What are your **se** words? What are your **ce** words? *(There will be some of each; include them on the chart.)*

5. Handout copies of <u>page xx</u> to each student. Invite kids to record the lists you just generated for **sa** and **ca.**

Try working with your partner and see where you can fill in words with the other patterns. *(The only patterns that will have /s/ words in the **c** column are **ce, ci,** and **cy.** You can refer to my list of /s/ sound words for more examples.)*

6. After kids have had a chance to talk again with their partners, ask:

What did you notice? *(Move them toward realizing that unless the second letter is an **e, i,** or **y,** the first letter has to be **s.** If the second letter is one of those three, the first letter could be either **s** or **c.**)* Any ideas about why this happens? *(If **sad,** for instance, started with a **c** it would read **cad,** since **c** represents a /k/ sound before most letters. Younger children may not have enough experience with language to grasp this, but the lesson can still proceed. It just means that getting /s/ sound words right won't come as naturally to them as it will in a year or two.)*

> The /s/ sound is usually spelled with **s.** It's sometimes spelled with **c,** but only before **e, i,** or **y.**

7. See if kids can generate a rule for deciding how to spell the /s/ sound.

So what's a good rule to use if you're writing a word that starts with the /s/ sound? *(Build on their ideas to end up with: if the second letter is **e, i,** or **y,** the word could start with either **s** or **c,** so you have to know the word to be sure it's right. The rest of the time it*

134

Next Steps

> Kids might want to keep their charts in their spelling journals for quick reference.

» Follow-up

Right away:

When you're reading and writing today, try to notice words that start with the /s/ sound and see how well our rule works. You can add words to your chart if you like.

A few days later: Revisit the rule and talk about whether it's working for them. If not, try to clarify any confusion, but remember that the rule doesn't provide definitive answers about how to spell these words; only a dictionary can do that.

✓ Assessment

As a journal topic, suggest a question like:

What have you learned (or what do you know) about how to spell words that start with the /s/ sound?

Also, look for invented spellings of these words in students' writing; see if they result from breaking the rule or are just words that could reasonably start with either **s** or **c.**

⊕ Extension

For older students, you can add the following:

Take a look at the words **psychology** and **scissors.** They don't fit our rule, do they? Who'd like to get a dictionary and find some other words that start with **ps** and **sc.** What do you think? Why do they break the rule? *(It has to do with their etymology; they typically come from Greek.)* You just have to know those words, don't you? Here's an interesting fact: in French, the **p** in **ps** words is pronounced (like in the word **psychologie,** meaning **psychology**).

Sample Words

The /s/ sound is spelled **s** before:

	Easy	Medium	Harder
a	sad, same, saw	safety, salt, saddle	safari, salute, sausage
e	see, sell, seat	secret, sentence, seem	separate, select, setting
i	six, silly, sister	sign, silent, silver	signature, situation, simplify
o	so, soon, song	soccer, solve, soil	social, solar, sorrow
u	sub, sun, super	sudden, summary, subject	subscription, surrender, suspense
y	syllable	symphony	system
other letters	sleep, snake, smile, swim	sports, ski, strong, square	scorpion, skeleton, station, struggle

...and sometimes **c** before:

e	celery, center, cereal	certain, central, celebrate	cement, cemetery, ceremony
i	city, circle, Cinderella	circus, citizen, cinema	cinnamon, circumference, cinch
y	cycle	cyclone	cyberspace

Pattern 1: How to Spell the /s/ Sound   135

When to Use the Lessons

It can be useful to think of this curriculum in terms of what it looks like during the course of a week, and then again during the course of a whole year. Picture a classroom where writers' workshop takes place every day. On Monday, a spelling strategy lesson could be part of that day's workshop: for instance, inviting children to work with a partner to see, after finding a particular word (chosen by them or provided by you) in the dictionary, how they know they've found the right word. The lesson would also include a bit of explicit teaching on your part that would help them carry out the task. After that lesson but before moving into the rest of the workshop, you might ask them to do a brief free-write about what they learned about using the dictionary.

On Wednesday, you might do a lesson about how to tell if words start with a *c* or a *k*, ask the class to keep an eye out for words starting with the /k/ sound as they read and write that week, and check in on Thursday. Thus you have two lessons, of about 15 minutes each, and two shorter "touching base" moments.

The lessons are written so that carrying them out in the order they're written works well, but you may also choose to teach lessons according to what you see in your students' invented spelling patterns and spelling strategies. Appropriate indicators are listed with each lesson, but here's one example: if your students suddenly start realizing that they're still not finding a lot of their misspellings when they edit, it would be the perfect teachable moment for a few lessons on how to find all the words whose spellings need fixing (Strategies 26, 28).

Not all lessons will work or be needed in every classroom or grade level. Although there are 65 lessons in this curriculum, your students probably won't need all of them; they're likely to either already know some of the material or not be ready for it yet, depending on grade level. Within a school, lessons can be repeated at different grade levels, with greater sophistication as kids get older. You also might start out the year with just one lesson a week, follow your instincts as to what's likely to be useful at any given time, and, particularly on weeks when no topic seems obvious, pick lessons that the kids just might be interested in. The suggested sequence is there for those who'd like it, but being spontaneous and responsive to what you see kids doing already can also be very effective.

The Spelling Journal

We're all familiar with writing across the curriculum, and spelling, just like other subject areas, can be a focus of writing. I'm therefore suggesting that you invite your students to keep a spelling journal. The spelling journal is intended to be both a resource collection (such as lists of common words, pages for the students to fill in words they want to remember, or activities done during your weekly lessons) and a home for children's thoughts and ideas about spelling. At the end of most of the lessons, I've included a writing topic for children to do in their journals. Each writing idea is meant to be a suggestion for reflecting on the lesson, and shouldn't be seen as a rigid prompt.

Here's how I'd introduce the journal: *Every week when we do spelling lessons, I'm going to ask you to write something about what you thought about the lesson or what you learned. We're going to have spelling journals to keep all these ideas in one place. This will also be a place to keep lists of words you want to learn or have trouble with, and anything else that relates to spelling. When I ask you to write about a lesson, I'll give you an idea or a title, but these are just starting points; you can go in your own direction, and might even want to come back a day or two later and add some more. At the end of the year, it'll be interesting to look back and see how your ideas and thoughts about spelling have changed.*

You may want to initiate the use of the journal at the beginning of the school year by asking students to write about one or more of these topics or others: What do you think about spelling? What are your spelling goals for this year? How did you learn to spell?

Writing entries in the spelling journal serves two purposes. First, it gets students thinking, in particular by reframing their new knowledge and putting it in their own words. Second, it's an assessment tool for the teacher. You can read every student's journal entry after a single lesson to get a sense of how it went and what they seem to have learned. Alternatively, you can read a single student's entire journal, particularly a student you're concerned about, to see whether she's grasping the knowledge contained in the lessons. Additionally, lists of words and other information in the journal are, of course, useful resource tools for kids.

Exploration, Not Mastery

One final point about how this curriculum is designed: the focus is on exploration rather than mastery. Let me explain. Have you, as an adult writer, mastered when to use double letters in words? Of course not. (Even if you think you have, you'll see!). Apropos of this, I recently attended the Broadway musical *The 25th Annual Putnam County Spelling Bee*, which is just what the title sounds like, except that it has adult actors playing the twelve-year-old characters. At one point one of the contestants was asked to spell a word, and he spelled part of it, and then thought out loud, "One *l* or two"? A woman in the audience in front of me whispered "one" to her companion, but I knew it was two, and so did the character. How did I (and he) know? Well, I just knew the word (as did the character, or rather, the playwright), and that's why adults generally get double letters right. The principles involved are too complicated to master beyond a certain point, but we can certainly explore them. For instance, a word that ends with a consonant-vowel-consonant (CVC) pattern usually doubles the consonant before a suffix starting with a vowel, as in *saddest*. That's worth teaching to elementary school students. But a lesson on it doesn't mean they'll always remember to do it, or that they'll know that *c* usually turns into *ck* when you double it, but not always, so that you'd write "We were *picnicking* when they *sicced* their dog on us." And why do the British write *travelled* when we write *traveled*? The double letters in other words serve functions like indicating a preceding short vowel (*comma*), but then why doesn't *delicate* have a double *l*? Surprisingly, linguists have theorized and convincingly demonstrated that *giraffe* has a double *f* to show that the stress is on the second syllable (Chomsky and Halle, 1968). But then there's *carafe*. Why do *kiss*, *hall*, and *puff* end with double letters? Because we usually don't end words with single *s, l,* or *f*. (Though only in some cases: they're single in *cats, awful,* and *half* because these are, respectively a plural, a suffix, and a blend).

Back to the idea of exploration versus mastery. If I were to teach you every single rule for consonant doubling in English, it would be very unlikely that you'd master them in the sense of always applying them correctly to a word you didn't already know how to spell, particularly given that any word could potentially have a double consonant. Be honest now—do you sometimes forget which letters are doubled or not in *accommodate*? I could tell you the rules involved (the *m*'s show that the preceding vowel is short, the *ac* is a suffix that remains intact when preceding another *c*), but would you have mastered them well enough to apply them the next time you got stuck on *accelerate*? (And hey, why isn't there a double *l* in *accelerate*?) You get the idea. The rules for many spelling patterns are complicated, and it's not always clear when they apply and when they don't.

Fortunately, as a literate adult you get the double letters right most of the time. Why? Two reasons: you've seen the words already, *and* you've absorbed information about how the pattern works, even if you can't put a rule into words. You use double *p*'s in *apple* and *poppy* because they just wouldn't look right otherwise (APLE and POPY—ugh!) But that doesn't mean it's not worthwhile, and sort of fun, to learn and speculate about why we have double letters and how they work. Kids tend to find these explorations interesting, since they know that they still have a lot to learn about written language, and any topic is interesting if you approach it in a way that promotes discovery. Understanding the value of what children will get out of these lessons can ensure that we don't have inappropriate expectations of mastery. (However, as we'll see, each lesson does have goals, and student learning can and should be assessed.)

Spelling Strategies and Patterns

STANDARDS, TESTING, AND SPELLING

I've provided a set of assessment tools for classroom evaluation of spelling, but would like to address here the role of spelling in standards and testing. If a state or school district has standards for writing, spelling and other conventions will almost always be part of them. Most frequently, there are multiple standards for writing that include an expectation that as students go through elementary school, their spelling will be increasingly readable and then increasingly correct. It's often included as part of a "conventions" standard, sometimes under the framework of the six traits of good writing (Culham, 2003).

Spelling used to be assessed by standardized tests, typically by asking the student to pick the one misspelled or correctly spelled word out of a group of four and bubble in the answer. Today, it's most common for spelling to be part of an assessment that involves writing to a prompt, so that spelling is considered in the context of the student's writing. This is, I believe, a positive change in the direction of more authenticity and relevance. Students may or may not be allowed to use dictionaries and other references when taking these state tests; I believe it's best if they are, since the assessment then measures kids' ability to spell under realistic conditions and isn't so dependent on their natural spelling ability and which words they happen to know.

How can teachers best work with standards and testing in the area of spelling? The good news is that asking students to work toward an age-appropriate level of spelling correctness is a perfectly reasonable expectation, much more so than asking them to know how to spell a fairly random selection of words. This entire curriculum is geared toward that goal, and, I believe, will help students do well with spelling when writing for a state assessment.

Is there anything more specific that teachers can be doing to help students prepare for the tests, not in the sense of skewing the results but rather in order to help them demonstrate well what they're able to do? As with all writing, good self-expression is the main point, but teachers can help children realize that this is a situation in which spelling does indeed matter, and that they want to show the test scorers how well they can spell if they're really trying to get it right. Should you encourage students to stick to words they know how to spell, particularly if dictionaries aren't allowed? Well, the trade-off is that their writing will be weakened if they aren't using the full expressive range of their vocabulary, and test scorers will presumably be forgiving if a fourth grader misspells *meteorologist*, while giving her credit for knowing the word in the first place.

Some teachers have told me that since spelling and other conventions are part of state standards and testing, they feel they should have a traditional, list-based spelling curriculum. But this, despite its other drawbacks, isn't even a good fit with contemporary assessment of writing. It seems most logical that if students are being assessed on how they spell when they write, the best preparation is a curriculum that helps them spell better when they write.

WORKING WITH PARENTS

So many teachers have told me that they've stuck to a traditional, word-list based spelling program because parents seem to expect or indeed demand it. They don't expect medicine or clothing for kids to be the same as when they were young, so why do they want spelling preserved in amber? I think it's not so much nostalgia (too many adults have bad memories of spelling tests!) as it is stereotypes. Spelling lists have an air of rigor, tough expectations of kids that may also seem to be prerequisite for them to get by in a world that prizes perfect spelling. When teachers don't follow this model, they're suspected of being lax or permissive.

In a phrase, here's what we need to do: share our knowledge with parents. The reason we're thinking about different approaches to spelling these days is more like why medicine has changed than why fashion has changed: we know more than we used to. The two big things that we've learned about are how spelling develops and how the writing process works. That's why this curriculum deals with patterns—since research (see Wilde, 1992, for citations) tells us that kids go through levels of acquiring them on their own as they go through the elementary school years—and strategies—since research, including my own (Wilde, 1987), shows that writers can use a number of different ways to come up with spellings and edit their work for correct spelling.

How should we go about telling parents what we're doing and why? Either in person or in writing is valuable. Wouldn't it be fun to do a parent night on spelling? You could work on a lesson or two with them; One-Second Words (Strategy 9) and The /k/ Sound (Pattern 2) work well with adults. The FAQs below can also be used for presentations to and discussions with parents.

We can talk with parents individually as well. I once had a very successful conference with a mom who was concerned about her son's spelling; all I did was walk her through a sample of his writing, pointing out why he spelled words the way he did and focusing on what his spellings revealed he knew about written language. (The CD-ROM included with this curriculum has examples of my conversations about kids' spellings.) This student wasn't a particularly strong speller compared to his classmates, but he was where he was, so what was most useful was to show evidence of knowledge and thinking, to reassure his mom that he wasn't just a bad speller but was an actively developing one.

If you have a newsletter for parents, you can include occasional information about your spelling program, as well as spelling stories and vignettes from your classroom (like the bananna story I began with). If using this curriculum is a big change from what you've done with spelling before, you may want to send a letter home at the beginning of the year—but I know you're wondering what exactly to say to parents, so I've provided answers to frequently asked questions to provide suggestions for your communications with them.

Spelling FAQ #1: Tell me about your spelling curriculum.

My spelling program focuses on really *teaching* kids; every week I'm teaching kids lessons that help them learn something new about how words are spelled and how to have better spelling in their writing.

Spelling FAQ #2: Will my child be learning lists of words?

No, because we've learned that this isn't a good use of time (Wilde, 1990). Kids given a big list of words may be able to learn them for the test, but they typically don't transfer them to their writing. What we *will* do is help your child figure out what words he's missing a lot in his writing and "learn them cold" so that he'll never get them wrong again. But we focus on only one word at a time so that it's really learned forever.

Spelling FAQ #3: What's this invented spelling I keep hearing about? Isn't spelling just supposed to be correct?

The term *invented spelling* came along in 1971 when some researchers (Chomsky, 1971; Read, 1971) realized that young kids, preschoolers in fact, were writing words before they started to read, when all they knew was the names of the letters. They were truly inventing these spellings, since they came up with them on their own without any teaching. We now use the term to talk about any spelling that a writer comes up with on her own; these spellings don't come out of thin air but are based on what the writer knows about language. The great thing about inventing a spelling rather than asking somebody is that it gets you to think; in fact, first graders who wrote with invented spelling did better on tests of phonics and spelling than those who didn't (Clarke, 1989).

Spelling FAQ #4: So when do you expect kids to spell correctly?

It's gradual. Here are the components, which are typically happening simultaneously: First, kids pick up a lot of words from their reading. Second, in class we explore how to get more words right in their first draft; for instance, maybe the word is on the word wall where they can see it quickly, or there are words they use a lot that they should just memorize. Third, they learn how to edit their writing for spelling. These processes are all going on all year, and kids still use invented spelling for words that they don't know when they're first writing.

Spelling FAQ #5: What can I do to help my child be a better speller?

Lots! The most important one is to encourage your child to read, because that's how we learn to spell most of our words. If she's writing at home, you can talk with her about how she comes up with her spellings and how she edits for spelling. You don't want to be too picky or heavy-handed about this; for most children, editing a few spellings makes more sense than trying to get every word right, which can be tedious until they're a little older. Dictionaries and spellcheckers make good gifts; I can recommend some. Check the annotated bibliography.

 # CONCLUSION

I hope that this introduction to *Spelling Strategies and Patterns* has put the curriculum in context for you, and gotten you eager to start using it. If you have questions—now or as you're exploring spelling with your students—feel free to email me at wildes@pdx.edu. I love hearing from readers!

STRATEGIES REPRODUCIBLES

Lesson at a Glance: WHAT KIND OF SPELLER ARE YOU?

What to Do	What to Say	What Kids Need to Know
INTRODUCE		
• Get kids thinking about what kind of spellers they are. • Hand out copies of page 266 and have kids fill out the questionnaire. • After they've finished, have them discuss their answers in small groups.	"Do you find it fun to notice the spellings of words and try to get them right, or do you find it boring? Does spelling come easy to you, or is it a bit of a struggle? Does it matter to you if words are spelled right, or do you not really care? Let's find out what kind of speller you are." "On the questionnaire I'm giving you, check one answer for each item. Just pick the one that's a better fit for you. When you're done, get in groups of three or four and discuss your answers."	There are all different kinds of spellers.
EXPLORE		
• Give the class time to discuss what their answers were, how they were similar and different, and so on. • You may want to share your own answers with them.	"So what do you think? What does this tell you? We're different from each other, aren't we? The answers to the first two questions show whether you think spelling is fun or boring, the third and fourth whether spelling is easy or hard for you, and the last two how much you care about spelling."	We all have different attitudes about spelling.
DISCOVER		
• Point out that kids can help each other with spelling.	"All this year, when we work on spelling, these differences will come out. Some of you might wish we spent more time on spelling, some of you less. Those of you who find spelling harder can ask the other kids for tips (and maybe give them tips on something you're good at). The people who aren't so fussy about getting it right can help those who want it perfect to loosen up on the first draft, and vice versa. But I know that all of you will become better spellers as the year goes on."	We should be understanding of different people's spelling abilities and attitudes. We can use our strengths to help others.

WHAT KIND OF SPELLER ARE YOU?

 We don't all feel the same way about spelling, just like we don't all feel the same way about math, or sports, or broccoli. It's important to recognize these differences, and be aware of them as writers.

Who, When, and Why

Materials
► copies of page 266

This lesson is very much for all students, because it's about recognizing diversity. It's a good lesson to do at the beginning of the school year.

Background Knowledge

Students differ in their interest in spelling (and other formal aspects of language), their ability with it, and how much they care about it. Some of these differences may well be differences of temperament and personality, as well as natural proficiency. Knowing what kind of speller you are can help you decide how you're going to approach spelling, and it's also valuable to realize that, as with anything else, there are individual differences in spelling.

The Lesson

1. Get kids thinking about what kind of spellers they are.

Do you find it fun to notice the spellings of words and try to get them right, or do you find it boring? Does spelling come easy to you, or is it a bit of a struggle? Does it matter to you if words are spelled right, or do you not really care? Let's find out what kind of speller you are.

Hand out copies of page 266.

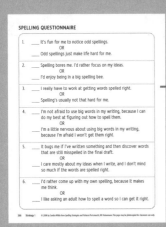

On the questionnaire I'm giving you, check one answer for each item. Just pick the one that's a better fit for you. When you're done, get in groups of three or four and discuss your answers.

2. Give the class time to discuss what their individual answers were, how they were similar and different, and so on.

So what do you think? What does this tell you? We're different from each other, aren't we? The answers to the first two questions show whether you think spelling is fun or boring, the third and fourth whether spelling is easy or hard for you, and the last two how much you care about spelling. *(At this point, you might want to share your own answers with them.)*

3. Point out that kids can help each other with spelling.

All this year, when we work on spelling, these differences will come out. Some of you might wish we spent more time on spelling, some of you less. Those of you who find spelling harder can ask the other kids for tips (and maybe give them tips on something you're good at). The people who aren't so fussy about getting it right can help those who want it perfect to loosen up on the first draft, and vice versa. But I know that all of you will become better spellers as the year goes on.

» Follow-up

These three dimensions of fun/boring, easy/hard, care/don't care can run through the year as an underlying theme or framework. Some students will be more engaged by spelling pattern lessons than others, but everyone can learn from them, and perhaps the enthusiasm of some children will infect the others a little.

✓ Assessment

As a journal topic, suggest a question like:

What kind of speller are you, and what does this mean for you as a writer?

Lesson at a Glance: DEVELOPING A REPERTOIRE OF SPELLING STRATEGIES

What to Do	What to Say	What Kids Need to Know
INTRODUCE		
• Discuss possible spelling strategies. • As students volunteer answers, make a list of them on chart paper.	"Has it ever happened to you that you're writing and don't know how to spell a word? So what do you do when that happens? Let's make a list."	You already use strategies to help you spell words you don't already know.
EXPLORE		
• When students run out of ideas, remind them of strategies you've seen them using and push their thinking a little.	"What did I notice you doing the other day when you wanted to spell **pterodactyl?** What could you do if you can't find a word in the dictionary?" "Can anyone think of a really unusual way to come up with the spelling of a word?"	There are many different strategies you can use to spell words.
DISCOVER		
• Help kids understand the idea of strategies that are "inside the head" versus those that are "outside the head." • Categorize the strategies on the class chart.	"Here's one other thing to think about. Some spelling strategies you can do all on your own, like trying it another way; you're spelling a word by using what's 'inside your head,' what you already know about spelling words. What's good about that? What's bad about it?" "You can use what's 'outside your head' if you're not sure, like asking a friend or looking in a book to find a spelling you don't know. Let's go through our list and see which strategies fall into each group."	Some strategies are "inside the head" and some are "outside the head." There are benefits and drawbacks to each type.

DEVELOPING A REPERTOIRE OF SPELLING STRATEGIES

 There are lots of ways to figure out how to spell a word.

Who, When, and Why

Materials
► chart paper

Just as we adults have a lot of choices about what we might do when we don't know how to spell a word, so do kids. This lesson has students generate the beginnings of a list of ideas for strategies to come up with the spelling of a word they don't know. A key part of this goal is resourcefulness: helping kids see all the choices they have when figuring out how to spell a word. This lesson works well early in the school year, to establish a foundation for future strategy work, and can be revisited throughout the year to expand and consolidate student strategies. It's recommended for every grade level; the children's responses will determine how far you can go with it. Fifth graders are likely to have a wider range of strategies than third graders, and the specifics of the lesson grow out of what they contribute in the class discussion.

Background Knowledge

Someone asked at random might say you either know how to spell a word, get it wrong, or look it up in the dictionary. But writers have a number of other options, as we'll explore in this lesson. I find that it's effective to talk to children about using what's "inside your head" (what kids already know about spelling) versus what's "outside your head" (resources they can use to find correct spellings) to think about how you can come up with a spelling.

1. To get kids thinking about the idea of spelling strategies:

   Has it ever happened to you that you're writing and don't know how to spell a word? *(This is said somewhat in jest, since it's a universal experience, especially for children.)* So what do you do when that happens? Let's make a list.

   As students volunteer answers, make a list of them on chart paper. Here are some common possible answers:

   > Sound it out.
   >
   > Look for it on the word wall.
   >
   > Look for it in a book where I saw it.
   >
   > Try to find it in the dictionary.
   >
   > Try writing it a couple of different ways.
   >
   > Ask someone (a friend, the teacher, a parent).

2. When students run out of ideas, remind them of strategies you've seen them using and push their thinking a little. For example:

   What did I notice you doing the other day when you wanted to spell **pterodactyl?** What could you do if you can't find a word in the dictionary? Can anyone think of a really unusual way to come up with the spelling of a word? *(This is a lesson where you really want to build on the kids' responses and take them a little beyond where they are already, as well as make them aware of the strategies they already use, as a foundation for strengthening their instincts and adding new ones.)*

3. To help kids understand the idea of strategies that are "inside the head" versus those that are "outside the head":

   Here's one other thing to think about. Some spelling strategies you can do all on your own, like trying it another way; you're spelling a word by using what's "inside your head," what you already know about spelling words. What's good about that? *(It's quick and easy.)* What's bad about it? *(You might not always get the right spelling.)* But then you can use what's "outside your head," like asking a friend or looking in a book to find a spelling you don't know. Let's go through our list and see which strategies fall into each group.

Categorize the strategies on the class chart.

Inside your head	Outside your head
Sound it out.	Look for it on a word wall.
Try writing it a couple of ways.	Try to find it in a dictionary.
Think of other words that might be similar.	Ask someone (a friend, the teacher, a parent).

Next Steps

» Follow-up

You might want to create a more permanent spelling strategies chart, either as a wall chart or in handout form for students to put in their spelling journals, and add to it as the year goes on and you explore more strategies. Alternatively, you may want to ask children to record the class list in their spelling journals and add to it as the year goes on. I would also do a brief touching-base discussion a couple of days after the original lesson.

✓ Assessment

As a journal topic, suggest a question like:

What are strategies you use to spell words?

The topic can also be discussed in individual writing conferences during the week.

How did you come up with this spelling?

Lesson at a Glance: WHY WRITE WITH INVENTED SPELLING?

What to Do	What to Say	What Kids Need to Know
INTRODUCE		
• Tell a personal anecdote about a time you didn't know how to spell a word. • Introduce the term **invented spelling** and ask students to think about the benefits and drawbacks of invented spelling.	"What are the pros and cons of just writing your best guess if you don't know how to spell a word? This kind of spelling is called **invented spelling.** We call it that because it's like what inventors do: you're coming up with your own idea."	**Pros:** If you just invent a spelling, you can keep on writing without losing your train of thought; it helps you think about the spelling of the word; it keeps you writing independently without needing anyone's help or a dictionary handy. **Cons:** If you invent the spelling, the word is spelled wrong and will have to be edited at some point if there's going to be a final draft; you might not remember what the word was (more true for younger children, whose invented spellings may be further off).
EXPLORE		
• Ask kids to think about when to use invented spelling.	"What words do you think it's best to use invented spelling for?"	Invented spelling is especially useful if you really don't know the word at all, or if you know the word but just can't remember it.
DISCOVER		
• Talk about how to invent a spelling. • If you think it's necessary, invite a couple of students to come up to the board to attempt words they think are "just too hard to spell," or words you provide.	"How exactly do you come up with a spelling when you don't know the word?"	When you try to invent a spelling, think about the sounds and about what you remember if you've seen it before, and then just do your best. If you're really stuck, the teacher might be able to help you figure out the spelling.

WHY WRITE WITH INVENTED SPELLING?

 Invented spelling is always useful when you don't know how to spell a word. As you become a better speller, you don't have to invent as many words.

Who, When, and Why

Materials
▶ none

If students don't want to write a word unless it's spelled right, this will limit both their choice of words (if they avoid words whose spellings they don't know) and their speed and fluency (if they feel they should always ask someone or use the dictionary if they don't know a word). These are the kids who need this lesson. It may be a small group rather than the whole class, but everyone can benefit from the ideas in this lesson.

Depending on their grade level and developmental level, students will have varying proportions of invented spelling in their writing. But the important focus of this lesson is that invented spelling is always appropriate if you don't know how to spell a word.

Background Knowledge

I'm often asked at what grade level students should be required to switch to standard spelling. A more useful way to look at the issue is to realize that invented spelling is *always* useful when you don't know how to spell a word. What changes over time is the proportion of words that students can get right in the first draft, and their ability to edit for a final draft. Also, invented spelling is valuable because it involves actively thinking about the sounds and patterns in a word.

The Lesson

1. Tell a personal anecdote about a time you didn't know how to spell a word. For instance, maybe you were making out a shopping list and weren't sure which vowel was in the middle of **cantaloupe,** but just took your best guess since you knew that it didn't really matter. (If you don't have any personal anecdotes, you can use this one as a "what if.")

2. Ask students to think about the benefits and drawbacks of invented spelling.

   > I prefer to use the term **invented spelling** with children because it's the "adult" term that educators use. But many teachers also like the term **guess-and-go spelling** (Snowball and Bolton, 1993), particularly for younger children. I also use the term **misspelling** in other contexts, such as when talking about editing.

   What are the pros and cons of just writing your best guess if you don't know how to spell a word? *(Pros: you can keep on writing without losing your train of thought; it helps you think about the spelling of the word; it keeps you writing independently without needing anyone's help or a dictionary handy. Cons: the word is spelled wrong and will have to be edited at some point if there's going to be a final draft; you might not remember what the word was—more true for younger children, whose invented spellings may be further off.)*

   This kind of spelling is called **invented spelling.** We call it that because it's like what inventors do: you're coming up with your own idea.

3. Ask kids to think about when to use invented spelling.

   > See Strategy 7 on one-second words for how to deal with words that you're pretty close to knowing.

   What words do you think it's best to use invented spelling for? *(Help students understand that invented spelling is especially useful if you really don't know the word at all, or if you know the word but just can't remember it.)*

4. Talk about how to invent a spelling.

   How exactly do you come up with a spelling when you don't know the word? *(You think about the sounds, about what you remember if you've seen it before, and then just do your best. If you're really stuck, the teacher might be able to help you figure out the spelling.)*

   > Possible words: ridiculous, mischievous, architecture, pneumonia

   If you think it's necessary, invite a couple of students to come up to the board to attempt words they think are "just too hard to spell," or words you provide. This is a chance to walk them through the process.

Next Steps

» Follow-up

After the lesson:

When you write today, notice what words you write invented spellings for, and think about how you come up with them. You can then have a sharing session about it at the end of that day's writers' workshop or a couple of days later.

✓ Assessment

As a journal topic, suggest a question like:

📓 What do you think about invented spelling?

A reduction in student requests to provide them with spellings is a good sign that this lesson has been effective. When they do ask for help, a good response is, "I'm not going to tell you how to spell the word, but I will help you figure it out." That way you can provide scaffolding without just providing the word.

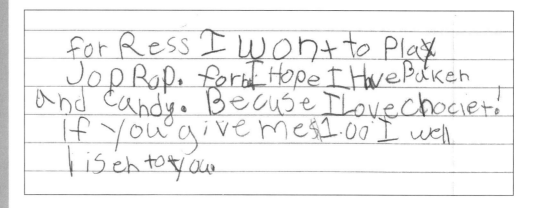

Lesson at a Glance: PERFECTIONISTS

What to Do	What to Say	What Kids Need to Know
INTRODUCE		
• Investigate why getting the spelling right is so important. • Help the student(s) understand the value of trying invented spellings.	"Let's talk about getting the spelling of words right when you're writing them. Why is it important to you?" "You know we've talked about invented spellings and how they can help you write faster. I understand that you'd rather get the words right even if it's not as fast. But what we're going to talk about today is another reason that invented spelling is a good strategy for writers. It helps you think about how a word might be spelled: what sounds are in it, have I seen it before, does this look right? So it's helping you become smarter at spelling."	Using invented spelling can be a helpful tool.
EXPLORE		
• Help the student(s) recognize other ways to check their spelling. • Help them remember recent words they struggled with. (An example is provided.)	"The bad news—maybe—is that I'm not going to tell you any more how to spell words—just like if you forgot what seven times eight is I wouldn't tell you but would ask you, to figure it out for yourself. But the good news is that we're going to talk about some ways that you can try to get the words right without my help." "I remember that three words you asked me how to spell recently were **umbrella, where,** and **cheetah.** I bet you can think of a good place to find each of those words somewhere in the room. Exactly! **Where** is on the word wall, **cheetah** is in the field guide to mammals we were looking at the other day, and **umbrella** is in the picture dictionary."	There are a number of places you can go to check your spelling.
SUMMARIZE		
• Summarize what you've discussed. • Explain that the editing phase may be a better time to worry about correct spelling.	"So if you want to spell words right, go for it, and it'll make you a better speller and writer to do it on your own. (I will help you if you get stuck, though.)" "And here's one other idea: think about whether it might be better to wait until you're editing to look for the words, instead of getting a dictionary when you're in the middle of writing your first draft."	If you are worried about getting a spelling right, try to spell it on your own, find it someplace else, or wait until editing.

PERFECTIONISTS

 It's important to try spelling words you don't know, and you can also look for the correct spellings in a number of places. Or you can wait until you edit your work to find the correct spellings.

Who, When, and Why

Materials
▶ **none**

See the section When Spelling Doesn't Come Easy *on page 119.*

This lesson is for students who say "I don't want to invent, I want to get it right." It is likely to be a lesson for an individual or small group, rather than a whole class. We often feel torn about these kids since they *are* wanting to spell words right, which is certainly to be encouraged. It's just that they want the teacher to do it for them. It's a little like asking you for the answers to their math problems so they'll get them right! Some of these kids are good students who like to have everything done right, but some of them are insecure and think it means they're stupid if they spell a word wrong.

For students who want you to tell them the words because they're insecure, particularly if they're weaker spellers, a different lesson would be more appropriate, one focusing not on how to get the words right but on developing the courage to invent your own spellings.

Background Knowledge

Oh, we all know those kids, don't we? "No, I don't want to do my own spelling; I want you to tell me how to spell it so I'll have it right." It's important, I believe, to honor the motivations and intentions of these students. But it's also important not to be swayed into doing their thinking and work for them. You'll see as we get into the lesson that success is dependent on having a variety of available resources where kids can find words.

The Lesson

1. Investigate why getting the spelling right is so important.

> Let's talk about getting the spelling of words right when you're writing them. Why is it important to you?

2. Help the student(s) understand the value of trying invented spellings.

> You know we've talked about invented spellings and how they can help you write faster. I understand that you'd rather get the words right even if it's not as fast. But what we're going to talk about today is another reason why inventing spelling is a good strategy for writers. It helps you think about how a word might be spelled: what sounds are in it, have I seen it before, does this look right? So it's helping you become smarter at spelling.

3. Help the students recognize other ways to check their spelling.

> The bad news—maybe—is that I'm not going to tell you anymore how to spell words—just like if you forgot what seven times eight is I wouldn't tell you, but would ask you to figure it out for yourself. But the good news is that we're going to talk about some ways that you can try to get the words right without my help.

Help them remember recent words they struggled with, for example:

> I remember that three words you asked me how to spell recently were **umbrella, where,** and **cheetah.** I bet you can think of a good place to find each of those words somewhere in the room. Exactly! **Where** is on the word wall, **cheetah** is in the field guide to mammals we were looking at the other day, and **umbrella** is in the picture dictionary. (*If you don't have your own examples, you can use these as a "what-if."*)

4. Summarize what you've discussed.

> So if you want to spell words right, go for it, and it'll make you a better speller and writer to do it on your own. (I will help you if you get stuck, though.) And here's one other idea: think about whether it might be better to wait until you're editing to look for the words, instead of getting a dictionary when you're in the middle of writing your first draft.

Follow-up

A discussion a few days later about how it's going would be useful. If you've given the student the spellings of words before, she may find it hard or annoying to go "cold turkey," so I'd check to see if she seems, a few days later, to have understood the value of the lesson.

Assessment

As a journal topic, suggest a question like:

How do you feel about getting the words right on your own?

Lesson at a Glance: WHY—AND WHEN—SPELLING MATTERS

What to Do	What to Say	What Kids Need to Know
EXPLORE		
• Ask students to look for spelling errors in published children's books. • Ask students to think about the amount of spelling errors in the writing of their peers.	"When you're reading a published book, how often do you find a word that's spelled wrong? Why do you think that is?" "If you're reading the first draft of a story one of your friends wrote, how often do you find a word that's spelled wrong? Pretty often, huh? Why do you think that is?"	Published books are expected to have the words spelled right, while children don't always spell as well as adults.
DISCOVER		
• Talk about why students may not take the time to get spelling right. • Discuss times when spelling is really important. • Point out that editing is a good time to attend to spelling.	"One reason we sometimes don't have all the words spelled right is that it's easier to just leave it than to proofread the whole thing and make sure you've corrected all the spellings." "But sometimes it's important to get the words right even if it's a bit of a pain. So when would it be important—for you or for an adult—to have all the words spelled right?" "Even if it's not easy for you to get all the words spelled right in the first draft, that's what editing is for."	Some important times to get spelling right include when something's going to be published; when it's going to be on a bulletin board in the hallway; and when you want to make a good impression, such as in a letter to someone or when applying for a job.
SUMMARIZE		
• Talk about developing a more mature attitude toward spelling.	"One other thing to think about, particularly as you get older and know how to spell more words, is that getting the words right is part of taking pride in your writing. When writers send books off to their publishers, most of them try to get the words spelled right even though they know the writing will be proofread. It's a more mature thing to do."	Having a more mature attitude toward spelling and taking pride in your work can help you improve your spelling.

WHY—AND WHEN—SPELLING MATTERS

 It's important to know when spelling really matters. As students' attitudes toward spelling mature, they'll care more about correct spelling.

Who, When, and Why

Materials
▶ a selection of children's books

Exploring this topic benefits all students, since it helps them become more consciously aware of how well they need to spell in a given situation.

Though this topic can be explored with students as young as third grade, expectations for them are different than they are for older kids and adults. It wouldn't be appropriate to expect them to get the spelling of all words right all the time. One option is to limit the amount of time students spend finding and fixing their mistakes, so the attention they give to spelling isn't disproportionate to the amount of time they spend attending to the other elements of the writing process. If the piece is going to be published, you can help them identify and fix the remaining errors. Many fifth graders, on the other hand, can be moving toward more adult-like achievements in their spelling.

Background Knowledge

Have you ever been in the position of reading job, scholarship, or other kinds of applications and come across an egregious misspelling, or—worse yet—discovered one in your own application after you've already sent it off? Ouch! On the other hand, if you're taking notes in a class, or writing in a personal journal, you'll probably invent if you don't know the word. (Even adults who are obsessive about spelling the words right don't always have a dictionary handy at

A useful perspective: many great writers haven't been very good spellers, and they turn in manuscripts riddled with errors. Fortunately, their publishers have copyeditors who are sticklers for correct spelling. Biographies of authors often reproduce original manuscripts with the invented spellings intact; these could be fun for kids to look at. You might also enjoy taking a look at my article, "The Spelling of Lewis and Clark," (Wilde, 2003), where I analyze the spelling in the explorers' journals and talk about how they were unlikely to have carried dictionaries on their expedition.

those times.) So instead of pretending to kids that you should *always* spell correctly or, a more recent variant, that spelling doesn't matter because the reader will be able to figure it out, let's help them develop the same situation-based understandings that we have.

The Lesson

1. Hand out some children's books and invite students to page through them to get them thinking about spelling in published writing.

   When you're reading a published book, how often do you find a word that's spelled wrong? *(It's extremely rare, and perhaps especially so in children's books.)* Why do you think that is? *(Bring out ideas such as the publisher wants people to be able to read it, and it would look like the author was careless if a word was spelled wrong. Also, that's just the way the world works: published books are expected to have the words spelled right.)*

2. Ask students to think about their friends' writing:

   If you're reading the first draft of a story one of your friends wrote, how often do you find a word that's spelled wrong? Pretty often, huh? Why do you think that is? *(Obviously it's in part because kids don't spell as well as adults; it may also have to do with not wanting to spend the time searching for errors, or being preoccupied with content. Do point out, though, that even adults are likely to have words spelled wrong in their first drafts.)*

3. Get kids thinking about times when spelling is important:

   One reason we sometimes don't have all the words spelled right is that it's easier to just leave it than to proofread the whole thing and make sure you've corrected all the spellings. But sometimes it's important to get the words right even if it's a bit of a pain. So when would it be important—for you or for an adult—to have all the words spelled right? *(Look for and encourage answers like when something's going to be published; when it's going to be on a bulletin board in the hallway; when you want to make a good impression, such as in a letter to someone or when applying for a job.)* Even if it's not easy for you to get all the words spelled right in the first draft, that's what editing is for.

4. Talk about developing a more mature attitude toward spelling:

   > I introduced and explained the word **mature** to a class of second graders in this context; I knew that one of them had understood when she commented, "It means that you're wiser."

   One other thing to think about, particularly as you get older and know how to spell more words, is that getting the words right is part of taking pride in your writing. When writers send books off to their publishers, most of them try to get the words spelled right even though they know the writing will be proofread. It's a more mature thing to do.

Spelling Strategies and Patterns

Next Steps

✓ Assessment

As a journal topic, suggest a question like:

📓 When does it matter for you as a writer to get the words spelled right?

➕ Extension

You might want to have kids talk to adults they know about spelling. If so, hand out copies of page 267 to each student.

> You might find it interesting to talk to your parents or other adults about when they try to get everything spelled right in something they write. This might even be an interesting research project for some of you: you could interview some adults and maybe kids of different ages about this and write an article about it. Feel free to use this organizer to keep track of your information. *(Help students identify appropriate people to interview, if necessary.)*

Lesson at a Glance: WHY READING HELPS YOU SPELL

What to Do	What to Say	What Kids Need to Know
INTRODUCE		
• Ask kids to come up with words they have heard but never seen. If there are no answers, suggest **avocado,** or **honeydew melon.** • Ask volunteers to try to spell the words. • Have a volunteer provide the correct spellings or do so yourself.	"Can anyone think of a word that you've heard but have never seen in print?" "Would somebody who's never seen this word come up to the board and try writing it? Is there someone who's seen this word but isn't completely sure of the spelling and would like to try writing it? Is there anyone who's sure of the spelling and would like to write it?"	It's hard to spell words we've never seen before.
EXPLORE		
• Help children understand that it is easier to spell a word if you've seen it before.	"What's the difference between writing a word you've never seen before and one that you have?" "Do you always get it right if you've only seen it once or twice?" "Did you ever have the experience of reading a word and noticing something about the spelling?" "You may be surprised to hear this, but we grownups learned most of the words we know how to spell just from reading them over and over again, without even trying, and you will too."	Having seen a word before doesn't mean you will know how to spell it for sure, but it does make it easier.
SUMMARIZE		
• Suggest a strategy for using reading to improve spelling.	"I'd like to give you two tips for using reading to become a better speller. First, read a lot. Second, pay a little extra attention to how words are spelled when you're reading, especially when you come across words that are new to you."	When you are reading, paying attention to the spelling of words can help you learn them better.

WHY READING HELPS YOU SPELL

 Reading is a big, big piece of how we learn to spell. Reading more can help you improve your spelling.

Who, When, and Why

This lesson is appropriate for everyone. Learning through reading will happen no matter what, but if students are aware of it, it can help them magnify its effects by "reading like a speller."

Younger children will, through their reading, be coming up with better invented spellings, while older ones will more likely be able to move from good invented spellings to correct spellings. The discussion during the lesson can be steered in these directions.

Background Knowledge

A student who doesn't read much is extremely unlikely to be a good speller. If you grew up in the days of traditional spelling programs, the twenty words a week that you were tested on (for six or so years) only come to a few thousand words, a small fraction of what you know how to spell as an adult (and you had probably picked up a lot of the spelling-book words on your own already).

The way we learn to spell through reading is incremental; we may not be able to spell a word correctly after the first time we've read it, but we're more likely to get it right than if we hadn't seen it at all. (See Krashen, 2004). With multiple readings, we're more likely to remember details like whether there was a double consonant or not, or what that vowel in the middle was. (Nagy, Herman, and Anderson, 1985, have shown how a similar process works for learning the meaning of words through reading.) Would this be even more true if we were *trying* to notice those details to help us spell better? Can't hurt.

The Lesson

1. To get kids thinking about the topic:

Can anyone think of a word that you've heard but have never seen in print? *(If there are no answers:)* How about **avocado?** Or **honeydew melon?** Would somebody who's never seen this word come up to the board and try writing it? Is there someone who's seen this word but isn't completely sure of the spelling and would like to try writing it? Is there anyone who's sure of the spelling and would like to write it? *(If no one is, do so yourself.)*

2. Help children understand that it's easier to spell a word if you've seen it before.

What's the difference between writing a word you've never seen before and one that you have? *(You have some information to go on; you usually remember some of the letters, and so on.)* Do you always get it right if you've only seen it once or twice? *(Not necessarily, but you may get better every time.)* Did you ever have the experience of reading a word and noticing something about the spelling?

You may be surprised to hear this, but we grownups learned most of the words we know how to spell just from reading them over and over again, without even trying, and you will too.

3. Suggest a strategy for using reading to improve spelling.

I'd like to give you two tips for using reading to become a better speller. First, read a lot. Second, pay a little extra attention to how words are spelled when you're reading, especially when you come across words that are new to you.

Next Steps

» Follow-up

Ask kids to pay a little more attention when they are reading to how words are spelled.

📓 Let's give a little extra attention to how words are spelled when we're reading over the next couple of days. If you notice the letters in a particular word, make a note of it in your spelling journal so we can talk about it. If all of a sudden you realize that you know how to spell a word that you didn't know before, make a note of that too, and we can talk about whether you think it's reading that did the trick.

✓ Assessment

As a journal topic, suggest a question like:

📓 What have you noticed about how reading helps you spell?

Lesson at a Glance: ONE-SECOND WORDS

What to Do	What to Say	What Kids Need to Know
INTRODUCE		
• Start off the discussion by asking kids to think of words they always spell correctly. • Then talk about words that kids are pretty sure they won't know. • Get kids thinking about words that they know but often spell incorrectly. • Allow some time for kids to volunteer their words. • Start a chart with their names and words, leaving a third column to fill in later.	"Are there some words you always spell right? How about **the?** And why do you always spell it right? You just know it!" "Are there some words you know you'd have to invent? Maybe it's names of dinosaurs, states, or countries. These are the words that you just don't know. They're big, they're hard, and you just invent them." "There's a third group of words, and these are the ones we're going to talk about today. Can you think of a word that you use a lot but still get wrong? Maybe one that you're finding you always have to fix when you edit, or that you're always getting confused on."	Sometimes there are a few tricky words that you use often but just can't remember how to spell.
EXPLORE		
You might want to wait for the next day to carry out this part of the lesson so you'll have plenty of time. • Explain the idea of one-second words. • Use **they** and **because** as examples of one-second words.	"Would it be worth it if you could take one extra second when you're writing and always get these words right? Here's how. It might be a little different for every word, but we'll use **they** and **because** as examples." (See page 28 for examples a and b.)	Using little tricks and visual reminders will help you remember how to spell words you frequently get wrong.
DISCOVER		
• Ask kids to think of one-second words. Have them look in their writing for ideas. • Have them come up with a way they can remember their words. • Record their responses on the chart.	"Does anyone have a word in mind that they would really like to be able to remember? Which part of the word do you have trouble remembering? What is a good way to remember it?"	It's a good idea to choose a word you have trouble with and think of a way to remember it.
SUMMARIZE		
• Have kids spend a week or so with their words and discuss how it went. The goal is to have 100% correctness for that word. • Have students keep a list in their spelling journals of their one-second words.	"How did it go? Do you always get your one-second words right now?" "Keep a list of your one-second words in your spelling journal so you can keep track of the words you've learned."	By taking an extra second to think about your word, you can usually remember how to spell it correctly.

ONE-SECOND WORDS

 By spending one extra second, you can remember the correct spelling for words you commonly misspell. Come up with a little trick for remembering the spelling or write the word in a place you can easily see.

Who, When, and Why

This lesson is appropriate for students who spell many if not most common words correctly, but have a few they frequently miss. Common examples (teachers tell me the same ones every time!) are *they, girl, where,* and *because.* The reason to wait to do this lesson until you see kids spelling common words correctly is that kids will pick up these high-frequency words through reading. This lesson is about "cleaning up" the few that are still persistently misspelled, typically for very understandable reasons. A good guideline for thinking about when kids are ready for this lesson is the Dolch words, the 220 most common words in English (see Sample Words). When kids are spelling the vast majority of the Dolch words correctly, they're ready to work on the few that they're still shaky on.

Many older students don't misspell common words anymore, only harder words. If so, this lesson may be appropriate only for part of your class. However, older students may find it fun to learn a hard word or two every week.

Background Knowledge

This may be your favorite lesson! Once kids understand the idea behind it, you'll be able to help them learn to spell the words they should know but are always missing.

High-frequency words are usually spelled right. In the study I did for my dissertation (Wilde, 1987), I found that the 37 words that made up 50% of six third and fourth graders' writing were misspelled only 2% of the time. Some of these were slips of the pen, like OT for *to,* but the rest probably won't surprise you.

These words are just tricky. **They** has a long **a** in it, so kids may well spell it as THAY. And here's the real challenge. As Frank Smith (1982) has commented, it's not that you can't remember the right spelling, it's that you can't forget the wrong one. For me, **cantaloupe** is the word I can't seem to remember. Is there an **a** in the middle and I think there's an **e,** or is there an **e** and I think it's an **a?** You can imagine kids doing the same thing with **they.** With **because,** the problem is that there're a lot of vowels in it and it's hard to remember which ones they're and where they occur.

The Lesson

1. Start off the discussion by asking kids to think of words they always spell correctly.

   Are there some words you always spell right, every time? How many of you always spell **the** correctly? Let me guess: everyone. And why do you always spell it right? It would be silly not to, wouldn't it? You just know it, so you get it right.

2. Then talk about words that kids are pretty sure they won't know.

   Are there some words you know you'd have to invent? Maybe it's names of dinosaurs; maybe it's the names of some states or countries. These are the words that you just know you don't know. They're big, they're hard, and you don't want to take the time to go and look them up, so you just invent them.

3. To get kids thinking about words that they know but often spell incorrectly:

   There's a third group of words, and these are the ones we're going to talk about today. Can you think of a word that you use a lot but still get wrong a lot? It might be a word that you're finding you always have to fix when you edit. It might be one that you think you know but you're always getting confused on.

   Allow some time for kids to volunteer their words. You could start a chart with their names and words, leaving a third column to fill in later.

4. You might want to wait for the next day to carry out this part of the lesson so you'll have plenty of time.

   Guess what! I have an idea so that you can always get these words right. Would it be worth it if you could take one extra second when you're writing and get them right? Here's how. It might be a little different for every word, so let's take some examples.

   a. For **they,** it's hard to remember what vowel it has. What would be an easy way to keep it straight? Here're two: it's just the word **the** plus a **y.** Or you can remember that **he** is part of **they,** so it has **he** in the middle. So if every time you go to write **they,** you can take one extra second to think of one of these, you can always get it right.

   b. What do you find hard about **because?** It's all those vowels, isn't it? Here's an idea. Write **because** somewhere that you can always see it when you're writing, maybe on a sticky note or strip of masking tape that you can stick on your desk or writing folder. That way, every time you go to write **because,** you can take that one extra second and look at it and get it right. And since you'll be looking at it so much, there's a good chance that within a week you'll be remembering it without having to look.

   These are the two basic strategies for one-second words: mnemonic devices and visual reminders.

5. The next step is for kids to spend some time deciding how they're going to make their word into a one-second word. This will be the third column on your chart. Ask for volunteers to offer some one-second words.

> Does anyone have a word in mind that they would really like to be able to remember? *(Allow time for kids to think or look over their writing.)* Which part of the word do you have trouble remembering? What's a good way to remember it? *(Record responses on the chart.)*

Then the next step is spending a week or so with their words and discussing how it went. The goal is to get to the point where they'll never get this word wrong again.

> How did it go? Do you always get your one-second word right now?

6. Have students keep a list in their spelling journals of the words they pick for one-second words.

> Keep a list of your one-second words in your spelling journal so you can keep track of the words you've learned.

Next Steps

» Follow-up

In a week or so, see if the children have achieved success with their one-second words. Then institute it as a regular practice: every week the students should pick a one-second word for that week, decide how they're going to get it right, and apply it in their writing. Within a few months, you should see quite a bit of improvement in the misspelling of common words, since there aren't very many of them that are problems.

✓ Assessment

From time to time, take a look at students' lists of their one-second words. By checking their lists against their recent writing, you can see if they're successfully using the strategy. Alternatively, suggest that they do this themselves.

Sample Words

See page 268 for Dolch Word List.

DOLCH WORD LIST

about	came	gave	keep	open	so	use
after	can	get	kind	or	some	very
again	carry	give	know	our	soon	walk
all	clean	go	laugh	out	start	want
always	cold	goes	let	over	stop	warm
am	come	going	light	own	take	was
an	could	good	like	pick	tell	wash
and	cut	got	little	play	ten	we
any	did	green	live	please	thank	well
are	do	grow	long	pretty	that	went
around	does	had	look	pull	the	were
as	done	has	made	put	their	what
ask	don't	have	make	ran	them	when
at	down	he	many	read	then	where
ate	draw	help	may	red	there	which
away	drink	her	me	ride	these	white
be	eat	here	much	right	they	who
because	eight	him	must	round	think	why
been	every	his	my	run	this	will
before	fall	hold	myself	said	those	wish
best	far	hot	never	saw	three	with
better	fast	how	new	say	to	work
big	find	hurt	no	see	today	would
black	first	I	not	seven	togeth-	write
blue	five	if	now	shall	er	yellow
both	fly	in	of	she	too	yes
bring	for	into	off	show	try	you
brown	found	is	old	sing	two	your
but	four	it	on	sit	under	
buy	from	its	once	six	up	
by	full	jump	one	sleep	upon	
call	funny	just	only	small	us	

Lesson at a Glance: HOW TO MEMORIZE WORDS

What to Do	What to Say	What Kids Need to Know
INTRODUCE		
• Ask students if there are some words they wish they knew how to spell.	"Are you finding that there are some words you use in your writing from time to time that you wish you knew how to spell and would get right every time? Maybe you write a lot about riding on your bike and would like to write **bicycle,** but can't remember how to spell it. What are some words you just wish you knew how to spell?"	Sometimes you might want to use a hard word in your writing, and it would be helpful to learn how to spell it right every time.
EXPLORE		
• Ask kids to think of words they'd like to learn. (Alternatively, you could give them a day or so to come up with a few words they'd like to learn.) • Have them write the word, look at the correct spelling and think about the parts they got wrong, and then try the word again.	"Today I'm going to teach you how to memorize a word so that you can always get it right, so it becomes pretty much automatic. Can everyone think of a word that you know you don't really know the spelling of but would like to learn?" "Okay, here goes. First, write your word. Next, just call out your words and I'll write them on the board. Look at the correct spelling and think about any parts you got wrong. Now, without looking at the board, write your word and see if you got it right this time."	If you look at the parts you got wrong and think about them, it will help you spell it right the next time.
DISCOVER		
• Ask kids what they noticed about the second time they tried to spell it. • Suggest that students try the word again in an hour or two to see if they can remember it. • (Save for the next day if you like.) Show kids the four steps they need to memorize a word. You can make a wall chart or handout copies of page 269 for children to keep in their spelling journals.	"One question: it was probably pretty easy to get the word right this time, since you just looked at it. Do you think you could get it right tomorrow morning if you hadn't seen it for a day? Here's what I'm going to suggest you do with your word. Everyone take the correct spelling of your word and hide it in your desk somewhere, and I'll erase the words on the board. Then, in an hour or two, I'm going to ask everyone to write your word again, and we'll see if you remembered it. Then we'll do the same thing tomorrow morning." "Here's how you can do this on your own, any time and for any word you want. 1. Write the word using your best guess. 2. Check and see if you got it right; if you didn't, think about the parts you got wrong. 3. Cover up the word and try spelling it again. 4. Repeat if you need to; check the next day and see if you can still get it right."	To memorize a word: 1. Write it. 2. Check and think. 3. Try again. 4. Check again tomorrow; repeat if you need to.

HOW TO MEMORIZE WORDS

To memorize a word, write it, check it and think about the parts you got wrong, and try it again. Then check again later and repeat until you always get it right.

Who, When, and Why

Materials

▶ copies of page 269

This lesson is good for kids who have a good stock of common words they know how to spell consistently, and are starting to use more sophisticated words in their writing.

Memorizing words will be easier for older students, since their first spelling of a word will usually be closer to the correct one. They're therefore more likely to correctly retain memorized spellings. Those of them who are very much into words (possible spelling bee contestants?) might like to learn a lot more words than average, and this lesson will give them a strategy to do so. With younger children, I wouldn't put much emphasis on memorizing, since most of the words they'd choose are ones they'd be picking up eventually from their reading anyway.

Background Knowledge

Gee, should memorizing words still be part of learning how to spell? Back in the day, it was the be-all and end-all of spelling curriculum, typically up to twenty words a week. (Could *you* memorize twenty new words every week? Yikes!) But I think it *is* reasonable for students to choose to memorize a word occasionally, whether it's one of their one-second words or just a word they realize they'd like to use in their writing from time to time and would like to get right. An analogy for adults: we sometimes choose to take the minute or so it takes to memorize a phone number if we're going to call it a lot. (Or not—we may just enter it in our cell phone directory!)

Back in the middle of the twentieth century, a number of researchers explored the best way to memorize words, since that was central to the spelling curriculum of that era. (See Fitzsimmons and Loomer, 1978, for a summary of those findings.) Common classroom practices like writing words in sentences, writing them five times, correcting them in proofreading exercises, and—these days—finding them in word search puzzles are of no use in learning them. What works is the procedure we'll see in this lesson.

The Lesson

1. **Introduce the idea by asking students if there are some words they wish they knew how to spell.**

   Are you finding that there are some words you use in your writing from time to time that you wish you knew how to spell and would get right every time? Maybe you write a lot about riding on your bike and would like to write **bicycle** but can't remember how to spell it. *(Or pick another, age-appropriate example.)* What are some words you just wish you knew how to spell?

2. **Ask kids to think of words they'd like to learn.**

   Today I'm going to teach you how to memorize a word so that you can always get it right, so it becomes pretty much automatic. Can everyone think of a word that you know you don't really know the spelling of but would like to learn? *(Alternatively, you could give them a day or so to come up with a few words they'd like to learn.)*

3. **Have students write the word they want to try, look at the correct spelling and think about the parts they got wrong, and then try the word again.**

   Okay, here goes. First, write your word. Next, just call out your words and I'll write them on the board. Look at the correct spelling and think about any parts you got wrong. Now, without looking at the board, write your word and see if you got it right this time.

4. **Suggest that students try the word again in an hour or two to see if they can remember it.**

   One question: it was probably pretty easy to get the word right this time, since you had just looked at it. Do you think you could get it right tomorrow morning if you hadn't seen it for a day? Here's what I'm going to suggest you do with your word. Everyone take the correct spelling of your word and hide it in your desk somewhere, and I'll erase the words on the board. Then in an hour or two, I'm going to ask everyone to write your word again, and we'll see if you remembered it. Then we'll do the same thing tomorrow morning.

5. **Save for the next day if you like.**

   Here's how you can do this on your own, any time and for any word you want.

   1. Write the word using your best guess.

   2. Check and see if you got it right; if you didn't, think about the parts you got wrong.

   3. Cover up the word and try spelling it again.

   4. Repeat if you need to; it also doesn't hurt to check the next day and see if you can still get it right.

You can make a wall chart or hand out copies of page 269 for children to keep in their spelling journals.

Next Steps

Follow-up

A few days later:

> I'm interested to hear two things: first, have you decided to try to memorize some words? Second, is it working?

Assessment

As a journal topic, suggest a question like:

When and why might you choose to memorize words?

Lesson at a Glance: TRY IT TWO WAYS

What to Do	What to Say	What Kids Need to Know
EXPLORE		
• Ask kids to look through their writing to find words they think might be misspelled. • Ask them to choose one and try spelling it another way. • Have them circle the way that looks right. If they think they still don't have it, they don't have to circle either one.	"I'd like to invite everyone to take out a piece of writing and pick three words that you think might be spelled wrong." "Next, for each one of those words, try spelling it another way, then circle the one you think is right, or don't circle any if you think neither one is right."	Sometimes you might have more than one idea about how a word could be spelled.
DISCOVER		
• Invite volunteers to come up and write both of their attempts for their word. • If they pick correctly, affirm this; if they don't, you can say they had it right the first time. Or if neither spelling is right, suggest that they try a third spelling.	"Who'd like to come up to the board and write their two spellings and show us which one they think is right?"	It's helpful to try spelling a word more than one way.
SUMMARIZE		
• Talk about the value of trying it two ways.	"What do you think of the "try it two ways" strategy? We'll talk another day about strategies for what to do when you still don't know what the right spelling is, but try this one today when you're writing or editing and see how you do with it."	When you try it two ways, you might not always know which one is correct, but it's a good first step.

TRY IT TWO WAYS

 Sometimes when you spell a word wrong, you're pretty close. If you try it again, you might get it right or at least get closer.

Who, When, and Why

Materials
▶ rough drafts or informal writing

This is a simple but remarkably effective strategy. When I tried it out with third graders, most of them got a misspelled word right on the second try and knew it was right. It's one of the most common strategies used by adults.

Any students who have at least a fair number of invented spellings that are pretty close to the correct one can benefit from this lesson. It's surprising how often, once kids are beyond early phonetic spelling, they'll be off by just one letter (AROWND for **around**) or just have the letters in the wrong order (PEPOLE for **people**).

Older students will have greater success than younger ones with this strategy, since their knowledge of individual words and spelling patterns is more developed, but the lesson is valuable for everyone, not just for producing more correct spellings but for the thinking involved. Realizing that a particular word could be spelled with a **c** rather than a **k** helps children activate knowledge about spelling patterns, both the ones you've been teaching about and the ones they're picking up through reading.

Background Knowledge

Spelling in English is both phonetic and visual. Letters and sounds are related, but there's often more than one way to spell a sound or a sequence of sounds. When children have seen a word, their spelling of it is likely to reflect what they've seen—even though they may have missed whether it has a double consonant or not, or what letter represents the schwa sound in the word (see Patterns 16 and 17 on these topics). Their memory—or their knowledge of spelling variations—may help them get it right on the second try. Knowing which attempt is right comes easier to some people than others, and will be covered in the next lesson.

The Lesson

1. **Ask kids to look through their own writing to find some words they think might be misspelled.**

    I'd like to invite everyone to take out a piece of writing and pick three words that you think might be spelled wrong. *(If some say they can't find any, take a look and see whether they're right or if they've just missed them.)*

    Next, for each one of those words, try spelling it another way, then circle the one you think is right, or don't circle any if you think neither one is right.

2. **Invite volunteers to write their two attempts of one word.**

    Who'd like to come up to the board and write their two spellings and show us which one they think is right? *(For children who pick correctly, affirm this; for the ones who don't, you can say "Guess what, the other one was right"; if neither spelling is right you can discuss that, and whether they'd like to try a third spelling. The point is not that this strategy will always produce the right spelling but that it's a good first step.)*

3. **Talk about the value of trying it two ways.**

    What do you think of the "try it two ways" strategy? *(Bring out the idea that sometimes when you try it two ways you know which one is right, sometimes you don't, and sometimes neither of them looks right. It may not work all of the time, but it's likely to work sometimes.)* We'll talk another day about strategies for what to do next when you still don't know what the right spelling is, but try this one today when you're writing or editing and see how you do with it.

Spelling Strategies and Patterns

Next Steps

» Follow-up

Invite students to make a record of every time they use this strategy for the next few days: what their first and second tries were, and whether they knew which one was right. You can distribute copies of page 270 and ask students to keep them in their spelling journals. Have a follow-up discussion on what they think of the strategy.

✓ Assessment

You can look for evidence that students are trying it two ways in their first or second drafts. After students have had a chance to use the strategy for a few weeks, you can suggest a question like the following as a journal topic:

> What do you think about the try it two ways strategy? Is it helpful for you? Why or why not?

> **Rough Draft**
>
> *really* This strange looking meercat has relly sharp claws OW! It has a dark belly with just a little hair. It has dark Brown fur like my hair. It aneime are eagles and Jackals. It ears insects if I was a meercat I would changl thing I would not eat insects I would rather eat a hamburger. I hope you learn a lot. hamburgers
>
> This strange looking meercat has really sharp claws Ow! It has a dark belly with just a little hair. It's enemies are eagles and Jackals. It eat's insects. If I was a meercat I would not eat insects I would eat a hamburger. I hope you lerd a lot about the meercat. learned

Lesson at a Glance: DOES IT LOOK RIGHT?

What to Do	What to Say	What Kids Need to Know
INTRODUCE		
• Get kids thinking about noticing misspellings.	"When we read books, the words are usually spelled right. But when you read something a friend has written, can you tell which words they've spelled wrong? How do you know? Have you ever seen a misspelled word somewhere else? How did you know?"	Sometimes we notice misspelled words.
EXPLORE		
• Ask kids to look through their writing to find misspelled words. • Have them try the words two ways. • Ask them which way looks correct. • Encourage a range of answers. Some kids will say that they can't really tell, and that's fine too.	"Let's try again what we did last week with trying it two ways; get out a piece of writing, see if you can find three misspelled words, and try writing each of them another way. Then see if you can tell which spelling is right. How did you know?"	When you try a word two ways, sometimes you can pick out the right spelling. You can't learn to see if a particular word is spelled right, only to make the effort to try to see.
DISCOVER		
• Discuss the idea that some people are better than others at knowing when a word is spelled right. • Have kids talk with a partner about whether or not they can easily spot misspellings.	"There are two times when seeing if a word looks right can help you: when you're trying to spot words you spelled wrong, and when you're trying to fix them. It's easier to spot other people's misspellings, but more important to catch your own. Some people are good at being able to tell if a word is spelled right just from looking at it; others not so good. If you do a lot of reading, that helps a lot, but it also just comes easier to some people than others." "Talk with a partner about how good you think you are at spotting if a word is spelled right."	Some people are better at finding misspellings than others.
SUMMARIZE		
• Help kids summarize the ideas that were discussed and think about how to apply their knowledge to their writing.	"So what do you think we've learned or discovered today? Here's an idea to think about: if you're good at noticing if a word is spelled right or wrong, you're lucky. If it comes harder to you, it may mean you'll have to work a little harder at editing, but everyone can learn to edit their own writing."	Sometimes you can tell from just looking at a word whether it's spelled right—and sometimes you can't. If you're good at spotting misspellings, then you're lucky. If it's a little harder for you, then you'll need to try some other strategies.

DOES IT LOOK RIGHT?

Sometimes you can tell from just looking at a word whether it's spelled right—and sometimes you can't. If you're good at spotting misspellings, then you're lucky. If it's a little harder for you, then you'll need to try some other strategies.

Who, When, and Why

Materials
▶ rough drafts or informal writing

Everyone can benefit from this lesson, as long as they're beyond the early, primarily phonetic levels of spelling. It can help identify students for whom spelling is a little more difficult. It can also help destigmatize them. (If they truly can't tell if a word is misspelled or not, they can't help it.)

Background Knowledge

When you're out in public, do you notice it when a word is misspelled? I especially enjoy spotting these in New York, where there are so many people who are speakers of other languages and write the signs for their stores. But some readers may not notice these at all. It appears that humans have different capacities for noticing whether words are spelled right or not (Frith, 1980), so kids will vary in how well they'll be able to do with this lesson, but I think everyone can benefit from asking themselves to pay attention to their instincts about a word's spelling.

Spelling combines the phonetic (how can this sound be spelled) with the visual. The visual relates to patterns such as how this sound has to be spelled if it's before this particular other letter. Or is there a word related in meaning to this word that has a similar spelling? But it works pretty much on an unconscious level: this word does or doesn't look right (although the patterns mentioned here are explored elsewhere in this book). This lesson focuses more on intuition than logic.

The Lesson

1. **To get kids thinking about noticing misspellings:**

    When we read books, the words are usually spelled right. But when you read something a friend has written, can you tell which words they've spelled wrong? How do you know? Have you ever seen a misspelled word somewhere else? How did you know? *(Even if this was an intentional misspelling, like Krispy Kreme, it'll work for purposes of the discussion.)*

2. **Ask kids to look through their own writing to find words they think might be misspelled.**

    Let's try again what we did last week with trying it two ways; get out a piece of writing, see if you can find three misspelled words, and try writing each of them another way. Then see if you can tell which spelling is right. How did you know? *(Encourage a wide range of answers, for instance: I just knew; I remembered when I saw it that it has a double **m**; when I see the two spellings together, I can see that one is right and one's wrong. You might add some ideas of your own: when I saw CEASAR SALAD on a menu I remembered that restaurants get it wrong a lot. Some kids will say that they can't really tell, and that's fine too; you can't learn to see if a particular word is spelled right, only to make the effort to try to see.)*

3. **Discuss the idea that some people are better than others at knowing when a word is spelled right.**

    There are two times when seeing if a word looks right can help you: when you're trying to spot words you spelled wrong, and when you're trying to fix them. It's easier to spot other people's misspellings, but more important to catch your own. Some people are good at being able to tell if a word is spelled right just from looking at it; others not so good. If you do a lot of reading, that helps a lot, but it also just comes easier to some people than others.

    Talk with a partner about how good you think you are at spotting if a word is spelled right.

4. **Help kids summarize the ideas that were discussed.**

    So what do you think we've learned or discovered today? Here's an idea to think about: if you're good at noticing if a word is spelled right or wrong, you're lucky. If it comes harder to you, it may mean you'll have to work a little harder at editing, but everyone can learn to edit their own writing.

Next Steps

» Follow-up

Encourage the class to try paying more attention to spotting words that are misspelled in their writing, and have a follow-up discussion in a few days.

✓ Assessment

As a journal topic, suggest a question like:

> ✎ Are you good at spotting if a word is spelled right or not? And what does this mean for you as a writer?

+ Extension

To get kids used to watching for misspellings, you might consider setting up a little spot in your classroom to record misspellings that kids catch, whether they are on signs, menus, letters, pieces of writing, or any other medium. Invite kids to share any misspellings they catch, and add them to the display. And you can keep their interest up by contributing to it as well.

Lesson at a Glance: FINDING SPELLINGS IN THE CLASSROOM

What to Do	What to Say	What Kids Need to Know
INTRODUCE		
• Get kids thinking about all of the different places they could find correct spellings of words.	"We all know about dictionaries and word walls, but there are other places we can find words to see how they're spelled; let's explore some! Were you ever looking for a word and then found it someplace other than the dictionary? Let's brainstorm all the places in our classroom where you might be able to find a word that you wanted to spell."	In addition to dictionaries and word walls, we can find correct spellings in indexes, charts, books, and a number of other places.
EXPLORE		
• Demonstrate how an index and a topical vocabulary book can help find words. • Discuss the idea that some sources will have more information than others.	"Here's a book on amphibians. I'm trying to write about them, but don't remember how to spell **salamander.** Look, here it is in the index. Here's another idea: I've got this big picture book of animals. When I look for amphibians in the table of contents and turn to the correct page, here are the pictures and names of twenty amphibians." "Which of the places are going to be the easiest to find a particular word? Which ones are going to have just about any word you look for?"	You can find spellings in many places, but some places will be more useful than others.
DISCOVER		
• Have kids work in pairs to think of three words they didn't already know. Or brainstorm words as a whole class. • Have kids write their best guess spelling for each word in their spelling journal. • Ask them to try to find those words somewhere in the classroom.	"With a partner, see if you can think of three words you didn't already know how to spell. Write the three words in your spelling journal, making your best first guess for each word. Then see if you can find each of the words somewhere in the room."	Sometimes it's faster to find a word somewhere in the room. Other times it might not be.
SUMMARIZE		
• After kids have had time to search for their words, discuss what they discovered. • Introduce the term "living off the land."	"Okay, let's report back. What did you discover? Were some of the words hard to find? Were some easy? Were there any that you never found? What did you learn from doing this?" "By the way, I have a name for what we can call this. When people are lost in the woods, if they know a lot about plants they can eat the right ones to stay alive. That's called 'living off the land.' All the places we can find words in our classroom are like plants we can feed off, so it's like we're living off the land as spellers!"	If you need to know the correct spelling of a word, you can "live off the land" and find it somewhere in the room. If you know about the different places you can look, you can decide the best place to go depending on what you want to find.

FINDING SPELLINGS IN THE CLASSROOM

When you're writing or editing, you can often find the correct spelling of a word on the classroom walls, in books other than dictionaries, and elsewhere in the room—and the same goes for your home and in the wider world.

Who, When, and Why

> **Materials**
> ▶ classroom resources, such as word walls, dictionaries, content-area books, posters, and so on

Everyone can benefit from this lesson, although it's somewhat more valuable for younger children who are still having to edit a lot of words and are less proficient with the dictionary (where you can, after all, find every word) than older ones.

This lesson is likely to be especially appealing to children who are more restless and fidgety! It gives them a good purpose for getting up and stretching their legs a little. It can also be helpful for students who find dictionaries hard to use and tedious. For Spanish speakers, bilingual dictionaries and word books are very useful resources: they can look up a word in Spanish to find the spelling of its English equivalent.

Background Knowledge

Don Graves suggests that children can "live off the land" as writers by using all the resources around them (1983), and in most classrooms, words (correctly spelled) are everywhere. You can provide your own background knowledge for this lesson by thinking about where those words are in your classroom and perhaps creating a center for good word sources ("Words on Parade"?) like atlases, thesauruses, topically arranged vocabulary books, dictionaries of all levels, and books with rich indexes. The annotated bibliography gives my choices of best dictionaries. You could create and promote awareness of more spelling sources in the classroom on an ongoing basis; a particularly useful one is a running vocabulary chart for content units. This is useful not only for concept development but for spelling as students write about the subject-area content. In fact, a chart on amphibians, for instance, will help students get words like **salamander** and **tadpole** right even in the first draft.

The Lesson

1. **Get kids thinking about all of the different places they could find correct spellings of words.**

   > *If word walls are unfamiliar to you, see the next lesson.*

   We all know about dictionaries and word walls, but there are other places we can find words to see how they're spelled; let's explore some! Were you ever looking for a word and then found it someplace other than the dictionary? Let's brainstorm all the places in our classroom where you might be able to find a word that you wanted to spell. *(Make sure that the discussion ends up including the word wall, indexes, dictionaries, charts, and books in general.)*

   > *Students may come up with some idiosyncratic ideas: I've seen kids run to the light switch to see how to spell off, and spot a school bus outside the classroom window that featured a word that was both part of a team name and the name of a local mountain that the student was writing about. This Native American word, Baboquivari, certainly wouldn't have been in the dictionary, so the student's strategy was not only ingenious but indispensable.*

2. **Spend a few minutes demonstrating how an index and a topical vocabulary book can help you find words. For instance:**

   Here's a book on amphibians. I'm trying to write about them, but don't remember how to spell **salamander.** Look, here it is in the index. Here's another idea: I've got this big picture book of animals. When I look for amphibians in the table of contents and turn to the correct page, here are the pictures and names of twenty amphibians. *(Or use another appropriate book and example.)*

3. **Discuss the idea that some sources will have more information than others.**

   Which of the places are going to be the easiest to find a particular word? Which ones are going to have just about any word you look for?

4. **Have kids work in pairs to think of three words they didn't already know how to spell. Then ask them to try to find those words somewhere in the classroom.**

   With a partner, see if you can think of three words you didn't already know how to spell. *(You might want to brainstorm words as a whole class to get ideas flowing.)*

   Write the three words in your spelling journal, making your best first guess for each word. Then see if you can find each of the words somewhere in the room. *(Encourage kids to find each word in a different place. If they go right for the dictionary, you might want to suggest that they try to find the words elsewhere first.)*

5. **After kids have had time to search for their words, discuss what they discovered.**

   Okay, let's report back. What did you discover? Were some of the words hard to find? Were some easy? Were there any that you never found? What did you learn from doing this?

   By the way, I have a name for what we can call this. When people are lost in the woods, if they know a lot about plants they can eat the right ones to stay alive. That's called "living off the land." All the places we can find words in our classroom are like plants we can feed off, so it's like we're living off the land as spellers!

Spelling Strategies and Patterns

Next Steps

» **Follow-up**

A few days later:

> Have you been living off the land to find words? How's it going? Have you done it anywhere else, like at home or when you're outside somewhere?

✓ **Assessment**

As a journal topic, suggest a question like:

> What would you tell other kids about living off the land to help them spell?

Lesson at a Glance: USING A WORD WALL FOR SPELLING

What to Do	What to Say	What Kids Need to Know
INTRODUCE		
This is intended for starting a word wall. You can modify it as needed if you're working with an existing word wall. • Ask students to think of words they might want to learn to spell. If necessary, probe with examples. (See page 48, step one, for example.)	"Can you think of some words that you find yourself wanting to use in your writing but aren't sure how to spell? Maybe some friends of yours need the same words?" "Are there other words you use a lot that are maybe pretty common but you are still having trouble getting them right?"	Sometimes there are words that are pretty common, but you still have trouble spelling them.
EXPLORE		
• Begin to generate a list of words that would be useful for children to learn. List the words anywhere that's handy for now, numbering the list. • Have kids add to the list over the next couple of days. Try to get about fifty words.	"Let's start by just making a list of as many of these words as we can think of. They should not be the really hard words that you might use once in a great while, but the words that at least a few of you think you're going to be using pretty often in your writing and aren't sure how to spell." "Let's all spend some time thinking over the next couple of days, and add any good words to the list. Try to get the spelling right if you can."	Listing words you want to be able to spell correctly can help you get them right.
DISCOVER		
A couple of days later: • Read through the list together and establish how the words will be posted. * Type up the words in a big font and ask a team of a few volunteers to cut them up, arrange them in alphabetical order, and hang them up on the wall.	"Okay, now we'll create a permanent spot for these words, although the actual words will change some from week to week. Then you can use the spot as a regular resource for spelling. We could call it a word wall, or does anyone have a better idea for a name for it?" "Let's read through the list and make sure we're happy that all the words on it will be useful to at least a few of you, and see if we want to add any more. Now here's a challenge: the words are on the list in the order that we thought of them, but what would be a good way to arrange them once they're up there so that you can find one faster?"	If the words on the word wall are in alphabetical order, they will be easier to find.
SUMMARIZE		
Next day: • After the word wall has been created, discuss why it is helpful.	Let's talk about how to use our word wall. Because you know what words are up there, all you have to do now is remember to look when you go to write one of those words. Why is that better than inventing a spelling? Why is it better than looking for the word in the dictionary? There are still going to be a lot of words you have to invent or look up, but these fifty you can get right in just a few seconds."	The word wall can be faster than a dictionary and is better than inventing spellings because you know you've got the word right. But there will still be words that you'll have to find elsewhere.

USING A WORD WALL FOR SPELLING

 A word wall is a fast and accurate way to check the spelling of common classroom words.

Materials

▶ empty wall or bulletin board space, current content-area materials

Who, When, and Why

Word walls, (known from the work of Cunningham, 1995, and others) are useful for spelling two kinds of words: common words that we don't know by heart, and words that students are going to be using in their writing because they're connected to current curriculum topics or are popular in their writing for other reasons (for instance, names of local stores and malls or other places that are part of children's lives).

Older students may reach a point where the words they need vary tremendously and there isn't enough commonality among them to justify a word wall, although it could still be useful for a small number of commonly misspelled words and curriculum vocabulary that they might use in writing.

Background Knowledge

An important part of learning to spell is seeing words in print and picking up their spellings not through formal memorizing but unintentionally through visual memory. Obviously not all words can be visible in the classroom at all times, but a small collection in the form of a word wall is useful for two reasons: if the kids know that particular words are up there, they'll be able to get them right in the first draft without much effort, and they get to see the spellings of the words regularly. This increases the chance that they'll retain them.

The biggest problem I've seen with word walls over the years is that many of them are dead; words that kids already know stay up there forever, new words may not be added, and the word wall fades into the mental background, taking up space but not being attended to or used. Therefore it's crucial to use a format where words can come and go, such as sticky notes or an erasable board. Before you teach the lesson, think about what format might work well in your classroom. For instance, you could print the words out in a large font, in bold type, and stick them up with a reusable adhesive, or with thumbtacks on a bulletin board, so they can easily be moved around.

The Lesson

1. This is intended for starting a word wall. You can modify it as needed if you're working with an existing word wall.

    Can you think of some words that you find yourself wanting to use in your writing but aren't sure how to spell? Maybe some friends of yours need the same words? *(If necessary, probe with examples.)* Do any of you ever write about Nickelodeon or skatboarding, but don't really know how to spell it, or words related to it? We're learning this week about Afghanistan; are there words you find yourself wanting to use when you write about that topic that you aren't sure how to spell? Are there other words you use a lot that are maybe pretty common but you are still having trouble getting them right?

2. Begin to generate a list of words that would be useful to learn.

    Let's start by just making a list of as many of these words as we can think of. They should not be the really hard words that you might use once in a great while, but the words that at least a few of you think you're going to be using pretty often in your writing and aren't sure how to spell. *(List the words anywhere that's handy for now, numbering the list.)* Let's all spend some time thinking over the next couple of days, and any time you think of a good word for the list, come up and add it. Try to get the spelling right if you can when you add it to the list. Let's try to get a list of about fifty words.

3. A couple of days later:

    Okay, we've got about fifty words. What we're going to do next is create a permanent spot for these words, although the actual words will change some from week to week. Then you can use the spot as a regular resource for spelling. We could call it a word wall, or does anyone have a better idea for a name for it?

4. Read through the list together and establish how the words will be posted.

    Let's read through the list and make sure we're happy that all the words on it will be useful to at least a few of you, and see if we want to add any more. Now here's a challenge: the words are on the list in the order that we thought of them, but what would be a good way to arrange them once they're up there so that you can find one faster? *(alphabetical order)* I'm going to type them up tonight *(or ask for typing volunteers)* in a big font, and I'd like a team of a few volunteers to cut them up, arrange them in alphabetical order, and hang them up on the wall over there.

5. Next day:

Okay, we've got our word wall. Let's talk about how to use it. The thing that helps is that you sort of know what words are up there, since we've read through the list. All you have to do now is remember to look when you go to write one of those words. Why is that better than inventing a spelling? *(Because you get it right and it's fast.)* Why is it better than looking for the word in the dictionary? *(It's much faster.)* There are still going to be a lot of words you have to invent or look up, but these fifty you can get right in just a few seconds.

Next Steps

» Follow-up

It's crucial to have regular follow-up to keep the word wall alive. I'd take a few minutes every week or so to ask what words the class feels they don't really need anymore, and what words they'd like to add. You could have a sheet of paper in a corner of the word wall where kids (or you) can write new candidates as they think of them, and then decide as a group which ones to type up and add. I'd recommend keeping it at about fifty words so that it stays simple to find the words kids are looking for. I'd also have a discussion about the word wall a week or two after you begin it to see how it's going.

✓ Assessment

As a journal topic, suggest a question like:

 Will a word wall be something you'd like to have around for the rest of your life, or will a day come when you don't need one? Share some thoughts about this.

Lesson at a Glance: HELPING EACH OTHER WITH SPELLING

What to Do	What to Say	What Kids Need to Know
INTRODUCE		
• Get kids thinking about resources that are outside the head. • If necessary, lead them to thinking about other people as resources.	"We've talked before about using what's inside your head and what's outside your head to help you spell words. Let's list again some resources you can use that are outside your head."	Sometimes what's outside your head can be another person.
EXPLORE		
• Discuss the difference between asking an adult and asking a classmate about correct spellings.	"What's the difference between asking an adult how to spell a word and asking another kid? If you ask me how to spell a word, I'll almost always help you figure it out rather than just tell you, because I want you to think about the spelling for yourself. If you asked a friend how to spell a word, if he knows it he might tell you. But could he still help if he didn't know how? Sure, he could share his ideas about it. What would you do then?"	If you ask an adult she probably knows; the other kid might not. If the kid doesn't know for sure, you could figure out for yourself if it makes sense, or try his idea and see if it looks right.
DISCOVER		
• Ask kids to try the strategy the next time they write. • Discuss ways you can help if a friend asks you.	"I'd like you to try an experiment in writer's workshop today. Every time you get stuck on a word, use 'check with a friend' as your first strategy." "Now, if you're the one being asked, what are some ways you can help?"	If you are asked to help someone, you can look at his spelling and see how it looks; try writing it yourself and see what you come up with; suggest changing a specific letter or two; if you know it, just tell him.
SUMMARIZE		
• Help kids develop strategies to use after they've asked a friend.	"If you're the one who asked for help, what should you do next?"	If you received help from a friend, you can see if his version looks better than yours; you might just realize she's right; consult with another friend or the dictionary if you're still not sure.

HELPING EACH OTHER WITH SPELLING

 One of the strategies that can help you spell a word is consulting with a friend; this is both a favor we do for each other and a tool for helping us think more about spelling.

Who, When, and Why

This lesson is appropriate for everyone. Everyone can contribute what they know about spelling, even if they don't know the exact spelling of a word. Kids will notice that some of their classmates are more likely than others to know the correct spellings of words, but it's important to emphasize that this isn't about having an authority who'll do the spelling for you; it's about having a consultation with someone who can help you think about the spelling.

Background Knowledge

Even as adults, if we don't know how to spell a word, and there's someone else in the room, we're likely to ask that person for help. Kids can and should do this too. But the downside is that you don't know if your friend knows the correct spelling either—especially true for kids—so it's more a collaboration than a check with an expert.

Learning often works well when it takes place in the learner's zone of proximal development (Vygotsky, 1978), which is simply the next step beyond where she is already. Children are well-suited to connect with each other's zones of proximal development since they're so close to each other in knowledge. We aren't looking to identify kids who are good spellers who then become walking dictionaries for everyone else; instead, we're helping students learn how to work together to figure out how a word is spelled.

The Lesson

1. **Get kids thinking about resources that are outside the head.**

   We've talked before about using what's inside your head and what's outside your head to help you spell words. Let's list again some resources you can use that are outside your head. *(If students don't suggest classmates, you can say the following:)* Sometimes what's outside your head can be another person.

2. **Discuss the difference between asking an adult and asking a classmate about correct spellings.**

   What's the difference between asking an adult how to spell a word and asking another kid? *(The adult probably knows; the other kid might not.)* If you ask me how to spell a word, I'll almost always help you figure it out rather than just tell you, because I want you to think about the spelling for yourself. If you asked a friend how to spell a word, if he knows it he might tell you. But could he still help if he didn't know how? Sure, he could share his ideas about it. What would you do then? *(Expect answers such as figure out for yourself if it makes sense, try his idea and see if it looks right.)*

3. **Ask kids to try the strategy the next time they write.**

   I'd like you to try an experiment in writer's workshop today. Every time you get stuck on a word, use "check with a friend" as your first strategy. Now, if you're the one being asked, what are some ways you can help? *(Encourage and develop answers such as look at her spelling and see how it looks; try writing it yourself and see what you come up with; suggest changing a specific letter or two; if you know it, just tell her.)*

4. **Help kids develop strategies to use after they've asked a friend.**

   If you're the one who asked for help, what should you do next? *(Encourage answers such as see if his version looks better than yours; you might just realize she's right; consult with another friend or the dictionary if you're still not sure.)*

» Follow-up

After writer's workshop that day:

> How did it go? Is this a strategy that you'll use again? When would you be most likely to use this strategy? *(When you're pretty stuck; when someone's right there handy.)* When someone asked you for help with a spelling, how do you think you did?

✓ Assessment

Watch to see how students use this strategy. It should definitely be used in moderation, so if some students become overly reliant on asking those around them, talk about how this is one of many strategies that can be used and you don't always have someone else around.

As a journal topic, suggest a question like:

> Did you like helping each other this way? What's good about it? Is there anything you don't like about it?

Lesson at a Glance: HOW TO USE A SPELL-CHECKER

What to Do	What to Say	What Kids Need to Know
EXPLORE		
• Hand out copies of page 271. • Have students pick three words that they don't already know how to spell and record the words on the chart. • Have pairs take turns looking up words on the spell-checker. • Ask them to record what they find on their charts.	"Start by picking three words that you aren't sure about the spelling of; you can either find them in a piece of your writing, or do your best invented spelling of a word you have in mind." "Take turns typing words into the spell-checker. You're likely to have one of four results: 1) The most likely is that it'll give you a list of words that your spelling might be. 2) It might tell you that you've already spelled the word right. 3) It might give you just one word. 4) It might be unable to find any words at all that work."	There are a variety of things that can happen when you enter a word in a spell-checker.
DISCOVER		
• After kids have finished looking up words, discuss what they found.	"For each of your three words, check which of these happened. If the spell-checker gives you a list, write a few of the words and see if you can tell which one you want." "Let's talk about what you found out. When was it helpful? When was it hard? Do you think using the spell-checker could be useful in helping you edit your writing? Did any of you get a big long list for any of your spellings? What's a good strategy if that happens?"	If you get a long list, you could see if you recognize any of them, or can narrow it down to a couple. If so, use the "say" button if you have one, or check elsewhere, like in the dictionary.
SUMMARIZE		
• Have kids enter LAUHG, LAF, RINOSERUS, and HERE on their spell-checkers so they can see the range of possible results. (See page 57, step 4, for sample results.) • Point out that spell-checkers won't help you catch the right spelling of the wrong word.	"There are some spellings I'd like you to try now so we can talk about the times the spell-checker would be really useful and times it wouldn't: LAUHG, LAF, RINOSERUS, and HERE." "What did you find out?" "Now I bet you wondered why I even asked you to check **here,** because it's already right. But if you were trying to write 'I hear you when you're talking,' it would have been wrong! It's the right spelling of the wrong word. The spell-checker won't catch those."	The spell-checker can't always help you find the right spelling, but sometimes it is really helpful.

HOW TO USE A SPELL-CHECKER

A spell-checker can help you if (1) you can get close enough to the right spelling that it knows what word you have in mind and (2) you can recognize the right spelling when you see it.

Who, When, and Why

Materials
► handheld spell-checkers
► copies of page 271

I once worked with a seventh grader who was an adequate reader and writer but a weak speller. His parents had bought him a spell-checker, and it was significantly more efficient for him than even a third-grade dictionary in correcting misspelled words. He corrected his spelling SATERN in a few seconds on the spell-checker after it took him a few minutes to find it in the elementary-school dictionary. He'd been unable to find it at all in the middle-school dictionary from his classroom.

Spell-checkers, even those marketed for elementary schools, don't do well at recognizing the invented spellings of younger children. Therefore, this lesson is most useful for students whose spellings are often within a letter or two of the correct one.

As long as their spelling developmental level is advanced enough for the spell-checker to decipher their attempts, this can be a very valuable strategy for students for whom spelling is more challenging. (They also need to read well enough to pick out the right spelling from the list provided.)

Background Knowledge

One of the questions I used to get asked all the time is "Do spell-checkers mean we don't need to teach spelling anymore?" (These days the question is "Has instant messaging wrecked spelling ability?") I think, though, that nobody now believes that spell-checkers are our salvation, since we still see misspellings from students and everyone else (although if the writer has spellchecked, it may be the right spelling of the wrong word, rather than the original, more creative spelling). But neither are spell-checkers worthless nor a device that makes writers lazy. With proper instruction, they can be a valuable part of the writer's toolkit.

The term **spell-checker** is typically used for two kinds of computer-driven devices: those that are part of a word-processing program, like Microsoft Word, and those that are handheld mini-computers, typically made by the Franklin company. The main difference between the two kinds is that a writer types a word into the handheld devices, while the spell-checkers embedded in word processing programs can highlight suspicious words in an existing document. Otherwise, both work by comparing words in their databanks to the spellings provided, finding matches when the writers' spelling is either close to the correct one or a phonetic rendition of the word. For example, in the program I'm using as I write this (WordPerfect 5.1 for DOS; I know, I'm a dinosaur!), I can get the spell-checker to produce **laugh** (along with other possibilities) by typing in either LAF, LAUG, or LAUPH (though not LAUHG). Then, except in the case of very close approximations to longer words (like PLANATARIUM for **planetarium**), it'll usually come up with a list of possible intended words.

Some of the high-end handheld spell-checkers have a feature that allows you to hear the word pronounced correctly if you aren't sure which of the words it provides is the right one. I recommend them for classroom use since they solve one of the problems young users often have with spell-checkers. Plus they're useful for reading as well; no need for phonics if you have a little computer to say the word for you.

I'm going to focus the lesson on the use of handheld spell-checkers, since students still write by hand most of the time. However, word processing programs include the option of typing in a single word for spellchecking, and this lesson can easily be adapted to spellchecking an entire piece of writing by having the computer flag the words for you. The lesson is best done with partners sharing a single spell-checker between them; if you don't have enough, you can either work with a few sets of partners in a small group or have four or so students use a single spell-checker.

The Lesson

1. Hand out a copy of page 271 to each child. To help students familiarize themselves with spell-checkers, have them pick three words that they don't already know how to spell and record the words on the chart.

    Start by picking three words that you aren't sure about the spelling of; you can either find them in a piece of your writing or do your best invented spelling of a word you have in mind.

2. Have pairs take turns looking up words on the spell-checker.

    Working with your partner, take turns typing words into the spell-checker and hitting "enter." You're likely to have one of four results:

    1) The most likely is that it'll give you a list of words that your spelling might be.

    2) It might tell you that you've already spelled the word right.

    3) It might give you just one word.

    4) It might be unable to find any words at all that work.

    For each of your three words, note on your chart which one of these happened. If it gives you a list, write down at least a few of the words and see if you can tell which one is the word you were looking for.

3. After kids have finished looking up words, discuss what they discovered.

    Let's talk about what you found out. When was it helpful? When was it hard? Do you think using the spell-checker could be useful in helping you edit your writing? Did any of you get a big long list for any of your spellings? What's a good strategy if that happens? (*See if you recognize any of them, or can narrow it down to a couple. If so, use the "say" button if you have one, or check elsewhere, like in the dictionary.*)

Note: Check on the spell-checkers you're using to see if the results are the same as I got; if not, pick different words.

4. Have kids enter LAUHG, LAF, RINOSERUS, and HERE on their spell-checkers so they can see the range of possible results.

There are some spellings I'd like you to try now so we can talk about the times the spell-checker would be really useful and times it wouldn't: LAUHG, LAF, RINOSERUS, and HERE.

What did you find out? LAUHG might be the spelling that someone would try for **laugh** if they knew what letters were in it but weren't sure of what order they were in. But the spell-checker didn't come up with anything; that just happens sometimes if you don't have the right spelling. But if you type in LAF, which is the way the word sounds, it'll come up with the right spelling. With RINOSERUS, even though I had a bunch of letters wrong, it found the word **rhinoceros** okay, so you don't always have to be super-close. Now I bet you wondered why I even asked you to check **here,** because it's already right. But if you were trying to write "I hear you when you're talking," it would have been wrong! It's the right spelling of the wrong word. The spell-checker won't catch those.

Next Steps

Follow-up

Two ideas for follow-up lessons:

1. What to do when the spell-checker comes up with a long list and none of them looks right (this is a good point for kids to ask the teacher for help).

2. How to use the asterisk (*) or question mark as wildcards in a possible spelling; the question mark substitutes for a single letter and the asterisk for one or more; so that you can type in PR?NOUNCE if it's just the first vowel letter that you're unsure of. However, this trick is of limited usefulness since all the other letters have to be correct; I tried to see if RIN*S*R*S would give me **rhinoceros**, but got only **ringmasters.**

Assessment

Encourage kids to try a spell-checker as one of their first strategies for the next few days and see how they do. Have a follow-up discussion if benefits or new problems emerge.

As a journal topic, suggest a question like:

What are your thoughts about using a spell-checker while you write? Do you think it will be helpful or not? Would you use one when you grow up? Why or why not?

Lesson at a Glance: SPELLING BETTER AS YOU GET OLDER

What to Do	What to Say	What Kids Need to Know
INTRODUCE		
• Get kids thinking about the idea of getting better at things over time.	"Can you think of something you do better now than you did in kindergarten? What's good about that? Here's a question: do you spell better than you did in kindergarten?"	As you get older and get more practice, you can improve at things.
EXPLORE		
• Discuss the number of words that kids can spell, and how that changes over time. • Talk about what it means to be mature.	"How many words do you think you know how to spell right now? How many words do you think I know how to spell? Someday you're going to know how to spell this many words too. How do you think you'll get there?" "When you're writing, some words you get right and some you get wrong. What's the difference between them?" "Here's a question: do you get some words right now that you got wrong in kindergarten or first grade? Why is that? Are there some words you get wrong now that you'll get right five years from now? You know what? Spelling more words right is part of being more mature, just like moving from a tricycle to a bicycle to driving a car."	Over time, you can pick up a lot of words through reading, learn how to edit better, work on the words that give you trouble, and so on.
DISCOVER		
• Talk about how kids can take a more mature approach to spelling.	"What could you do right now to be a little more mature as a speller? How about paying a little more attention to spelling, trying a little harder to get the words right if you can in your first draft, being a little more careful with editing? Wouldn't it be fun if a stranger looked at your writing and said, 'Gee, I'm surprised this is a third grader. She spells like a fifth grader!' This doesn't mean you have to stop inventing spellings when you don't know a word, but older kids and grown-ups often try to get spellings right even in the first draft if they can."	If you take a little more mature approach to spelling, it can help you improve.

SPELLING BETTER AS YOU GET OLDER

 Learning to spell is something that you get better at over time, and getting better at it and taking responsibility for it are a part—even though a small part—of growing up and becoming more mature.

Who, When, and Why

Materials
▶ none

This is a fairly brief lesson that focuses primarily on students' understanding of the role of spelling and their attitudes toward it. It's appropriate for students who are ready to take on more responsibility for spelling words correctly in their writing, particularly final drafts. That is, they know a lot of common words and are perhaps missing some words they could be getting right with just a little extra effort. This is also a good lesson for kids who don't have much ownership of the idea of correct spelling and feel it's something they're doing just for the teacher.

It's important not to stigmatize children that spelling is harder for. This isn't about spelling as well as your friend does; it's about taking a more sophisticated attitude to spelling that acknowledges how you'll change over time and how you can support your own growth.

Background Knowledge

I'm often asked when children should make the transition from invented spelling to correct spelling, but it's not a one-shot deal; it's a gradual process. The process involves knowing more words, having multiple strategies for spelling words, knowing how to edit for spelling, and (the topic of this lesson) trying to get the words right when you can. Sometimes when students have been using invented spelling from the beginning, they aren't even aware that it's a good idea to get the words right when you can. (Hey, if you can read it, what's the problem?) One of our responsibilities is to develop their sophistication about spelling and move them toward a more adult view of it.

The Lesson

1. **Get kids thinking about the idea of getting better at things over time.**

   Can you think of something you do better now than you did in kindergarten? *(Possible examples: ride a bike, swim, read.)* What's good about that? *(The answer is obvious— you get more out of anything that you do better—but give kids time to explore it.)* Here's a question: do you spell better than you did in kindergarten? *(Again, the answer is obvious, but allow some time for discussion.)*

2. **Discuss the number of words that kids can spell and how that changes over time.**

   How many words do you think you know how to spell right now? *(A reasonable answer in elementary school is in the hundreds.)* How many words do you think I know how to spell? *(For literate adults, it's tens of thousands.)* Someday you're going to know how to spell this many words too. How do you think you'll get there? *(In this discussion, build on students' responses to bring out the ideas that they'll pick up a lot of words through reading, they'll learn how to edit better, they'll work on the words that give them trouble, and any other relevant responses.)*

   When you're writing, some words you get right and some you get wrong. What's the difference between them? *(Responses are likely to include some words I just know; some are too hard; some I almost get right but forget part of it.)* Here's a question: do you get some words right now that you got wrong in kindergarten or first grade? Why is that? Are there some words you get wrong now that you'll get right five years from now? You know what? Spelling more words right is part of being more mature *(define if necessary)*, just like moving from a tricycle to a bicycle to driving a car.

3. **Talk about how kids can take a more mature approach to spelling.**

   What could you do right now to be a little more mature as a speller? How about paying a little more attention to spelling, trying a little harder to get the words right if you can in your first draft, being a little more careful with editing? Wouldn't it be fun if a stranger looked at your writing and said, "Gee, I'm surprised this is a third grader. She spells like a fifth grader!" This doesn't mean you have to stop inventing spellings when you don't know a word, but older kids and grown-ups often try to get spellings right even in the first draft if they can.

Next Steps

>> Follow-up

This would also be a good topic to encourage kids to reflect on in small groups. It could be part of a broader discussion about growing up and maturity: what it's all about, how it happens.

✓ Assessment

As a journal topic, suggest a question like:

📓 What do you think about being more mature as a speller? How can you be a more mature speller?

Lesson at a Glance: USING DIFFERENT KINDS OF DICTIONARIES

What to Do	What to Say	What Kids Need to Know
INTRODUCE		
• Ideally, for this part of the lesson pairs of children will each have three to four different dictionaries: one designed for their grade level; one or two easier ones (preferably including a picture dictionary, at least through fourth grade or so); and one or two harder ones (including a high-school or adult one for upper grades).	"I'd like to see if you can find the same word in all three dictionaries. Either pick a word with a partner, or you can use one of my words: **umbrella** or **vegetable**. It's okay if it's a word you already know how to spell. I'll ask you to report back on how quickly you found it in each dictionary (if you like, one partner can be the timer while the other ones looks) and how much information it gave you about the word."	Different dictionaries include different kinds of information.
EXPLORE		
• After kids have had a chance to search, discuss what they've discovered.	"What did you find out? There are trade-offs, aren't there? You could find **umbrella** in the picture dictionary very quickly, but it didn't teach you anything new since it just gave a simple definition. It took longer to find it in the bigger dictionaries, but (if you were able to find the word at all), they gave you more information. Did anyone learn something new from a definition, or learn about where a word comes from?"	Some dictionaries are better than others, depending on what you are looking for.
DISCOVER		
• Talk about how to know which dictionary to use at any given time. • Write the words **surround** or **diplodocus** on the board (or other suitable words) and have kids locate them in the dictionary.	"What's some advice you might give to another kid about how to decide which dictionary to use to look up a word? But here's one more thing to think about. Look for one of these words: **surround** and **diplodocus.** What did you find out?"	For spelling purposes, it might be helpful to use the easy dictionary, unless you want to find out more about the word.

USING DIFFERENT KINDS OF DICTIONARIES

 Different dictionaries are good for looking up different kinds of words. Bigger ones have more words, but it takes longer to find them. Simpler ones don't have as many words, but you can find them fast. It's useful to know which words you're likely to be able to find in the easier dictionaries.

Who, When, and Why

Materials
▶ a variety of dictionaries

I'd use this lesson at every age, with changes in how sophisticated the lesson is and how far you can take it.

For younger students: include some exploration of topically arranged word books, where words are arranged not in alphabetical order but by categories, such as a double-page spread of captioned pictures of foods or zoo animals. These are, of course, especially useful as spelling resources if you're writing about a topic that's illustrated in the word book.

For older students: invite them to explore an adult dictionary to see all the ancillary material that's included: *Webster's Collegiate* includes sections on the history of English, the sounds of English and how they're spelled, and so on. It would also be valuable to explore some features that go beyond spelling but are interesting in their own right, such as how to read the etymology information.

Background Knowledge

Dictionaries are obviously useful for a lot of purposes, but they can be a little challenging as a tool for finding the spelling of a word since your best guess at the spelling may lead you to the wrong place, plus there are just so many darn words! This is, of course, the reason for children's dictionaries, with their greatly reduced word counts. When looking for common, concrete words, a dictionary marketed to younger children can end up being an efficient choice.

If your classroom is typical, you're likely to have a set of twenty or more identical dictionaries; publishers typically develop them to suit a few major levels of markets: primary, elementary, middle school, high school, and adult. (The high-school versions are usually very close to the adult ones, but with the vulgar words omitted!) What I would strongly recommend is working to build a classroom dictionary library with several dictionaries designed for your grade level, but also a few each of easier ones, harder ones, and specialized ones. You can also include word books that are different in format from dictionaries. Maybe you can start by trading some of the ones for your grade level with teachers from higher and lower grades (see page 318 for an annotated bibliography of recommended dictionaries). Recalling the previous lesson, I'd also recommend half a dozen handheld spell-checkers, especially for grades three and up.

The Lesson

Note: before you begin the lesson, you may want to check your classroom dictionaries to see if they include your sample words.

1. Ideally, for this part of the lesson pairs of children will each have three to four different dictionaries: one designed for their grade level; one or two easier ones (preferably including a picture dictionary, at least through fourth grade or so); and one or two harder ones (including a high-school or adult one for upper grades). If you don't have this many available, work with small groups rather than pairs or make other adaptations.

   I'd like to see if you can find the same word in all three dictionaries. Either pick a word with a partner, or you can use one of my words: **umbrella** or **vegetable.** It's okay if it's a word you already know how to spell. I'll ask you to report back on how quickly you found it in each dictionary (if you like, one partner can be the timer while the other one looks) and how much information it gave you about the word. *(If you want to take the time, encourage the students to look up a few words, including some they don't know how to spell. Don't worry at this point if their search strategies are weak; this will be covered in future lessons.)*

2. After kids have had a chance to search, discuss what they've discovered.

   What did you find out? There are trade-offs, aren't there? You could find **umbrella** in the picture dictionary very quickly, but it didn't teach you anything new since it just gave a simple definition. It took longer to find it in the bigger dictionaries, but (if you were able to find the word at all), they gave you more information. Did anyone learn something new from a definition, or learn about where a word comes from?

3. Talk about how to know which dictionary to use at any given time.

   What's some advice you might give to another kid about how to decide which dictionary to use to look up a word? *(Use the easy dictionary, unless you don't think the word will be in there, or you want to find out more about the word.)* But here's one more thing to think about. Look for one of these words *(write them on the board to make them easier to find)*: **surround** *(or pick another word that's not in the picture dictionary)*, **diplodocus** *(or pick another word that's not in the elementary school dictionary)*. What did you find out? *(The easier dictionaries don't have as many words—that's why they're easier—so they might not help if you're looking for a harder word.)*

surround

diplodocus

Next Steps

» Follow-up

Students might enjoy spending time over the next few days browsing through different dictionaries to get a sense of how they're set up, what they're like, how they use pictures, and so on. (This could also be done before conducting this lesson, as an exploratory introduction to dictionaries in general.)

✓ Assessment

As a journal topic, suggest a question like:

What do you think about dictionaries and when would you use different ones?

Lesson at a Glance: ALPHABETICAL ORDER IN THE DICTIONARY: FIRST LETTERS

What to Do	What to Say	What Kids Need to Know
EXPLORE		
• Have kids work in pairs to quickly locate the word **potato** in the dictionary. (Or students can pick their own word to look for.) • Invite students to share how they located the words.	"Get a partner, get a dictionary, and see how quickly you can find the word **potato.** Raise your hand when you've found it." "Let's talk about how you went about finding your word. What's the first thing you did to try to get to the right part of the dictionary?"	Children may say they looked until they spotted the **p** words, thought about or looked at the alphabet, or "just knew" where they'd be.
DISCOVER		
• Help students develop a strategy for getting to the right part of the dictionary. • Give pairs an opportunity to try locating a few more words. Have them begin by planning what course of action they will take.	"Let's talk about developing a good strategy for getting to the right part of the dictionary quickly. If you were looking for **apple,** roughly where would it be in the dictionary? What about **zebra?** What about **monkey?**" "Let's see how fast you can get with this. I'll call out some words, and see how quickly you can get to the first letter in the dictionary. Partners can take turns doing the looking. But before we start, let's talk about how you'll do it. If I say the letter **h,** do you have a good sense in your head of where it comes in the alphabet? If not, what's a good way to remember or figure out quickly? Would it be useful for each of you to write the alphabet on a piece of paper before we start, so you can take a quick look to remember about where each letter comes in alphabetical order? Okay, let's go. Raise your hand when you've gotten to the right first letter."	If the word starts with a letter near the beginning of the alphabet, you can look for it near the beginning of the dictionary, and so on.
SUMMARIZE		
• Invite students to summarize how it went and ask them how they'll apply what they've learned.	"So how did that go? What have you learned today that'll help you the next time?"	When looking up a word in the dictionary, thinking about where the first letter of the word comes in the alphabet can help you find it more quickly in the dictionary.

ALPHABETICAL ORDER IN THE DICTIONARY: FIRST LETTERS

 The words in dictionaries are in alphabetical order. You'll have an easier time finding a word if you can get quickly to the right first letter.

Who, When, and Why

Materials
▶ dictionaries

Here's a very simple pre-assessment: ask students to pick a word to try to find in the dictionary, and watch to see how quickly they get to the section of words beginning with the right first letter and whether they seem to have a strategy for doing so. Anything less than a very efficient process suggests that this lesson would probably be useful.

Some students will already be pretty good at this and older ones may not need the lesson at all. But if your students don't already have this strategy, the lesson will be helpful for them, since it's a simple principle to follow.

Background Knowledge

I was once asked by a teacher to carry out a lesson with third graders about using guide words in the dictionary. I started by asking them to work with a partner to find a word, and discovered that easily half the class had trouble getting to the right first letter in the dictionary, many of them looking up at the alphabet chart over the blackboard to see where a particular letter fell in the alphabet. I realized that they weren't ready to learn about using guide words yet, and I proceeded instead with the lesson that follows.

Pretty simple: the words in dictionaries are in alphabetical order, and getting to the right first letter quickly will really speed up the whole process. By the way, a dictionary with a thumb index (that is, a small labeled indentation on the page where words with a particular letter begin) can make a tremendous difference for kids. Since this adds expense, children's dictionaries don't typically have them, but it would be a valuable feature to look for if you're buying a single adult dictionary for your classroom.

The Lesson

1. **Have kids work in pairs to quickly locate a word in the dictionary.**

   👥 Get a partner, get a dictionary, and see how quickly you can find the word **potato.** *(Alternatively, students can pick their own word to look for.)* Raise your hand when you've found it.

2. **Invite students to share how they located the words.**

   Let's talk about how you went about finding your word. What's the first thing you did to try to get to the right part of the dictionary? *(Children's answers will of course reveal how efficient and informed their strategies are, and are likely to vary across the class. They may say they looked until they spotted the p words, thought about or looked at the alphabet, or "just knew" where they'd be.)*

3. **Help students develop a strategy for getting to the right part of the dictionary.**

   Let's talk about developing a good strategy for getting to the right part of the dictionary quickly. If you were looking for **apple,** roughly where would it be in the dictionary? *(It should be pretty obvious that it would be near the beginning.)* What about **zebra?** *(It should be obvious that it would be near the end.)* What about **monkey?** *(Since m's in the middle of the alphabet, an **m** word would be pretty much in the middle of the dictionary.)*

4. **Give pairs an opportunity to try locating a few more words.**

   👥 Let's see how fast you can get with this. I'll call out some words, and see how quickly you can get to the first letter in the dictionary. Partners can take turns doing the looking. But before we start, let's talk about how you'll do it. If I say the letter **h,** do you have a good sense in your head of where it comes in the alphabet? If not, what's a good way to remember or figure out quickly? Would it be useful for each of you to write the alphabet on a piece of paper before we start, so you can take a quick look to remember about where each letter comes in alphabetical order? *(This may seem babyish, but if kids truly don't realize automatically, as adults do, that h is about a quarter of the way into the alphabet, they'll be unnecessarily slowed down in trying to find **h** words. Also, it's easier to use a piece of paper, which will be right at hand, than an alphabet chart high on the wall.)* Okay, let's go. Raise your hand when you've gotten to the right first letter. *(See Sample Words for suggestions.)*

5. **Invite students to summarize how it went and ask them how they'll apply what they've learned.**

   So how did that go? What have you learned today that'll help you the next time?

Spelling Strategies and Patterns

Next Steps

» Follow-up

Suggest that students try turning to the dictionary more frequently.

> Over the next week or so, you might want to try using the dictionary a little more than you usually do, either when you're editing or when you come across words you don't know when you're reading.

✓ Assessment

As a journal topic, suggest a question like:

📓 What do you now know about finding words faster?

Sample Words

Words that are located roughly in the...

first part of the dictionary	middle of the dictionary	last part of the dictionary
flavor	queen	slipper
cone	jail	volcano
hotel	playful	zero
dozen	lime	tiger
bacon	nine	yellow
angry	octopus	umbrella
eyelash	moose	rise
glow	kangaroo	wash

Lesson at a Glance: ALPHABETICAL ORDER IN THE DICTIONARY: SECOND LETTERS

What to Do	What to Say	What Kids Need to Know
EXPLORE		
• Prepare and distribute copies of page 272 as shown on page 72 to pairs of kids. • Distribute a dictionary to each pair. • Have pairs find each word on the list and check it off.	"Work with a partner to find each word on this list in the dictionary, as fast as you can. Make sure you've found the right one. Then check off each one as you find it, and move on to the next one. Today it's all about speed, so don't stop to read the definitions."	There are lots of words in the dictionary that begin with the same letter.
DISCOVER		
• Discuss how the word search went. • Invite students to share any strategies they used to locate words. • Lead them to understand that they can look to the second letter to find the word faster.	"So how did it go? And why do you think I had you do this? You probably noticed that the words all started with **s,** so you were able to stay within one section of the dictionary. What strategies did you use to find words faster within that section?" "If a word starts with **a,** it's going to be near the beginning of the dictionary. So if a word starts with **sa,** where could you find it?"	You can use the second letter of a word to help you locate it faster.
SUMMARIZE		
• Have students summarize what strategies they can use to find words in the dictionary.	"So if you're looking up a word in the dictionary, what's a good way to do it?"	You can look at the first letter to get close, and then you can get closer by thinking about whether the second letter will be at the beginning, middle, or end of that section.

ALPHABETICAL ORDER IN THE DICTIONARY: SECOND LETTERS

 Using the second letter of a word can help you find it more quickly in a dictionary.

Who, When, and Why

Materials
▶ page 272
▶ dictionaries
▶ stopwatches

This lesson is the first step in working with kids who can get to the **s** words okay but then will start at the beginning of the section and read every word until they find the one they're looking for (or pass right over it because their eyes have started to glaze over). It's also appropriate for any students who haven't realized in an operational sense that the **sa** words will be toward the beginning of the **s** section, the **sm** words will be in the middle, and so on. Asking kids to look for a word and watching what they do is the easiest way to get a sense of this.

This will benefit all students, but will come more easily to some than others, so don't have them compete against each other to see who can find words fastest. It's fine, however, for them to use a stopwatch to monitor their own (hopefully increasing) efficiency at finding words. Finding words quickly in the dictionary is probably one of the few aspects of spelling for which practice can directly improve ability, since every time they hunt for words they're getting more familiar with the dictionary and its layout.

Background Knowledge

As adults, we aren't even conscious of using this principle most of the time, but students often need some instruction on it.

1. Prepare copies of page 272 as shown below and ask pairs of students to locate each word on the list in the dictionary:

   👥 Work with a partner to find each word on this list in the dictionary, as fast as you can. Make sure you've found the right one. Then check off each one as you find it, and move on to the next one. Today it's all about speed, so don't stop to read the definitions.

BLANK CHECKLIST

Checklist for ___S Words___

- ☐ smith
- ☐ synonym
- ☐ salad
- ☐ shoot
- ☐ stegosaurus
- ☐ snob
- ☐ slipper
- ☐ spoon

270   Strategy 18   © 2008 by Sandra Wilde from *Spelling Strategies and Patterns* Portsmouth, NH: Heinemann. This page may be photocopied for classroom use only.

2. After students have finished:

   So how did it go? And why do you think I had you do this? You probably noticed that the words all started with **s,** so you were able to stay within one section of the dictionary. What strategies did you use to find words faster within that section?

   Lead students to understand:

   If a word starts with **a,** it's going to be near the beginning of the dictionary. So if a word starts with **sa,** where could you find it? *(Near the beginning of the s words.)* Would any of you like to talk about this or any other strategies that you used?

3. Invite students to summarize what strategies they can use to find words in the dictionary.

   So if you're looking up a word in the dictionary, what's a good way to do it? *(Students should mention that they begin by looking at the first letter, and then pay attention to the second letter. They can hone in on the word by thinking about whether the second letter will be at the beginning, middle, or end of that section.)*

Spelling Strategies and Patterns

Next Steps

Follow-up

If students need more practice:

> If you'd like to spend time getting better at this, I'll make up some more lists of words like the one we did today and when you have a few free minutes you can do a speed-hunt for them by yourself or with a partner. Or you can make up your own lists, by yourself or with a partner. *(See Sample Lists. On another copy of page 272, students can record additional words to locate.)* This is something you can probably get faster at with practice. Borrow my stopwatch if you like! You can even record your times next to each word to see if you are getting faster.

Assessment

As a journal topic, suggest a question like:

> What strategies can you use to find words in the dictionary?

Sample Lists

B	P	T
blacksmith	purchase	temper
biscuit	peculiar	trap
backward	philosopher	thirsty
beggar	pajamas	toss
bureau	prey	tank
bone	pierce	tune
by	plantation	twice
breakfast	poison	tight

Lesson at a Glance: USING GUIDE WORDS IN THE DICTIONARY

What to Do	What to Say	What Kids Need to Know
EXPLORE		
• On the board or on chart paper, write the words **bicycle, headlight, pedal,** and **chain.** • Have kids work with a partner to locate the words in the dictionary. • Point out the guide words for students' reference at the top of each page.	"Work with a partner to find these words in the dictionary. As you look, notice the two words in bold type at the top of every page in the dictionary, and see if you can use them to help you find the words."	Sometimes it's hard to locate words in the dictionary. The words at the top of each page might be helpful for finding words faster.
DISCOVER		
• After students have located the words, talk about how helpful the guide words were (if at all). Encourage every response you get. • Introduce the term **guide words** and allow time for students to connect with the idea.	"So let's talk about whether those words at the top of the page helped you." "These words at the top of the page are called **guide words;** why do you think that is?"	Guide words guide you to knowing what words are on each dictionary page.
SUMMARIZE		
• Ask kids to summarize what they know about guide words. • You can compile some lists of words with interesting definitions, good pictures in the dictionary, and so on. (See Sample Lists for suggestions, but you'll need to preview your class dictionaries to make sure the words are in there.)	"So let's sum up: would you recommend that other kids use these guide words, and what tips would you give them? Are there any problems with using them? You might want to use the dictionary a little more than usual over the next few days to practice using guide words. I can give you some lists of words to look up if you like."	Using guide words can help you more efficiently find the word you are looking for.

USING GUIDE WORDS IN THE DICTIONARY

 Every page in a dictionary has two guide words at the top; one of them is the first word on the page and the other is the last word. Using this simple feature can speed up finding words.

Who, When, and Why

Materials
▶ dictionaries

This lesson should definitely be carried out after the two previous ones, or when kids are otherwise pretty good at getting to the right general section of the dictionary.

Children will differ in their ability to use guide words effectively, but most of them should be able to benefit from this lesson.

Background Knowledge

Guide words are pretty useful once you know how to use them. I was always a little underwhelmed by the lessons on guide words in traditional spelling books; they'd reproduce perhaps two pages from a dictionary with guide words on top, and ask students to tell which page each of a list of words would be found on. But the hard part with guide words isn't narrowing it down between two pages, it's getting to the right section of the dictionary in the first place. But of course the traditional spelling books couldn't assume that you had dictionaries in the classroom!

Note: Some dictionaries only include one guide word on each page. The word on the left-hand page is the first word on that page. The word on the right-hand page is the last word on that page. Before you begin the lesson, you might want to check your classroom dictionaries to see how the guide words are done.

Every page in a dictionary has two guide words at the top, one of them the first word on the page and the other the last word. Knowing how to use this very simple feature can speed up your finding of words. However, as you'll see from the way I've structured the lesson, there isn't an easy way to put into words how to use them.

bicycle
headlight
pedal
chain

1. Begin by writing the following words on the board or on chart paper: **bicycle, headlight, pedal,** and **chain.**

   Work with a partner to find these words in the dictionary. As you look, notice the two words in bold type at the top of every page in the dictionary, and see if you can use them to help you find the words.

2. After students have located the words, talk about how helpful the guide words were (if at all).

   So let's talk about whether those words at the top of the page helped you. *(Encourage every response you get; some are likely to be more useful than others, and some students may say they weren't any help at all. That's fine; this is about hearing their responses, whatever they are.)*

3. Introduce the term **guide words** and allow time for students to connect with the idea.

   These words at the top of the page are called **guide words;** why do you think that is? *(The answer should be obvious; they guide you to knowing what words are on the page.)*

4. Ask kids to summarize what they know about guide words.

   So let's sum up: would you recommend that other kids use these guide words, and what tips would you give them? Are there any problems with using them? You might want to use the dictionary a little more than usual over the next few days to practice using guide words. I can give you some lists of words to look up if you like. *(You can compile some lists of words with interesting definitions, good pictures in the dictionary, and so on. See Sample Lists for suggestions, but you'll need to preview your class dictionaries to make sure the words are in there.)*

Next Steps

» Follow-up

A few days later:

How's it going with guide words?

✓ Assessment

As a journal topic, suggest a question like

📓 What advice would you give about using guide words to find a word?

Sample Lists

List 1	List 2	List 3
crocodile	falcon	guitar
gymnastics	tuba	igloo
eel	anchor	prowl
knit	starfish	canoe
wig	lily	mosaic
hoof	giggle	satellite
balloon	lifeguard	drum
railroad	joust	jaguar
pizza	ballet	trophy
tadpole	peanut	unicycle

Lesson at a Glance: FINDING WORDS YOU DON'T KNOW HOW TO SPELL

What to Do	What to Say	What Kids Need to Know
EXPLORE		
• Have pairs look up words that have spellings they're unsure about. • Suggest they first write down their best guess at the spelling and then search for the word. • Talk about the experiences kids had while looking for their words.	"Working with a partner, think of a word you don't know how to spell, write down your best first guess, and use what you've written down to see if you can find the word in the dictionary. Because of what we're going to focus on today, you might try to use words you think might be hard to find. Remember to use the guide words to help you." "How many people managed to find their words? Did it help to have it written down?"	When looking for a word that you're not sure how to spell, it can be helpful to write down your best guess first.
DISCOVER		
• Discuss what kids can do if they can't find the word. • Ideally, build the discussion on student examples. (See page 80, step 3, for examples.) • Lead them to understand that if you guess the wrong letter, or are looking for a proper name or new term, you'll have trouble finding them in the dictionary.	"Who couldn't find their word? Let's talk about what to do if this happens."	It can be difficult to find a word in the dictionary if you don't already know how to spell it.
SUMMARIZE		
• Help students summarize what they've learned.	"So you've got two good ideas here: try spelling it another way and look again, or think about whether there's a reason the word might not be in the dictionary. But sometimes if you get stuck, the best strategy is to ask an adult for help, if there's one around. Your teacher or parent can then help you figure out if you're looking in the wrong place or if you need to look somewhere besides the dictionary."	Take your best guess about how to spell the word and try to find it in the dictionary. If that doesn't work, think about why. Turn to another reference source, like an atlas, an encyclopedia, other books, the Internet, or an adult, if you get stuck.

FINDING WORDS YOU DON'T KNOW HOW TO SPELL

 A good strategy to find a word you don't know how to spell in the dictionary is to start with your best first guess. The best strategy if you still can't find it is to get help.

Who, When, and Why

Materials
▶ dictionaries

This lesson is most useful for kids who have had the previous dictionary lessons, since they will have learned some good tools to make searching more efficient. However, you could also do it early in the year in a shorter version, just to give them a starting point if they want to use the dictionary.

All students can benefit from this lesson, although those who are already stronger spellers are likely to have better luck finding their words in the dictionary.

Background Knowledge

Have you ever given up on finding a word in the dictionary that you didn't know how to spell? Sometimes we're looking in the wrong place (maybe we don't realize that the word starts with a silent letter), and sometimes it's just not in there (maybe it's too new). It's even harder for kids, since they're less likely, for one thing, to think of possible alternative spellings if their first one doesn't pan out.

Kids seem to do better at looking for a word in the dictionary if they have their best guess written down where they can see it; it gives them a reference point to compare to. A certain number of dictionary searches are going to be futile, particularly for children. The best strategy when you can't find a word is to ask an adult for help, since the adult will know if the student is looking in the wrong place or if the word just isn't in the dictionary (because it's a proper name, for instance), and where it might be found instead. I've also, however, included a couple of other strategies to use if you reach a dead end.

The Lesson

1. Invite children to work in pairs to look up words that have spellings they're unsure about. Have them first write down their best guess at the spelling and then search for the word.

   Working with a partner, think of a word you don't know how to spell, write down your best first guess, and use what you've written down to see if you can find the word in the dictionary. Because of what we're going to focus on today, you might try to use words you think might be hard to find. Remember to use the guide words to help you.

2. After kids have had time to search for their words:

   How many of you managed to find your word? Did it help to have it written down?

3. Discuss what kids can do if they can't find the word.

   Who couldn't find their word? Let's talk about what to do if this happens. *(Ideally, build the discussion on student examples: for instance, if someone has a letter wrong early in their spelling of the word or was looking for a proper name. I've used possible examples here.)*

   Wrong Letter:

   Okay, you couldn't find **crocodile.** Let's see what your best first guess was: KROKODILE. *(Try to prevent other kids from jumping in with the correct spelling!)* Let me show you an example that will give you a hint about a strategy. If you tried ELEVATORR as a spelling for **elevator,** you'd probably find it anyway. But if a letter near the beginning of a word is wrong, you may miss finding it. Is there something near the beginning of your spelling you could try changing? Yes, try changing the **k** to a **c,** and look again. Does anyone else think that changing something near the beginning of your spelling might help?

   Proper Names or New Terms:

   You were looking for *Pokémon* and couldn't find it. This time it's for a different reason. Any ideas? I think there are two: first of all, proper names often aren't in the dictionary. *(Though it depends on the dictionary; let's figure out later if it's true for the ones in our classroom.)* Also, this may be just too new a word. When new words come along, people have to use them for a while before the dictionary writers put them in. But here's a question: if you're looking for a proper name, or a new word, where else might you be able to find it? *(Possibilities: a reference book like an atlas or encyclopedia; other books; the Internet; or ask an adult like a teacher or librarian.)*

4. Help students summarize what they've learned.

So you've got two good ideas here: try spelling it another way and look again, or think about whether there's a reason the word might not be in the dictionary. But sometimes if you get stuck the best strategy is to ask an adult for help, if there's one around. Your teacher or parent can then help you figure out if you're looking in the wrong place or if you need to look somewhere besides the dictionary.

Next Steps

» Follow-up

Over the next few days:

Make a point of looking up some words you don't know, even if you aren't using them in your writing right away, just to get some practice.

A few days later, discuss how it's going.

✓ Assessment

As a journal topic, suggest a question like:

How can you have success at finding words in the dictionary when you don't know how to spell them?

Lesson at a Glance: DEFINITIONS IN THE DICTIONARY

What to Do	What to Say	What Kids Need to Know
INTRODUCE		
• Introduce the lesson by getting kids thinking about how they know that they've found the right word in the dictionary.	"Here's a question for you: when you're looking up a word in the dictionary, how do you know you've found the right word?"	Sometimes you just know you've found the right word in the dictionary.
EXPLORE		
• Invite students to talk about the definitions in dictionaries and how they can be used. • Suggest some words for children to look up in a dictionary. (Either write them on the board, or just say them orally to provide a little more challenge. Include at least one word that your classroom dictionaries have a picture for.)	"Do you all know what the definitions in a dictionary are? Have you used the definitions in the dictionary? What for? Did you know that they can be helpful when you're looking up words for their spelling, too? They can help you know if you've found the right word." "Let's look up some words that it might be fun to read the definitions of. Why don't we look up **crossword, ostrich,** and **avocado?** Pick a word of your own, too, if you like."	The dictionary definitions can help you know if you've found the right word.
DISCOVER		
• After kids have had some time to search, discuss what they found. • Get kids thinking about what happens when a word has more than one definition.	"So how did it go? Were you able to read and understand all the definitions? If any of the definitions were a little hard, did they sort of make sense anyway? Could you tell from the definition that you'd found the right word? Of course sometimes a picture will tell you that you've found the right word." "Here's one other tip. Sometimes a word will have more than one definition. Let's all take a look at the definitions for **quarter.** It can mean 'a coin,' or 'one-fourth of something,' or even 'a room to stay in.' So don't think you've found the wrong word just because the first definition doesn't fit. Sometimes there'll even be two separate entries for one word. For instance, **branch** can be a noun, in this case a thing, like a part of a tree or a river. But **branch** can also be a verb, like when you say the road branched off in two directions. The dictionary will usually list those separately."	Looking at the definitions will help you know whether you've found the right word, but watch for words with more than one definition. You may have to read more than one of the definitions to find the correct one.

DEFINITIONS IN THE DICTIONARY

 When looking up words in the dictionary, reading the definition of the word can help you make sure you've found the right spelling.

Who, When, and Why

Materials
▶ dictionaries

Definitions may not seem like an important part of dictionary use for spellers, since they're most useful when you're looking up a word when you do have the spelling but don't know the meaning. But I think that a lesson on this topic can be not only fun but useful in helping kids make sure they've found the right word when they're looking for a spelling.

All students who use dictionaries can benefit from this lesson, but those who are primarily using picture dictionaries are less likely to need it since pictures obviate the need for definitions.

The success of this lesson is contingent on students' ability to read and understand the definitions in the dictionaries they're using. Weaker readers will likely need extra support, but can still make partial sense out of definitions even if they can't read every word.

Background Knowledge

Obviously, defining words is one of the central functions of a dictionary. I've found that in picture dictionaries the definitions are often beside the point, since the words are almost always in children's oral vocabularies, and the definitions may be a lot harder to read than the word is; for instance, imagine a second grader trying to make sense of the definition, "The soft fleshy edges around your mouth"—yes, lips! (Root, 1993)

Children's dictionaries have gotten better at writing kid-friendly definitions. This was brought home to me in a classroom where one child wanted to look up **leukemia** because he'd had a friend with the disease. When he found a definition, in an older dictionary, that referred only to a disorder of the leucocytes, his response was a big "Huh?" The classroom also had newer dictionaries, where we found reference to a disease that affects white blood cells—far more useful.

1. **Get kids thinking about how they know that they've found the right word in the dictionary.**

   Here's a question for you: when you're looking up a word in the dictionary, how do you know you've found the right word? (*Students are likely to respond that they just know it when they've found it, which is usually true, but this lesson is designed to show them that there's a further resource there for them to use.*)

2. **Invite students to talk about the definitions in dictionaries and how they can be used.**

   Do you all know what the definitions in a dictionary are? (*It's the part that tells you what the word means.*) Have you used the definitions in the dictionary? What for? (*They're especially useful when you're reading and don't know what a word means.*) Did you know that they can be helpful when you're looking up words for their spelling, too? They can help you know if you've found the right word.

3. **Suggest some words for children to look up in a dictionary.**

   Let's look up some words that it might be fun to read the definitions of. (*You can either write them on the board so that they can remember them and find them without having to come up with the spelling, or just say them orally to provide a little more challenge. Include at least one word that your classroom dictionaries have a picture for.*) Why don't we look up **crossword, ostrich,** and **avocado?** Pick a word of your own, too, if you like.

4. **After kids have had some time to search, discuss what they found.**

   So how did it go? Were you able to read and understand all the definitions? If any of the definitions were a little hard, did they sort of make sense anyway? Could you tell from the definition that you'd found the right word? Of course sometimes a picture will tell you that you've found the right word.

5. **Get kids thinking about what happens when a word has more than one definition.**

   Here's one other tip. Sometimes a word will have more than one definition. Let's all take a look at the definitions for **quarter.** It can mean "a coin," or "one-fourth of something," or even "a room to stay in." So don't think you've found the wrong word just because the first definition doesn't fit. Sometimes there'll even be two separate entries for one word. For instance, **branch** can be a noun, in this case a thing, like a part of a tree or a river. But **branch** can also be a verb, like when you say the road branched off in two directions. The dictionary will usually list those separately.

❯❯ Follow-up

Encourage students to go a step further when they look up words in the dictionary:

> When you're looking up words for spelling, try taking a minute to read the definition just as a way to double-check. You might also find it fun to look up the definitions of some words you know just to see exactly what they mean and how well you know them.

I sometimes like to browse through the dictionary a little (okay, I do; my readers may not!) to discover new words or pick up information about familiar ones. This idea could be fun to mention to kids: would you ever look through the dictionary if you weren't looking for something specific? What might you find?

Lesson at a Glance: PRONUNCIATION GUIDES IN THE DICTIONARY

What to Do	What to Say	What Kids Need to Know
INTRODUCE		
• To get kids thinking about pronunciations, have them look up a simple word.	"Do you ever come across a word when you're reading, that you don't know how to pronounce? The dictionary can help you with this. Let's all get dictionaries and start with an easy one: **cat.** Look it up and see if you can find where it tells you how to pronounce it. What do the symbols tell you?"	Dictionaries often include a pronunciation to show you how to say each word. The pronunciation usually looks different than the other information (typically it's between slashes and/or in a different font).
EXPLORE		
• Point out the main ideas of a pronunciation and see if students can find the pronunciation guide. • Have pairs use the table of contents in the dictionary to find the pronunciation guide and talk about what they've found.	"Why do you think there's a **k,** even though the word is spelled with **c?** We know that some words that start with this sound use a **k,** like **kite,** and some use a **c,** like **cat.** But when the dictionary is showing you how to pronounce words, it uses the same symbol for the same sound every time. And there's a list of what those symbols are."	When the dictionary is showing you how to pronounce words, it uses the same symbol for the same sound every time. You can refer to the dictionary's pronunciation guide to help you know what the symbols mean.
DISCOVER		
• After pairs have discussed, ask them to share with the class what they noticed. • Lead them to any generalizations they didn't make on their own. • Ask students to look up a two-syllable word and talk about what they find. (See page 88 for examples.) • Repeat with an even longer word. (See page 89 for examples.)	"What did you notice? See if you noticed this: a lot of the symbols for consonants are the single letters we usually spell them with. But the vowel symbols are more complicated. We know, for instance, that words can have either long **a** or short **a,** and the dictionary has to be able to tell us which one it is. Let's look up **cape** to see how it shows us when a word has long **a.** Did you notice that even though **cape** has four letters, the pronunciation for it just has three symbols? That's because it only has three sounds; the **e** is silent." "Let's try a two-syllable word…" "I'd like to have us look up a longer word now…"	There are a few tricky things about pronunciations, but by getting familiar with them you can learn how to pronounce words better.
SUMMARIZE		
• Ask students how they did and see if they can use pronunciations more regularly.	"How did you do? This is one of the hardest parts of the dictionary to use. Here's an idea: as you're reading over the next few days, when you come across a word you don't know, try looking it up to see if the dictionary is useful in helping you pronounce it. You can check with me or another adult to see if you get it right."	Using the pronunciation guide in the dictionary can be helpful with unfamiliar words.

PRONUNCIATION GUIDES IN THE DICTIONARY

 Dictionaries help us spell words, but they can also help us pronounce words we see in print but don't know.

Who, When, and Why

Materials
▶ dictionaries

I wondered about even including this lesson, since it's not really part of using the dictionary for spelling, but since dictionary pronunciation guides are so hard to use, even for adults, I figured it could be helpful for teachers.

Students who are comfortable with the dictionary and who have had a number of lessons on different spelling patterns will benefit from this lesson the most. Since pronunciation guides require being able to use symbols somewhat abstractly, not all kids may be able to negotiate them very well and will choose to use other ways to find out how a word is pronounced. This is fine, since adults do the same thing!

The lesson is the same for everyone, but outcomes will vary depending on students' ability to handle abstract symbols and the difficulty of the words they're looking up.

Background Knowledge

English has about 40 sounds and only 26 letters, so if a dictionary is going to show how words are pronounced, it has to use symbols or letter combinations to represent some of the sounds. To further complicate matters, different dictionaries have made different choices. So before you carry out this lesson, it's good to get familiar with the pronunciation system used by the dictionaries in your classroom; there may be more than one if you have multiple titles. You'll want to check and make sure that everything in the text of this lesson fits with your dictionaries and make any necessary changes, though I've kept it general enough (and checked it against some common children's dictionaries) so that it should work in most cases.

The Lesson

Before beginning the lesson, take a look at the format of the pronunciations in your classroom dictionaries and modify the lesson as needed.

1. To get kids thinking about pronunciations, have them look up a simple word.

    Do you ever come across a word when you're reading that you don't know how to pronounce? The dictionary can help you with this. Let's all get dictionaries and start with an easy one: **cat.** Look it up and see if you can find where it tells you how to pronounce it. *(Typically, between slashes and/or in a different font.)* What do the symbols tell you? *(In this case, that there are three sounds; each one corresponds to a letter of the word.)*

2. Point out the main ideas of how dictionaries represent pronunciation, and see if students can find the pronunciation guide.

    Why do you think there's a **k,** even though the word is spelled with **c?** We know that some words that start with this sound use a **k,** like **kite,** and some use a **c,** like **cat.** But when the dictionary is showing you how to pronounce words, it uses the same symbol for the same sound every time. And there's a list of what those symbols are. See if you can use the table of contents in the dictionary to find the pronunciation guide. *(Some dictionaries will have the guide, and some a portion of the guide, at the bottom of every page.)* Then look it over with a partner and talk about what you notice.

3. After kids have had a chance to take a look, ask them to generalize about what they noticed.

    What did you notice? *(Allow time for students to offer their observations.)* See if you noticed this: a lot of the symbols for consonants are the single letters we usually spell them with. But the vowel symbols are more complicated. We know, for instance, that words can have either long **a** or short **a,** and the dictionary has to be able to tell us which one it is. Let's look up **cape** to see how it shows us when a word has long **a.** Did you notice that even though **cape** has four letters, the pronunciation for it just has three symbols? That's because it only has three sounds; the **e** is silent. What's the difference between how the dictionary shows us the **a**'s in **cat** and **cape?**

4. Ask students to look up a two-syllable word.

    Let's try a two-syllable word: look up **chicken.** What do you notice that's different in the pronunciation guide from the one-syllable words? *(Allow time for students to offer their observations.)* A couple of things. First, there's a dash to divide it into two syllables. Second, there's a mark to show which syllable is accented; that's so you'll know it's CHICK-en and not chick-EN. Also, here's something you'll find a lot of the time when you look up longer words. The schwa symbol, /ə/, is used for the vowel in the second syllable. *(If you haven't done the lesson on schwa with them, explain that it's sort of a weak vowel sound that you can't hear very well.)*

Spelling Strategies and Patterns

5. Repeat with an even longer word.

> I'd like to have us look up a longer word now. Let's try **catastrophe.** Look it up and see if the pronunciation guide for it makes sense to you. Can you see how each part of the word is represented? I'm going to ask you next to look up a word you don't know and see how you do at figuring out how to pronounce it from the dictionary: *(write on board but don't say)* **lexicographer.** *(Check first to see if your students' dictionary includes it; if not, use another word.)*

6. Ask students how they did.

> How did you do? This is one of the hardest parts of the dictionary to use. Here's an idea: as you're reading over the next few days, when you come across a word you don't know, try looking it up to see if the dictionary is useful in helping you pronounce it. You can check with me or another adult to see if you get it right.

Next Steps

» Follow-up

A few days later:

> Now that you've had some time to try it out on your own, do you think the dictionary pronunciation guide is going to be useful for you? Are there any problems that you ran into in using it? Maybe we can figure out a way to deal with them.

✓ Assessment

As a journal topic, suggest a question like:

> Would you recommend using the dictionary pronunciation guide to a friend? Why or why not? What makes using the pronunciation guide a challenge for you?

Lesson at a Glance: USING INDEXES AND OTHER PLACES TO FIND WORDS

What to Do	What to Say	What Kids Need to Know
INTRODUCE		
• Before starting the lesson, gather up enough nonfiction books with indexes for each pair of students to have one. • Invite kids to share words they want to use in their reports but don't know how to spell.	"You're all working on writing reports right now. I know that sometimes when you're writing about something you're learning about, like amphibians, there are words you don't know how to spell because you're learning new words when you learn new information. Can anyone share an example of a word you're going to be using in your report that you'll probably have to look up to get right?"	Sometimes when you are writing about what you are learning, there are new words that you don't know how to spell.
EXPLORE		
• Invite students to talk about what indexes are and what is included in them. • Have students work in pairs to look through the index of their book.	"Do you all remember what the index of a book is?" "Take a look with your partner at the index of the book I've given you. How is it different from the table of contents?"	The table of contents of a book shows topics in the order they appear, but the index is in alphabetical order. Also, the index usually has a lot more detail.
DISCOVER		
• Ask students to think about how indexes can be helpful for spelling.	"We just talked about the harder words you're going to be using in reports. Why do you think I had you look at an index just now? What's the advantage over using the dictionary?" "Looking at the index you have, do you see some words that you might want to write if you were doing a report on that subject, but wouldn't have known how to spell? Let me give you one more tip. Pick a topic in the index and turn to the page it refers you to. Do you see some words on that page that you don't know how to spell? What does this suggest to you about another way the index can help you with spelling?"	The index can be a place to find words that you want to use in your report, but don't know how to spell. There's a good chance that you'll find the word you need if you're looking at the index of a book on your topic, and you only need to look through maybe a few dozen words instead of the whole dictionary. Even if the index doesn't have the word you're looking for, it might get you to a page that does.
SUMMARIZE		
• Finish up the discussion by talking about how books other than dictionaries can be helpful resources.	"So an index is a good place to find words you can use for spelling. Here are a few other ideas. Sometimes if you're looking for a proper name and it's not in the dictionary, an encyclopedia might have it. If you're writing about something that's been in the news, particularly a name of a person or place, check the newspaper. For place names, check the atlas (which has an index) or the globe if it's a country or big city. Any other ideas?"	Using books other than dictionaries might be a faster way to find the word you are looking for. In some cases, it might be the only way to find the word.

USING INDEXES AND OTHER PLACES TO FIND WORDS

 The books that you're using to get the information for your nonfiction piece are also good sources to help you spell the technical words that you're using in your writing.

Who, When, and Why

Materials
▶ nonfiction books
with indexes

For informational writing in particular, there are often more efficient sources than the dictionary to find the spelling of a word, particularly since children are often already using reference books to gather the material for their writing on these topics.

This is an obvious lesson to use when students are writing nonfiction based on knowledge they're gaining from their reading. It's useful for all ages, but perhaps particularly for younger children who won't know how to spell many of the harder words they want to use in this writing. Younger or less proficient students will need a bit more hand-holding and coaching.

Background Knowledge

Indexes, which nonfiction books even for children are likely to have, are very accessible sources of spellings of words related to a particular topic. Either the specific word you're looking for will be there, or it will lead you to a page that contains the word. (For instance, you could find the spelling of **rhinoceros** either in the index of a book on mammals or on the mammal pages of a book on animals.)

The Lesson

1. Before starting the lesson, gather up enough nonfiction books with indexes for each pair of students to have one.

    You're all working on writing reports right now. I know that sometimes when you're writing about something you're learning about, like amphibians *(or pick an example that reflects what your students are doing)*, there are words you don't know how to spell, because you're learning new words when you learn new information. Can anyone share an example of a word you're going to be using in your report that you'll probably have to look up to get right?

2. Invite students to talk about what indexes are and what's included in them.

    Do you all remember what the index of a book is? *(Or, if they're unfamiliar with indexes:* "The index is a list, in alphabetical order and almost always in the back of the book, that shows you what pages you can find different topics on.")

    Have students work in pairs to look through the index.

    Take a look with your partner at the index of the book I've given you. How is it different from the table of contents? *(The table of contents shows topics in the order they appear; the index is in alphabetical order. The index usually has a lot more detail.)*

3. Ask students to think about how indexes can be helpful for spelling.

    We just talked about the harder words you're going to be using in reports. Why do you think I had you look at an index just now? *(The index can be a place to find words that you don't know how to spell.)* What's the advantage over using the dictionary? *(There's a good chance you'll find the word you need if you're looking at the index of a book on your topic, and you only need to look through maybe a few dozen words instead of the whole dictionary.)*

    Looking at the index you have, do you see some words that you might want to write if you were doing a report on that subject, but wouldn't have known how to spell? Let me give you one more tip. Pick a topic in the index and turn to the page it refers you to. Do you see some words on that page that you don't know how to spell? What does this suggest to you about another way the index can help you with spelling? *(Even if it doesn't have the word you're looking for, it can get you to a page that does.)*

4. Finish up the discussion by talking about how books other than dictionaries can be helpful resources.

    So an index is a good place to find words you can use for spelling. Here are a few other ideas. *(Adjust this part so it fits the resources you have available.)* Sometimes if you're looking for a proper name and it's not in the dictionary, an encyclopedia might have it. If you're writing about something that's been in the news, particularly a name of a person or place, check the newspaper. For place names, check the atlas (which has an index) or the globe if it's a country or big city. Any other ideas?

Note: I haven't included the Internet as an example because not all classrooms (or homes) have web access.

Spelling Strategies and Patterns

Next Steps

» **Follow-up**

A few days later:

> Have you been using indexes and other sources to find spellings for your report writing? How has it gone?

✓ **Assessment**

As a journal topic, suggest a question like:

> How does using places other than the dictionary to find words work for you?

Lesson at a Glance: THE IMPORTANCE OF SPELLING IN PUBLISHED WRITING

What to Do	What to Say	What Kids Need to Know
INTRODUCE		
• Begin by getting kids thinking about spelling in published writing.	"When you read a book, are the words always spelled right? Why do you think that is? Do you ever find words spelled wrong in books? Sometimes people mention the Junie B. Jones books (by Barbara Park), where Junie spells words wrong because she's just a little kid, but other than cases like that, it's not very often you'll find a word spelled wrong in a book."	Spelling in published writing is generally 100% correct.
EXPLORE		
• Invite students to think about the process that might be behind correct spelling in published work.	"How do you think the publishers get all the words right? Do you think that every author is a perfect speller? No, they're not. Even adults don't always spell the words right. Sometimes publishers get manuscripts with a lot of words spelled wrong. But publishers have people who work for them who are really good spellers. They're called copy editors, and they do a lot of checking of the manuscript to make sure everything's done right, including checking the spelling."	Published writing is often read and carefully copyedited by specialists to make sure there aren't any spelling errors.
DISCOVER		
• Explain why correct spelling is so important to authors and publishers.	"Could you still read a book if one word or so on every page was spelled wrong? Sure. But publishers try to get the spelling 100% correct because they're proud of the books they publish. Most authors will try to get the spelling all correct before they send the manuscript in too, because they're proud of what they've written. But they know that if they miss a few words, the copy editor will catch them."	Because authors and publishers take pride in their work, they want the spelling to be 100% correct.
SUMMARIZE		
• Talk about the idea of applying publishing roles to the classroom. • Encourage kids to move towards 100% correctness, or, for younger children, trying to fix as many misspellings as possible.	"Do you know what? I'm the copy editor for the classroom. When you're publishing your writing, I'm the one who does a final check to see that everything's spelled right. But what do you think about doing what most adult authors do—trying to fix any misspellings when you do the final draft of your manuscript before it gets published? Do you like the idea of taking pride in your work that way?"	By taking pride in your work, and looking for more spelling errors to fix, you can get closer to 100% correct spelling.

THE IMPORTANCE OF SPELLING IN PUBLISHED WRITING

 Words are almost always spelled correctly in books for a number of reasons: it makes the text easier to read, it's part of the pride authors take in their work, and that's just the way the adult world works.

Who, When, and Why

Materials
▶ none

This lesson is appropriate for all students, though older ones are likely to have more interest and understanding in how the copy-editing process works. The lesson will be especially meaningful in classrooms where students publish their work in some form, and will work well when talking about the publishing process.

Background Knowledge

Misspelled words are very, very rare in published books (although a little more common in newspapers, which have much tighter deadlines). This isn't, however, because all published writers are good spellers; far from it! But, publishers hire copy editors, who are good spellers, and are also experts in finding and fixing misspellings. The goal is 100% correct spelling in published writing; at this level, it's not just about communication, but also about expectations and creating an impression of careful work.

The Lesson

1. To get kids thinking about spelling in published writing:

   When you read a book, are the words always spelled right? Why do you think that is? *(Student answers are likely to include: so people can read it, and so they know you aren't stupid.)* Do you ever find words spelled wrong in books? Sometimes people mention the Junie B. Jones books (by Barbara Park), where Junie spells words wrong because she's just a little kid, but other than cases like that, it's not very often you'll find a word spelled wrong in a book.

2. Invite students to think about the process that might be behind correct spelling in published work.

   *If necessary, you can give the definition of a **manuscript**: the version of the book the author sends in before it's published.*

   How do you think the publishers get all the words right? Do you think that every author is a perfect speller? No, they're not. Even adults don't always spell the words right. Sometimes publishers get manuscripts with a lot of words spelled wrong. But publishers have people who work for them who are really good spellers. They're called copy editors, and they do a lot of checking of the manuscript to make sure everything's done right, including checking the spelling.

3. Explain why correct spelling is so important to authors and publishers.

   If kids seem interested: What kind of person do you think makes a good copyeditor? (knows how to spell really well; likes writing to be "perfect") Do any of you think you'd enjoy the job of a copyeditor?

   Could you still read a book if one word or so on every page was spelled wrong? Sure. But publishers try to get the spelling 100% correct because they're proud of the books they publish. Most authors will try to get the spelling all correct before they send the manuscript in too, because they're proud of what they've written. But they know that if they miss a few words, the copy editor will catch them.

4. Talk about the idea of applying publishing roles to the classroom.

   Do you know what? I'm the copy editor for the classroom. When you're publishing your writing, I'm the one who does a final check to see that everything's spelled right. But what do you think about doing what most adult authors do—trying to fix any misspellings when you do the final draft of your manuscript before it gets published? *(Or, for younger students: trying to fix as many of the misspellings as you can.)* Do you like the idea of taking pride in your work that way?

Spelling Strategies and Patterns

Follow-up

Continue to use the vocabulary of **manuscript** and **copy editor** as you work with students in their writing. Also, I believe that taking pride in your work and operating like an adult author are the best motivators for correcting spelling in writing that's going to be published, and more honest than presenting it as an issue of communication. Also, it gives the ownership to students and avoids having them feel as though proofreading is something to do because the teacher requires it.

Assessment

As a journal topic, suggest a question like:

What kind of author do you think you'd be? Would you want to send in "perfect" manuscripts? Or would you rather rely on a copy editor?

Lesson at a Glance: HOW MANY SPELLINGS SHOULD I EDIT?

What to Do	What to Say	What Kids Need to Know
EXPLORE		
• Have kids bring a first draft of a piece of writing about a page long. • Have them read through their writing and count the words they think they spelled wrong.	"Read through the piece of writing you brought with you and try to count how many words you think you spelled wrong. This is just one of the differences between writers; some of us are better than others at getting words right in the first draft. But we'll learn today about how to work on getting more of them right for a final draft."	Different people have different spelling strengths and weaknesses.
DISCOVER		
• First, address the students who have 100% correct spelling. (Take a look later to make sure they haven't missed any.) • Next, address those students with only a few misspellings. • Finally, address the students with many misspelled words in their first draft.	"Did any of you have all the words spelled correctly? Congratulations, your spelling is ready for a final draft! Are any of you pretty good at spelling everything right in the first draft? How do you think you manage to do that?" "How many of you found between one and five words misspelled on your page? Do you think you could manage to fix all of them for your final draft? Are some of them words you know but just happened to get wrong by accident? Are some of them words you could find quickly on the word wall, or try another way and probably get right? Are some of them words that would take longer to fix, maybe by looking them up in the dictionary? How long do you think it would take you to fix all of them, and do you think it would be reasonable to ask you to?" "How many of you found more than five words spelled wrong? It might be a lot of work to fix all of them, but I think it would be fair to ask you to edit some of them. How many do you think would be a good number?"	If you've only got a few words wrong, it might not be a bad idea to try to fix them all. If you've got many words wrong, you may want to set different goals.
SUMMARIZE		
• Review the suggested approach to correcting spelling. • Talk about the benefits of correct spelling in the first draft.	"Does this seem like a good idea, then? You each do some editing for spelling when you're going to do a final draft, but nobody has to do so much of it that they get really sick of it." "Another idea about this: the better you can get at getting words right in the first draft, the less editing you'll have. Sometimes just taking an extra second to think about the spelling is enough to get it right."	It is important to try to spell as many words correctly as possible, but not to the extent that it makes writers frustrated.

HOW MANY SPELLINGS SHOULD I EDIT?

 Editing for spelling is an important part of being a writer, but each person needs to know how much time and attention they should spend on correcting their spelling.

Who, When, and Why

Materials
▶ first drafts

This lesson is valuable for all children, and will be slightly different at different ages, ranging from finding and fixing a few invented spellings to trying to catch them all.

Even at a single grade level, children can vary quite a bit in how correct their first-draft spelling is; this is due not only to their literacy development in general, including how much they've read, but to their natural spelling ability. Spelling simply comes easier to some people than others. We may be inclined to think that the weaker spellers really need to be pushed hard to edit their mistakes, but this is likely to be counterproductive. Later lessons will focus on how to make sure your spelling in a piece is completely correct, but the usual expectation for weaker spellers should be more modest so that they don't get overwhelmed. (The lessons on struggling spellers revisit these issues as well—see Strategies 30–32.)

Background Knowledge

An important component of making the transition from invented to correct spelling is editing spellings for a final draft. But asking students to correct too many spellings can be intimidating and may lead them to choose simpler words to cut down on the editing burden; this lesson will help everyone establish reasonable expectations for editing that reflect children's developmental levels as spellers.

As is obvious to any teacher, children's spelling in their first-draft writing gets better as they get older. But all writers need to proofread as well; the words come out wrong sometimes even for good spellers. But proofreading shouldn't take up too much time or it'll become a burden that discourages writing with your full vocabulary. Students can be engaged in the *process* of proofreading, however, even if they're not yet ready to fully perfect the final *product.* Even a first grader can pick a couple of the words she wrote with invented spelling and find them somewhere in the classroom.

The Lesson

1. **Have kids bring a first draft of a piece of writing about a page long.**

    Read through the piece of writing you brought with you and try to count how many words you think you spelled wrong. *(Answers will vary widely within and across grade levels, from zero to lots.)* This is just one of the differences between writers; some of us are better than others at getting words right in the first draft. But we'll learn today about how to work on getting more of them right for a final draft.

2. **First, address the students who have 100% correct spelling.**

    Did any of you have all the words spelled correctly? Congratulations, your spelling is ready for a final draft! (But I'll take a look to make sure you haven't missed any.) Are any of you pretty good at spelling everything right in the first draft? How do you think you manage to do that?

3. **Next, address those students with only a few misspellings.**

    How many of you found between one and five words misspelled on your page? Do you think you could manage to fix all of them for your final draft? See what kinds of words they are: are some of them words you know but just happened to get wrong by accident? Are some of them words you could find quickly on the word wall, or try another way and probably get right? Are some of them words that would take longer to fix, maybe by looking them up in the dictionary? How long do you think it would take you to fix all of them, and do you think it would be reasonable to ask you to?

4. **Finally, address the students with many misspelled words in their first draft.**

    How many of you found more than five words spelled wrong? It might be a lot of work to fix all of them, but I think it would be fair to ask you to edit some of them. How many do you think would be a good number? And then I can be the final copy editor before your piece is published and I'll catch the rest of them. *(A good answer for expectations is three to five, or as many as you can do in five minutes or so.)*

5. **Review the suggested approach to correcting spelling.**

    Does this seem like a good idea, then? You each do some editing for spelling when you're going to do a final draft, but nobody has to do so much of it that they get really sick of it. Another idea about this: the better you can get at getting words right in the first draft, the less editing you'll have. Sometimes just taking an extra second to think about the spelling is enough to get it right.

Next Steps

>> **Follow-up**

Establish what you've discussed as an expectation for spelling in students' future writing, working with individuals as needed if they're having trouble either finding or fixing their misspellings.

✓ **Assessment**

While moving through the writing process, it is really important to strike an appropriate balance between content and correctness. You may want to spend some time monitoring each student's attention to spelling while drafting, so you have a feeling for what kind of direction they'll need from you. If you find some students are focusing too much attention on correct spelling at the expense of ideas and organization, help them develop a plan to get the big ideas down first and focus in on the smaller things later. If you see other students who would not be slowed down by spending a little extra time on spelling in early drafting stages, you can encourage them to do so.

As a journal topic, suggest a question like:

📓 Is editing your spelling an important part of being a writer? Why or why not? Do you have any difficulties in editing for spelling?

Lesson at a Glance: HOW TO FIND ALL OF YOUR MISSPELLINGS

What to Do	What to Say	What Kids Need to Know
EXPLORE		
• Have kids bring a first draft of a piece of writing about a page long. • Ask them to identify any words they think they misspelled. • Then have them identify any words they aren't sure about. • Ask kids to spend some time checking the spellings of the words they were unsure of. Circulate around the room to help kids who have many words to check. • Alternatively: have volunteers list their words on the board and have the class help them figure out which ones were right. The rest of the kids can then do their own or work with a partner.	"Take your first-draft piece of writing and go through it fairly quickly, marking all the words you think might be spelled wrong. How many of you are pretty sure you caught them all? Next I'd like you to go through again, but more slowly; stop and think about whether each word is spelled right. For instance, if you wrote 'The grapefruit was as yellow as a banana,' you might be positive about **the, was, as, yellow,** and **a,** but not be 100% sure about **grapefruit** and **banana.** Put a little mark by those words." "After you're done, take five minutes or so to check the spellings of the words you weren't completely sure of. Do as many as you can. I'll come around and tell you some too."	Sometimes you know you've spelled a word wrong; other times you aren't sure if it's right or wrong.
DISCOVER		

• Talk about what kids discovered.	"So what did you discover?
	  • You may have spotted some of the words you got wrong but missed some others. That means that you need to try a little harder to catch all your misspellings.
	  • You caught most of the misspelled words the first time through. That means that you're doing a good job with editing.
	  • You thought words were spelled wrong when they were right. You're a better speller than you think you are!"
	
	"It would be too much work to think about every word every time you edit, but what we did today should give you a good sense of how well you spot your misspellings."
		Some people are really good at finding their own misspellings, and others will have to work harder to find them.

SUMMARIZE		
• Teach students the strategy of reading backwards.	"I'd like to teach you a new strategy for proofreading your writing, which you may or may not want to use. Take a first draft and try reading it backwards word by word and see if that helps you catch more misspellings." "What did you think? Probably some of you liked it and some of you didn't, but now that you know about this strategy you can use it if you want to if you think it'll help."	Reading your draft backwards can sometimes help you spot misspellings.

HOW TO FIND ALL OF YOUR MISSPELLINGS

 It's good to know if you're the kind of writer who doesn't always catch all your misspellings, and there are strategies to help you get better at it.

Who, When, and Why

This lesson is good for students who are getting a lot of their spellings right in the first draft, doing a pretty good job of editing, but still missing some of their incorrect spellings when they proofread. So, this lesson may only be needed by some of the students in your class, or you could do the lesson with everyone and follow up in conferences with those who need more scaffolding.

You might want to do the two parts of the lesson (Steps 1–3 and 4) on two different days.

Background Knowledge

If a spelling is close to correct, or is a real word even if it's not the one you intended, it's harder to catch it when you're proofreading. Two useful strategies, however, are to have a sense of how likely you are to miss seeing these words, and to read your piece backwards.

We've all had students come up to us with a piece of writing that they think is finished but actually still has a number of misspelled words. But this can happen even with adults; it's hard to catch all of them, and, ironically, the better speller you are the harder it is to find your lingering misspellings because they're usually pretty good. This lesson should help.

The Lesson

1. **Have kids bring a first draft of a piece of writing about a page long.**

   Take a first-draft piece of writing about a page long and go through it fairly quickly, marking all the words you think might be spelled wrong. How many of you are pretty sure you caught them all? Next I'd like you to go through again, but more slowly; stop and think about every word, whether you know for sure it's spelled right. For instance, if you wrote "The grapefruit was as yellow as a banana," you might be positive about **the, was, as, yellow,** and **a,** but not be 100% sure about **grapefruit** and **banana.** Put a little mark by those words.

2. **Ask kids to spend some time checking the spellings of the words they were unsure of.**

   After you're done, take five minutes or so to check the spellings of the words you weren't completely sure of. Do as many as you can. I'll come around and tell you some too.

   Or alternatively: have some volunteers come up to the board and list both the words they weren't sure of and the ones they were pretty sure were wrong, and have the class help them figure out which ones were right. The rest of the kids can then do their own or work with a partner.

3. **Talk about what kids discovered.**

   So what did you discover? Here are three possible outcomes:

   - You may have spotted some of the words you got wrong but missed some others. That means that you need to try a little harder to make sure you've caught all your misspellings.

   - You caught pretty much all the words you misspelled the first time through. That means that you're doing a good job with editing.

   - You thought words were spelled wrong when they were right. You're a better speller than you think you are!

   It would be too much work to go through and think about every word every time you edit, but what we did today should give you a good sense of whether you're doing a good enough job of spotting your misspellings.

4. **Teach students the strategy of reading backwards.**

   I'd like to teach you a new strategy for proofreading your writing, which you may or may not want to use. Take a first draft and try reading through it backwards word by word and see if that seems to help you catch more misspellings, since you aren't focusing on the meaning. *(Allow time for them to try this out.)* What did you think? Probably some of you liked it and some of you didn't, but now that you know about this strategy you can use it if you want to if you think it'll help.

> When I did this lesson with a fifth-grade class, one student said she liked it because she thought it really did work, where another thought it was boring and confusing.

Spelling Strategies and Patterns

Next Steps

» **Follow-up**

See if students are indeed getting better at catching all their misspellings when they edit.

✓ **Assessment**

As a journal topic, suggest a question like:

▶ What do you think works best for you to catch all of your misspellings?

Lesson at a Glance: THE RIGHT SPELLING OF THE WRONG WORD

What to Do	What to Say	What Kids Need to Know
INTRODUCE		
• Begin by identifying the problem.	"Sometimes there are correctly-spelled words in your writing that are still wrong, because you've written a real word, spelled correctly, but it's the wrong word. Do you think these are harder or easier to find than other misspellings?"	Sometimes you write the right spelling of the wrong word. Those mistakes are usually harder to find, because they're real words, so they sort of look right.
EXPLORE		
• Invite children to share their own experiences. • Use examples from your own class. You may want to ask kids to look back through their drafts. • If necessary, you can review the **here/there/where** pattern. (See Pattern 20.)	"Are you aware of some words that you do this with a lot? I've noticed that some of you write **their** for **there,** or **where** for **were,** or vice versa. Do you know the difference between them? If there are any that you really don't know which is which, ask me and I'll help you figure out a way to remember."	Sometimes you just write the wrong word, but if you don't really know the difference between the two words, you can come up with a trick to remember which is which.
DISCOVER		
• Talk about how to find these kinds of mistakes.	"But do you find that even if you know which word is which, you still sometimes write the wrong one? If so, what you need to get better at is catching them when you proofread. Here's how we'll do it. Over the next few days, every time you realize that you've written the right spelling of the wrong word, make a note of it in your spelling notebook. I'll keep an eye out for them in everyone's writing too. From that point on, when you're proofreading, keep an eye out especially for whether you've written one of those words, and take a moment to check if you've gotten it right."	It's a good idea to keep a list of words you use in your own writing that are the right spellings of the wrong words. Then you can check your writing for those specific words when you proofread.

THE RIGHT SPELLING OF THE WRONG WORD

 Sometimes you write the right spelling of the wrong word. You can keep a list of words that you sometimes confuse in this way, and look especially for those words when you proofread.

Who, When, and Why

Materials
▶ marked-up drafts for each student

Do this lesson if your kids seem to need it; the form the problem is most likely to take is homophone substitution. They'll get most out of it if they're already fairly good at proofreading. But realize also that it's one of those little glitches of spelling that even adults have trouble with, so I wouldn't expect mastery, just a little more awareness of how to catch these errors. You may also want to do some individual coaching after the lesson with students who are still having a hard time catching these words.

Background Knowledge

These days, the few misspellings one finds in published books often involve the right spelling of the wrong word, often but not always homophones. This is to some extent a consequence of the age of the spellchecker; if you've written **grizzly** instead of **grisly** (as one writer did in a book about a murder), your computer won't catch it.

Substituting one homophone for another is a common spelling error that can persist even in good adult spellers; even for those who know the difference, the wrong one sometimes just comes out. (Would you believe that I just, in the last sentence, typed **no** instead of **know?** Proves my point.) As I've discussed elsewhere (see Pattern 20, on homophones), I don't think focusing on pairs of homophones is a good idea since it's likely to associate the two words with each other even more. But this does need to be dealt with as an editing issue. Before the lesson, you might want to skim through some writing samples from your class to see who has a problem with this and what words it's most likely to occur on.

The Lesson

1. **Begin by identifying the problem.**

   Sometimes there are correctly-spelled words in your writing that are still wrong, because you've written a real word, spelled correctly, but it's the wrong word. Do you think these are harder or easier to find than other misspellings? *(They're usually harder to find, because they're real words, so they sort of look right.)*

2. **Invite children to share their own experiences.**

   Are you aware of some words that you do this with a lot? I've noticed that some of you write **their** for **there,** or **where** for **were,** or vice versa. *(Use examples from your own class; these are common ones. You may want to ask kids to look back through their drafts to find examples.)* Do you know the difference between them? *(If necessary, you can review the **here/there/where** pattern at this point. See Pattern 20.)* If there are any where you really don't know which is which, ask me and I'll help you figure out a way to remember.

3. **Talk about how to find these kinds of mistakes.**

   But do you find that even if you know which word is which, you still sometimes write the wrong one? If so, what you need to get better at is catching them when you proofread. Here's how we'll do it. Over the next few days, every time you realize that you've written the right spelling of the wrong word, make a note of it in your spelling notebook. I'll keep an eye out for them in everyone's writing too. From that point on, when you're proofreading, keep an eye out especially for whether you've written one of those words, and take a moment to check if you've gotten it right.

» **Follow-up**

A few days later:

> Do you think this lesson helped you get better at finding and fixing the right spelling of the wrong word?

✓ **Assessment**

As a journal topic, suggest a question like:

> How do you keep straight the words you tend to confuse? How do you catch them if you've missed them?

theatre review
I thout the play was good but the acting wasent that great. thay probly coud of done better and the costumes **wear** somewhat good.

Lesson at a Glance: HOW TO ACHIEVE 100% CORRECT SPELLING

What to Do	What to Say	What Kids Need to Know
INTRODUCE		
• Begin by asking kids to think about the idea of 100% correct spelling in a piece of writing.	"How many of you wish you could write a final draft of a piece and have all the words spelled correctly: 100%? What percent do you think you're at now for your final drafts? When would you especially like to aim for this goal? I think it makes most sense for a piece that's going to be published, or if you're writing a letter to someone, which is almost like another way of publishing, since it gets an audience beyond the classroom. I'd like to teach you a series of steps that will help you get as close to 100% correct as possible."	If you are going to publish a piece of writing, it's a good idea to try to get all the words spelled correctly.
EXPLORE		
• Hand out copies of page 273 and review the steps with children. • This portion of the lesson includes a long stretch of teacher talk, so be sure to give kids opportunities to react and respond.	**"Step one: Try to get words right in your first draft.** When you're drafting, sometimes if you take a second or two to get a word right the first time, then you don't have to worry about trying to catch it when you're editing." **"Step two: Mark your invented spellings when you write them.** If you know you're inventing a spelling, put a little mark by it to make sure you check it when you're editing." **"Step three: Read through your piece, focusing just on spelling.** After you've revised your piece and you're ready for the final draft, do a read-through just focusing on the spelling. Try reading a little slower than usual or even go through backwards if this works for you." **"Step four: Have an adult look over your piece.** Bring the piece to me or another adult who's a good speller. If you find that you're often missing some of your misspellings, think about which of the other steps you could do better on."	The four steps to 100% correct spelling are: Step one: Try to get words right in your first draft. Step two: Mark your invented spellings when you write them. Step three: Read through your piece, focusing just on spelling. Step four: Have an adult look over your piece.
SUMMARIZE		
• Give children a chance to review the steps in their own words and to think about what they might add to the steps.	"Who can say what the steps are in their own words? Do these steps sound good to you? Any ideas you want to add? Put your copy of the steps in your spelling journal so you can refer to it later."	Even if using the four steps doesn't produce 100% correctness, it can still help you get closer.

HOW TO ACHIEVE 100% CORRECT SPELLING

 It's not always possible to spell every word right, but if you try to get words right in your first draft, mark your invented spellings when you write them, read through your piece while focusing just on spelling, and have an adult look over your piece, you'll be well on your way.

Who, When, and Why

Materials
▶ spelling journals

This lesson is most appropriate for students who are already spelling and proofreading pretty well. Students who are somewhat weaker spellers may still want to aim for 100% correctness and may be able to do so with extra support from you. ("Show me your piece when you think all the spellings are correct and I'll see if you've missed any.")

Background Knowledge

Brain surgery and spelling: the two endeavors where we expect a 100% success rate! All kidding aside, though, most adults do try to get their spelling completely correct, even though human error frequently creeps in anyway. Some students in the upper grades of elementary school will be able to spell most if not all words correctly in their first drafts, some will do less well in their first drafts but will do a good job of editing, and others will find 100% correctness a struggle. However, all students can learn a procedure that will maximize their chances of good spelling in their final draft. This lesson consolidates ideas from previous lessons and will give students a series of steps to follow so that when they're trying to do their best, they can.

> My university recently had a graduation ceremony for a few hundred of our students, and on the front page of a program where all the proper names had been meticulously proofread, there in large type was the spelling *Acadmic.* This was obviously a typo, not a misspelling, since no one would spell the word that way. It had originally been spelled correctly, so someone must have made a stray keystroke that nobody caught.

1. Begin by asking kids to think about the idea of 100% correct spelling in a piece of writing.

   How many of you wish you could write a final draft of a piece and have all the words spelled correctly: 100%? What percent do you think you're at now for your final drafts? When would you especially like to aim for this goal? I think it makes most sense for a piece that's going to be published, or if you're writing a letter to someone, which is almost like another way of publishing, since it reaches an audience beyond the classroom. I'd like to teach you a series of steps that will help you get as close to 100% correct as possible. *(The following includes a long stretch of teacher talk, so be sure to give kids opportunities to react and respond.)*

2. Hand out copies of page 273 and review the steps with children.

   Step one: Try to get words right in your first draft.

   This is a step that starts when you're first writing your piece. Sometimes if you take a second or two to get a word right the first time—if you're pretty sure about the spelling—then you don't have to worry about trying to catch it when you're editing.

   Step two: Mark your invented spellings when you write them.

   If you know you're inventing a spelling, put a little mark by it to make sure you check it when you're editing. This is for the harder words that you know you don't know and don't want to take the time to look up while you're writing.

   Step three: Read through your piece, focusing just on spelling.

   After you've revised your piece and you're ready for the final draft, do a read-through just focusing on the spelling. You may have already caught some in earlier read-throughs, but this is a time to just think about spelling. Try reading a little slower than usual or even go through backwards if this works for you.

   Step four: Have an adult look over your piece.

   Bring the piece to me or another adult who's a good speller to check to see if you've caught them all. If you find that you're often missing some of your misspellings, think about which of the other steps you could do better on. Or it may still be a little bit hard for you to get 100% because you don't know enough words yet; talk to me if you think that's the case.

3. Give children a chance to review the steps in their own words and to think about what they might add to the steps.

   Who can say what the steps are in their own words? Do these steps sound good to you? Any ideas you want to add? You can put your copy of the steps in your spelling journal so you can refer to it later.

Follow-up

A few days later:

> Are the four steps for 100% spelling working well? Any problems we need to discuss?

I'd also keep an eye out to see if students are indeed improving in their final drafts. If not, you may want to talk about the steps again, but realize they may be at the limit of their competence.

 ### Assessment

As a journal topic, suggest a question like:

> What's challenging for you about getting every word spelled correctly?

Lesson at a Glance: WHEN IT REALLY, REALLY HAS TO BE RIGHT

What to Do	What to Say	What Kids Need to Know
INTRODUCE		
• Get kids thinking about when correct spelling really matters.	"If you think about the world around you, and all the adults out there, when do you think spelling matters most?"	Correct spelling is more important some times than others.
EXPLORE		
• Ask kids to think about what kind of effects could result from spelling errors. • Point out that while correct spelling isn't always crucial, there are some times when it's really important. • You may want to share some sample resumes or job applications and have a brief discussion about them, just so kids have an idea about what this kind of writing looks like.	"Can the everyday person out there get away with spelling words wrong sometimes? For instance, if you were in charge of making up the menu for a restaurant, and you spelled a word wrong one day, how much trouble do you think you'd get into? What if you made up new menus every day, and every day spelled a different word wrong? That would be more serious, and you'd probably need some better strategies if you wanted to keep your job." "Almost always, if you've spelled a word or two wrong, people can still read what you wrote. But they may dis you anyway, because sometimes people think—even though it's not true—that misspelling words means you're not smart or you're lazy. Because of that, do you know when it matters most? When you're trying to make a good impression on someone, especially if you're applying for a job."	There are times when spelling errors can have some negative consequences.
DISCOVER		
• Talk about ways you can make sure you have correct spelling for those times when it really matters.	"So when you're trying to make a good impression, and the spelling really, really has to be right, how can you make sure that it is? First of all, you'd go back to your four steps for getting your spelling 100% correct. If this is one of those cases where spelling is a lot more important than usual, it's worth taking a little extra time to check. Maybe even ask a few good spellers to take a look. Lots of people haven't even gotten interviewed for a job they wanted because they spelled one word wrong in their application."	You can use the four steps to 100% correct spelling and spend extra time on your writing to make sure you have all the words spelled correctly when it really matters.

WHEN IT REALLY, REALLY HAS TO BE RIGHT

In the world outside of school, sometimes spelling matters a lot, and it's important to know when that is and what to do about it.

Who, When, and Why

This lesson will have the most practical applications for students who are able to proofread well enough so that their spelling can be correct when it matters, but it makes for an interesting discussion even with less advanced students. Be sure to maintain a tone that won't stigmatize those who have a harder time getting their spelling right. A good time to do this lesson would be during a careers unit.

Background Knowledge

This is a capstone lesson that helps children think ahead to the adult world where people are judged on their spelling and sometimes correct spelling is very important. The lesson also maintains the perspective that gee, it is just spelling, and maybe people make too much of a fuss over it sometimes.

Out in the world, spelling is often used as a very harsh judgment call. You may recall when, in 1992, Vice President Dan Quayle mistakenly told an elementary school student that his correct spelling of **potato** needed an **e** on the end. Editorial cartoonists thought they'd died and gone to heaven! The twelve-year-old was invited to appear on David Letterman. For those of us whose lives are less prominent, misspelling can still draw negative reactions on anything more public than a shopping list. Kids need to know this and understand how to cope with it.

This is especially important for poor and working-class students, whose economic futures can be more damaged by spelling errors. A teacher I know had once had in a job that involved screening candidates for secretarial jobs, and he said that, since there were usually a lot of applications, a misspelling was an immediate disqualifier. A group of teachers once told me that in their school district, screening for all jobs, including bus driver, contained a spelling component. Yet Dan Quayle (assuming he is indeed not a particularly strong speller) made it through law school and to the position of vice president. At that level, the only spelling strategy you really need is a good assistant!

1. **Get kids thinking about when correct spelling really matters.**

   If you think about the world around you, and all the adults out there, when do you think spelling matters most? *(Allow time to discuss. Answers are likely to include examples like needing words spelled right if you're trying to sell something, if you're writing a book for people to read, and so on.)*

2. **Ask kids to think about what kind of effects could result from spelling errors.**

   Can the everyday person out there get away with spelling words wrong sometimes? For instance, if you were in charge of making up the menu for a restaurant, and you spelled a word wrong one day, how much trouble do you think you'd get into? *(Probably not too much.)* What if you made up new menus every day, and every day spelled a different word wrong? That would be more serious, and you'd probably need some better strategies if you wanted to keep your job.

   > A restaurant near my office has a neon (i.e., expensive) sign in its window advertising VEGETERIAN food; if they haven't realized it's wrong, I don't have the heart to tell them! I wonder if any heads would roll.

3. **Point out that while correct spelling isn't always crucial, there are some times when it's really important.**

   Almost always, if you've spelled a word or two wrong, people can still read what you wrote. But they may dis you anyway, because sometimes people think—even though it's not true—that misspelling words means you're not smart or you're lazy. Because of that, do you know when it matters most? When you're trying to make a good impression on someone, especially if you're applying for a job. *(You may want to show kids some sample resumes or job applications and have a brief discussion about them, just so they have an idea about what this kind of writing looks like.)*

   > A second grader once commented, on seeing a photo of SHCOOL stenciled in large letters on pavement, that maybe it had been done by an evil person who didn't want the cars to stop for kids.

4. **Talk about ways you can make sure you have correct spelling for those times when it really matters.**

   So when you're trying to make a good impression, and the spelling really, really has to be right, how can you make sure that it is? First of all, you'd go back to your four steps for getting your spelling 100% correct. If this is one of those cases where spelling is a lot more important than usual, it's worth taking a little extra time to check. Maybe even ask a few good spellers to take a look. Lots of people haven't even gotten interviewed for a job they wanted because they spelled one word wrong in their application.

Next Steps

» Follow-up

Invite the students to keep an eye out for any misspelled words in the world around them, sharing how they reacted to them and how important or unimportant they thought the mistakes were in the grand scheme of things.

✓ Assessment

As a journal topic, suggest a question like:

📓 Do you think people make too big a fuss about spelling or not enough of a fuss? Why?

Lesson at a Glance: IS SPELLING HARD FOR YOU?

What to Do	What to Say	What Kids Need to Know
INTRODUCE		
• Get kids thinking about how hard spelling is for them.	"What do you remember about first learning to spell? What do you think is helping you get better at spelling now? How many of you feel that spelling comes to you pretty easily? How many find it hard to remember how to spell words?"	Spelling is easier for some people than others.
EXPLORE		
• Explain the three parts of being a good speller.	"There're three main parts to being a good speller: First, you have to read a lot. Why do you think that is? And the great thing is, you don't really have to work at memorizing a lot of words; you just pick them up as you read. Second, when you're writing, you can work at trying to get the words right, either in your first draft or when you're editing. Those two things, reading and paying attention to spelling when you're writing, are things you can control. But you know what? The third part of being a good speller is something that you can't really control; it's whether spelling just comes easily to you or not. Here's a couple of comparisons. Some of you wear glasses. Did you decide whether you were going to have bad vision? Of course not; it's just part of who you are. How many of you are pretty fast runners? Did you decide to be a fast runner? You may have worked at it, but some people are always going to be faster runners than others. It's also just part of who you are, and so is spelling ability."	People who are good at spelling tend to read a lot, try to get words right when they are writing, and have a natural ability to spell. The first two characteristics are things everyone can work on. But being a naturally good speller isn't something you can control.
SUMMARIZE		
• Ask kids to think about what it means if you're a good speller, and what it means if you're not.	"So what does this mean for us? If you're a naturally good speller, your life is going to be a little bit easier; if you're not, you're going to have to work harder at it, but there are a lot of tools you can use to spell words right when it matters. And the good spellers can help the not-as-good spellers, too."	If you don't happen to have a natural ability for spelling, there are still many things you can do to improve your spelling.

IS SPELLING HARD FOR YOU?

Some kids are just better spellers than others. There are three things that make up how good a speller you are: whether it comes naturally to you; how much you read; and how effectively you work at getting spelling right in your writing.

Who, When, and Why

Materials
▶ none

This lesson is a good one for the whole class, so that everyone can understand what goes into effective spelling. It can work well early in the year to provide a framework for other instruction. Also, the principles of this lesson are especially important for struggling spellers, particularly at a point when many students in a class have become very strong spellers. You therefore might want to bring up these ideas again in working with those weaker spellers.

Background Knowledge

Weak spellers generally fall into two groups (though in practice perhaps there's more of a continuum): those who are weak spellers *because* they don't read very much, and those who are weak spellers *despite* being good readers. Someone who doesn't read much can't be a very good speller because he hasn't seen enough words in print often enough to learn the spellings. But we all know people who are good readers and poor spellers; they just have a harder time retaining a spelling once they've seen it, and are less likely to be able to tell if a spelling is correct from looking at it.

In working with students who are struggling with spelling, it's important to keep your expectations realistic. If they don't read much, improving their reading will eventually improve their spelling. A child who already reads quite a bit but does not have a natural spelling ability needs to learn and carry out the process of proofreading, but with expectations that focus more on a reasonable number of words to edit for spelling than on a perfectly spelled final product.

It's also important to use this lesson to destigmatize those who aren't natural spellers.

The Lesson

1. **Get kids thinking about how hard spelling is for them.**

   What do you remember about first learning to spell? *(Allow time for discussion.)* What do you think is helping you get better at spelling now? *(Again, take time to discuss.)* How many of you feel that spelling comes to you pretty easily? How many find it hard to remember how to spell words?

2. **Explain the three parts of being a good speller.**

   The three characteristics of a good speller:
   1) Spends lots of time reading.
   2) Tries to get the words right when writing.
   3) Spelling just comes easily.

   There're three main parts to being a good speller:

   First, you have to read a lot. Why do you think that is? *(You have to see words in print to know what they look like.)* And the great thing is, you don't really have to work at memorizing a lot of words; you just pick them up as you read.

   Second, when you're writing, you can work at trying to get the words right, either in your first draft or when you're editing. Those two things, reading and paying attention to spelling when you're writing, are things you can control.

   But you know what? The third part of being a good speller is something that you can't really control; it's whether spelling just comes easily to you or not. Here's a couple of comparisons. Some of you wear glasses. Did you decide whether you were going to have bad vision? Of course not; it's just part of who you are. How many of you are pretty fast runners? Did you decide to be a fast runner? You may have worked at it, but some people are always going to be faster runners than others. It's also just part of who you are, and so is spelling ability.

3. **Ask kids to think about what it means if you're a good speller, and what it means if you're not.**

   So what does this mean for us? If you're a naturally good speller, your life is going to be a little bit easier; if you're not, you're going to have to work harder at it, but there are a lot of tools you can use to spell words right when it matters. And the good spellers can help the not-as-good spellers, too.

Spelling Strategies and Patterns

Next Steps

» Follow-up

This lesson has provided a vocabulary to use with students, especially the weaker spellers. In talking with them about their spelling, you can have expectations for them, but with a neutral and helpful tone, rather than a nagging one. Also, this lesson should help create a climate where students are accepting of each others' differences rather than disparaging towards weaker spellers.

✓ Assessment

As a journal topic, suggest a question like:

✎ Does spelling come easily to you or not? What can you do to be the best speller you can be?

Lesson at a Glance: THE CHOICES YOU MAKE WHEN YOU SPELL

What to Do	What to Say	What Kids Need to Know
INTRODUCE		
• Begin by getting kids thinking about their spelling in a first draft.	"When you write a first draft, you almost always spell some of the words right and some wrong. Why? And you probably get some words right even though you don't already know them, because your best guess turns out to be right."	You don't always know how to spell all the words you want to use in your writing.
EXPLORE		
• Help students recognize that they are making spelling choices all the time. • If necessary, suggest the idea that taking an extra minute to think about the spelling or find it somewhere can help get it right.	"Every time you write a word you don't know, you have a choice: you can invent a spelling, or you can use a strategy like trying it two ways or looking for it somewhere in the room. How do you make that choice?"	Sometimes when you are writing, you don't know how to spell a word and you have to decide what to do.
DISCOVER		
• Suggest that when students are drafting, they choose a few words they might normally invent and add the extra time to try to get them right. • Help students set reasonable goals for correct spelling.	"I'd like to invite you to try something: the next time you're writing, on a few words that you don't know, make the choice to try to get it right the first time. Even if you still don't get it right, it's a way of paying a little more attention to spelling without slowing down your whole writing process." "Let's talk about reasonable expectations for editing spelling in your writing. If spelling doesn't come easily to you, it could take you a long time to correct all the spellings in your final draft. Let's make a deal. If you agree to work on becoming a better proofreader, I'll agree to be the final copy editor for anything you're going to publish. Let's set a goal for how many words you can reasonably edit for spelling when you're doing a final draft, or set a reasonable amount of time to spend editing for spelling. That way, you're making a choice to care about getting the words spelled right, and I'm agreeing to not ask you to do more proofreading than what's reasonable."	It's a good idea to choose to spend a little extra time on a few words here and there. But not so much that it prevents you from spending time on other important parts of writing.
SUMMARIZE		
• Summarize what you've talked about.	"So, you're making two choices: how much to try to get words right in the first draft, and how much editing for spelling to do with a final draft. It's important to remember that most of your energy should go into what you want to say in your writing, but even though spelling doesn't come easy to you, you can still make the choice to try to do a little better at it."	Part of being a good writer is choosing to attend to spelling. Choose to spend a reasonable amount of time on getting the words right in the first draft, and a reasonable amount of time correcting misspellings while editing.

THE CHOICES YOU MAKE WHEN YOU SPELL

 When you write, you have two choices to make about your spelling: how hard should I try to get words right in the first draft, and how much editing for spelling should I do? The answers to these questions won't be the same every time you write.

Who, When, and Why

Materials
▶ none

This lesson is especially aimed at students who struggle with spelling, and provides a greater focus on concepts that have been explored in previous strategy lessons. However, it could also be done as a whole-class lesson. One point to focus on is that if spelling is a struggle for you, your choices will be appropriately different than if spelling comes easily to you and you know a lot of words.

Background Knowledge

For students who don't spell well, strategies are especially important, and they need to think about how much energy they should be putting into spelling as compared to other aspects of their writing. For them, focusing on correct spelling could consume much of the time and energy that goes into writing. They need to learn to be selective. We need to focus on what's useful for these writers' literacy development as a whole, not just on the final product.

Spelling words right is a function of how many words you've seen in print, your natural ability to remember the spellings of words, and the choices you make about trying to get words right. The first of these is contingent on how much reading you do, the second is out of your control, and the third is the focus of this lesson.

The Lesson

1. **Begin by getting kids thinking about their spelling in a first draft.**

   When you write a first draft, you almost always spell some of the words right and some wrong. What's the reason for this? (*Some words you know and some you don't.*) And there are probably some words that you get right even though you don't already know how to spell them, because your best guess turns out to be right.

2. **Help students recognize that they are making spelling choices all the time.**

   Every time you go to write a word you don't know, you have a choice: you can invent a spelling, or you can try to get it right by using a strategy like trying it two ways or looking for it somewhere in the room. How do you make that choice? (*Allow time for responses: students are likely to say they always invent because it's faster, but try to also evoke some responses—or suggest the idea—that sometimes if you take an extra moment to think about the spelling you can get it right, or maybe you can find it quickly in the room—such as on the word wall—and get it right quickly.*)

3. **Suggest that when students are drafting, they choose a few words they might normally invent and add the extra time to try to get them right.**

   I'd like to invite you to try something: the next time you're writing, on a few words that you don't know, make the choice to try to get it right the first time even if it would be a little quicker to just invent the spelling. Even if you still don't get it right, it's a way of paying a little more attention to spelling without slowing down your whole writing process.

4. **Help students set reasonable goals for correct spelling.**

   Let's talk about reasonable expectations for editing spelling in your writing. If spelling doesn't come easily to you, it could take you a long time to correct all the spellings in your final draft. You could even end up avoiding writing hard words because it would be so much work to get them spelled right. Let's make a deal. If you agree to work on becoming a better proofreader, I'll agree to be the final copy editor for anything you're going to publish. Let's set a goal for how many words you can reasonably edit for spelling when you're doing a final draft, or set a reasonable amount of time to spend editing for spelling (*perhaps ten minutes*). That way, you're making a choice to care about getting the words spelled right, and I'm agreeing to not ask you to do more proofreading than what's reasonable.

5. **Summarize what you've talked about.**

   So, you're making two choices: how much to try to get words right in the first draft, and how much editing for spelling to do with a final draft. It's important to remember that most of your energy should go into what you want to say in your writing, but even though spelling doesn't come easy to you, you can still make the choice to try to do a little better at it.

Next Steps

» Follow-up

You might choose to follow up this lesson with individual conferences focusing on reasonable expectations for each student, remembering that you should be looking for incremental improvement and focusing on process and ownership, not a dramatic improvement in spelling, which will only come over time.

✓ Assessment

As a journal topic, suggest a question like:

How much effort does it make sense for you to put into your spelling?

Lesson at a Glance: WHAT TO FOCUS ON TO BECOME A BETTER SPELLER

What to Do	What to Say	What Kids Need to Know
INTRODUCE		
• Begin by talking about how adults get to be good spellers. Allow time to explore theories.	"Okay, we all know that adults spell better than kids, right? How do you think they get there?"	Adults are typically better spellers because they work at it, they just pick up more words, they've had more years in school, and so on.
DISCOVER		
• Discuss the idea that there are things kids can do now to help them be better spellers, such as spending more time reading. • Point out that paying extra attention to spelling while reading and writing can also be worthwhile. • Remind students that working towards correct spelling when it really matters is another way to improve.	"You know what? Some of it just happens, because you have more years to see words and notice how they're spelled. But you can also make it happen more by doing a few simple things. Do you know what the most important one is? Reading! Every time you read and see a word you don't know how to spell, you have a better chance of spelling it right the next time. So if you already like to read and read a lot, you're helping yourself be a better speller too. If you don't read much now, let's see if we can find some ways to get you reading more." "Another way to become a better speller is to pay a little bit of extra attention to spelling. When you read, if you notice a word you don't know how to spell, you can pay a little extra attention to the letters in it. When you write, check to see if the words look right." "The third way to become a better speller is to get really good at spelling correctly when it really matters. That means using a lot of spelling strategies, and also realizing that sometimes you're going to need some help. If you're writing a letter to the editor of a newspaper, to increase the chances that it'll be published you could have a good adult speller look it over. You don't have to know all the words yourself to get them right in a final draft; what does matter is that you care and that you know how to use all the resources that you have."	Spending more time reading and paying attention to spelling while reading and writing are both ways to improve spelling. Another way to improve is to focus on being the best speller you can be when it really matters.
SUMMARIZE		
• Summarize the discussion.	"Remember, whether spelling comes easy to you or not is just the way you are; it's not something you can control. But what you *can* control is what you do to try to get better at spelling: read, pay attention, and know how to get it right when it matters."	Even if spelling doesn't come easy to you, you can still find ways to improve.

WHAT TO FOCUS ON TO BECOME A BETTER SPELLER

 You'll get better at spelling as you grow older, and you can have a hand in making it happen.

Who, When, and Why

Materials
► none

This lesson is designed for weaker spellers who need and would like to improve. It may be best done as an individual conference, though it could also be useful for a whole class, regardless of current proficiency in spelling.

Be aware that by upper elementary school, students who don't spell as well as others may be feeling more self-conscious and insecure about it; it may seem babyish to them to still get so many words wrong, particularly words that other students have mastered. The best approach with them is to be direct, acknowledging that this is a problem area for them but making it clear that there's a lot they can do for themselves.

Background Knowledge

What a shame that everyone isn't just naturally a good speller! But that's just life, isn't it? I'd love to be a good singer, but I can't even carry a tune. But at least weaker spellers don't need to feel stupid and hopeless. They can be well-served if you help them feel a sense of ownership about their development as spellers. Their weakness in spelling isn't their fault, and there's no need to be helpless in the face of it.

The Lesson

1. **Begin by talking about how adults get to be good spellers.**

    Okay, we all know that adults spell better than kids, right? How do you think they get there? *(Allow time to explore theories. Students might have responses like they work at it; they just pick up more words; they've had more years in school.)*

    You know what? Some of it just happens, because you have more years to see words and notice how they're spelled. But you can also make it happen more by doing a few simple things. Do you know what the most important one is? Reading! Every time you read and see a word you don't know how to spell, you have a better chance of spelling it right the next time. So if you already like to read and read a lot, you're helping yourself be a better speller too. If you don't read much now, let's see if we can find some ways to get you reading more.

2. **Point out that paying extra attention to spelling while reading and writing can also be worthwhile.**

    Another way to become a better speller as the years go by is to pay a little bit of extra attention to spelling. When you read, if you notice a word you don't know how to spell, you can pay a little extra attention to it and notice the letters in it. When you write, you can pay a little bit of extra attention to whether the words look right or not.

3. **Remind students that working towards correct spelling when it really matters is another way to improve.**

    The third way to become a better speller is to get really good at spelling correctly when it really matters. That means using a lot of spelling strategies, and also realizing that sometimes you're going to need some help. If you're writing a letter to the editor of a newspaper, to increase the chances that it'll be published you could have a good adult speller look it over, particularly if you know that you have trouble catching your misspellings. You don't have to know all the words yourself to get them right in a final draft; what does matter is that you care and that you know how to use all the resources that you have.

4. **Summarize the discussion.**

    Remember, whether spelling comes easy to you or not is just the way you are; it's not something you can control. But what you *can* control is what you do to try to get better at spelling: read, pay attention, and know how to get it right when it matters.

Spelling Strategies and Patterns

Next Steps

» Follow-up

I'd follow up with individual chats with struggling spellers, with a focus on encouragement and ownership; bad spelling isn't something you're condemned to, but rather it's just a difference between people, and spelling is only a small part of literacy.

✓ Assessment

As a journal topic, suggest a question like:

> What do you think is going to be most important for you in becoming a better speller? How are you going to work on it?

Patterns

PATTERNS REPRODUCIBLES

Lesson at a Glance: HOW TO SPELL THE /S/ SOUND

What to Do	What to Say	What Kids Need to Know
INTRODUCE		
• Write the words **sad, send, cent, sit, city, sock,** and **sun** on the board or on chart paper. • Discuss as a class what sound the words start with. • Have students work in pairs to create a list of words that start with the /s/ sound.	"Let's read these words together. What do you notice about what sound they start with? What do you notice about what letter they start with?" "Work with a partner and see how many words you can write that start with the /s/ sound. Write them in your spelling journals in two groups, depending on which letter they start with. If you aren't sure, make your best guess."	Lots of words start with the /s/ sound, but sometimes they start with an **s** and sometimes they start with a **c.**
EXPLORE		
• Ask students to share their word lists. • Say the words **sit** and **city** aloud. Discuss how to know whether the words start with **c** or **s.** Repeat with **celery** and **secretary.** • Write the words **sit, city, celery,** and **secretary** on the board or on chart paper. • Ask students to think about how to spell those words. Have them discuss with a partner whether there is a way to tell if the words start with an **s** or a **c.**	"Let's share the words you've written. Now, close your eyes and listen to me say these two words: **sit, city.** Is there any way that you can tell just from listening to them which one starts with **c** and which one starts with **s?** If you do know which one starts with each letter, how do you know? Let's try it with another two words. Close your eyes and listen again: **celery, secretary.** Can you tell what letter they start with?" "Here's something to think about with a partner: when you listen to the words **sit, city, celery,** and **secretary,** you can't tell whether they start with an **s** or a **c.** So then how do you know which letter to use when you write them?"	Just from listening to a word with the /s/ sound, you can't tell whether it starts with an **s** or a **c.**
DISCOVER		
• As a class, share what partners discussed. • Distribute copies of page 274. • Review initial word lists and, as a class, sort them under the headings **sa, ca, se,** and **ce.** • Have students work with a partner to fill in /s/ words that start with the remaining patterns. (See Sample Words for examples.)	"Let's share what you came up with. Is there any way—besides just knowing the word—to tell whether to use **s** or **c?** Let's try something. Look back at the lists you did with your partner, and let's list all the /s/ words that start with **sa.** Okay, now let's list all the /s/ words that start with **ca.** Let's try another pattern. What are your **se** words? What are your **ce** words?" "Try working with your partner and see where you can fill in words with the other patterns."	Some /s/ words start with **sa,** but not **ca** (unless students have mistakenly included some words that start with the /k/ sound). There are words that start with both **se** and **ce.** The only patterns that have words in the **c** column are **ce, ci,** and **cy.**
SUMMARIZE		
• Discuss the sorting results. • Invite children to offer a rule for writing words that start with the /s/ sound.	"What did you notice? Any ideas about why this happens?" "So what's a good rule to use if you're writing a word that starts with the /s/ sound?"	If the second letter is **e, i,** or **y,** the word could start with either **s** or **c,** so you have to know the word to be sure it's right. The rest of the time it has to start with **s.**

HOW TO SPELL THE /S/ SOUND

 The most common way to spell the /s/ sound is, of course, with the letter **s**, but sometimes it's spelled with **c** before **e, i,** and **y.**

Who, When, and Why

Materials
- spelling journals
- copies of page 274

Since there are so many words using the letter **s**, and since you can hear the sound in the name of the letter *(ess)*, children make the connection very early in their spelling. But the letter **c** can also represent the /s/ sound, and you can also hear the sound in its letter name *(cee)*, even though **c** can represent the /k/ sound too. Therefore, particularly as children become familiar with words like **cent** and **city,** you'll see them sometimes using **c** to spell the /s/ sound. When kids have this awareness—that there's more than one way to spell /s/—they're ready to do some exploration of it. Younger students might not be able to grasp and apply the rule very well; in their case, the lesson is more about developing some awareness of the pattern than applying it consistently.

Background Knowledge

The /s/ sound is usually spelled with **s,** and sometimes with **c.** The **c** spelling occurs only before **e, i,** or **y,** and the **s** spelling is more common. Beyond that, it's a matter of knowing the specific word. For Spanish speakers, the same rule applies in Spanish. Other English spellings of /s/, as in **scissors** and **psalm,** are rare.

The Lesson

sad, send, cent, sit, city, sock, sun

1. To get kids thinking about different spellings for the /s/ sound, write **sad, send, cent, sit, city, sock,** and **sun** on the board or on chart paper.

   Let's read these words together. What do you notice about what sound they start with? What do you notice about what letter they start with?

   Work with a partner and see how many words you can write that start with the /s/ sound. Write them in your spelling journal in two groups, depending on which letter they start with. If you aren't sure, make your best guess.

2. After they've done this:

   Let's share the words you've written.

Then:

Close your eyes and listen to me say these two words: **sit, city.** Is there any way that you can tell just from listening to them which one starts with **c** and which one starts with **s?** If you *do* know which one starts with each letter, how do you know? *(Probably just from knowing that specific word.)* Let's try it with another two words. Close your eyes and listen again: **celery, secretary.** Can you tell from listening what letter they start with?

> sit   celery
>
> city   secretary

3. Write the words **sit, city, celery,** and **secretary** on the board or on chart paper.

   👥 Here's something to think about with a partner: when you listen to the words **sit, city, celery,** and **secretary,** you can't tell whether they start with an **s** or a **c.** So then how do you know which letter to use when you write them?

4. After they've finished their discussion:

   Let's share what you came up with. Is there any way—besides just knowing the word—to tell whether to use **s** or **c?** Let's try something. Look back at the lists you did with your partner, and let's list all the /s/ words that start with **sa.** *(Record the **sa** words they offer in the correct section of the chart.)* Okay, now let's list all the /s/ words that start with **ca.** *(There won't be any, unless they've mistakenly included some words that start with the /k/ sound.)* Let's try another pattern. What are your **se** words? What are your **ce** words? *(There will be some of each; include them on the chart.)*

5. Handout copies of page 274 to each student. Invite kids to record the lists you just generated for **sa** and **ca.**

   👥 Try working with your partner and see where you can fill in words with the other patterns. *(The only patterns that will have /s/ words in the **c** column are **ce, ci,** and **cy.** You can refer to my list of /s/ sound words for more examples.)*

6. After kids have had a chance to talk again with their partners, ask:

   What did you notice? *(Move them toward realizing that unless the second letter is an **e, i,** or **y,** the first letter has to be **s.** If the second letter is one of those three, the first letter could be either **s** or **c.**)* Any ideas about why this happens? *(If **sad,** for instance, started with a **c** it would read **cad,** since **c** represents a /k/ sound before most letters. Younger children may not have enough experience with language to grasp this, but the lesson can still proceed. It just means that getting /s/ sound words right won't come as naturally to them as it will in a year or two.)*

The /s/ sound is usually spelled with **s.** It's sometimes spelled with **c,** but only before **e, i,** or **y.**

7. See if kids can generate a rule for deciding how to spell the /s/ sound.

   So what's a good rule to use if you're writing a word that starts with the /s/ sound? *(Build on their ideas to end up with: if the second letter is **e, i,** or **y,** the word could start with either **s** or **c,** so you have to know the word to be sure it's right. The rest of the time it has to start with **s.**)*

/S/ SOUND WORDS

sa	ca
se	ce
si	ci
so	co
su	cu
sy	cy
s + any other letter	c + any other letter

Spelling Strategies and Patterns

Next Steps

Kids might want to keep their charts in their spelling journals for quick reference.

›› Follow-up

Right away:

> When you're reading and writing today, try to notice words that start with the /s/ sound and see how well our rule works. You can add words to your chart if you like.

A few days later: Revisit the rule and talk about whether it's working for them. If not, try to clarify any confusion, but remember that the rule doesn't provide definitive answers about how to spell these words; only a dictionary can do that.

✓ Assessment

As a journal topic, suggest a question like:

> 📓 What have you learned (or what do you know) about how to spell words that start with the /s/ sound?

Also, look for invented spellings of these words in students' writing; see if they result from breaking the rule or are just words that could reasonably start with either **s** or **c**.

⊕ Extension

For older students, you can add the following:

> Take a look at the words **psychology** and **scissors.** They don't fit our rule, do they? Who'd like to get a dictionary and find some other words that start with **ps** and **sc.** What do you think? Why do they break the rule? *(It has to do with their etymology; they typically come from Greek.)* You just have to know those words, don't you? Here's an interesting fact: in French, the **p** in **ps** words is pronounced (like in the word **psychologie**, meaning **psychology**).

Sample Words

The /s/ sound is spelled *s* before:

	Easy	Medium	Harder
a	sad, same, saw	safety, salt, saddle	safari, salute, sausage
e	see, sell, seat	secret, sentence, seem	separate, select, setting
i	six, silly, sister	sign, silent, silver	signature, situation, simplify
o	so, soon, song	soccer, solve, soil	social, solar, sorrow
u	sub, sun, super	sudden, summary, subject	subscription, surrender, suspense
y	syllable	symphony	system
other letters	sleep, snake, smile, swim	sports, ski, strong, square	scorpion, skeleton, station, struggle

...and sometimes *c* before:

	Easy	Medium	Harder
e	celery, center, cereal	certain, central, celebrate	cement, cemetery, ceremony
i	city, circle, Cinderella	circus, citizen, cinema	cinnamon, circumference, cinch
y	cycle	cyclone	cyberspace

Lesson at a Glance: HOW TO SPELL THE /K/ SOUND

What to Do	What to Say	What Kids Need to Know
INTRODUCE		
• Ask students to generate a list of words that start with the /k/ sound. • Write the words on the board or on chart paper, grouped by first letter, but don't label the groups. (See Sample Words.) • Discuss what students notice about the groups of words. • Prompt any key understandings that aren't volunteered.	"Let's think of a bunch of words that start with the same sound as **cat.**" "What do you notice?" "How and why did I group these /k/ words? Which group is the biggest? What do all of the **q** words have in common?"	There are more **c** words that start with the /k/ sound than **k** words. There aren't many **q** words, and those all have **u** as the second letter.
EXPLORE		
• Ask kids to think about a strategy for spelling the /k/ sound. Have them record a few ideas in their spelling journals. • Work with students to develop a multipart strategy.	"What's a good strategy to use if you're writing a word that starts with the /k/ sound and you don't know which letter to use?"	There are a lot more **c** words than **k** words, so **c** is a good first guess. But if the second letter is an **e, i,** or **y,** the first letter in all /k/ words has to be **k.** If the word starts with a /kw/ sound, like **queen,** use **qu.**
DISCOVER		
• Help kids discover why the /k/ sound is spelled with a **k** when followed by an **e, i,** or **y.** • If students can recognize that the spellings look strange, continue with a few other examples. If not, move on by saying that the /k/ rules can help them get these words right.	"Did you notice that whenever the second letter is an **e, i,** or **y,** the first letter is **k?** Why do you think that is? If we write **kitten** with a **c,** what looks funny about it?"	Students may or may not be able to tell that it looks like it says **sitten.**

HOW TO SPELL THE /k/ SOUND

 There are three main ways that /k/ is spelled in English: most commonly with **c**, sometimes with **k**, and with **q** when the /k/ is followed by a /w/ sound at the beginning of words.

Who, When, and Why

Once students get beyond the point where their spelling is mainly phonetic, you'll start seeing different spellings of the /k/ sound in their writing; they'll use **k** because the sound appears in the name of the letter *(kay)*, **c** because it's the most common spelling of the sound, and **q** in the **qu** words that they've seen. This lesson works well after the one on spelling the /s/ sound, since there's a connection between their spelling patterns; /s/ and /k/ spellings depend on the letter that follows them.

Background Knowledge

Your best bets:
* *Try **k** when the /k/ sound is followed by **e, i,** or **y**.*
* *Try **qu** if the second sound in the word is /w/.*
* *Try **ck** if the /k/ sound occurs at the end of short-vowel syllables.*
* *The rest of the time, **c** is your best bet.*

As we saw with /s/, the spelling of the /k/ sound is affected by the second letter in the word. Since **c** makes the /s/ sound when it's followed by **e, i,** or **y,** the letter **k** has to be used at the beginning of those words (**keep, king, Kyle**). If the second sound in the word is /w/, the /kw/ blend is almost always spelled **qu.** The rest of the time, **c** is most common, though **k** still appears sometimes. A **ck** spelling for /k/ occurs at the end of short-vowel syllables (**kick**) or (pretty rare) when doubling a final **c** (**picnicking**). There are a few words with a **ch** spelling of /k/ (**chorus**). A lesson with younger kids would probably just deal with the first part of all this.

For Spanish speakers: Spanish doesn't have the letter **k** except in a few borrowed words, and uses **qu** to spell /k/ before **e** and **i** (**queso, quiero**). **Cu** is used to spell /kw/ (**cuando, cuidar**). Don't be surprised, then, to see some invented spellings that reflect this.

The Lesson

1. To get kids thinking about words that start with the /k/ sound:

   Let's think of a bunch of words that start with the same sound as **cat.** *(Write them on the board as they're mentioned, grouping them according to first letter but not labeling the groups. Make sure some **qu** words are included. See Sample Words for more examples.)*

   What do you notice? *(The ideas you'll be looking for—you can prompt those that aren't volunteered—include: they're grouped by the first letter; there are more **c** words than **k** words; there aren't many **q** words, and those all have **u** as the second letter. Just use natural language to prompt these if needed, as follows:)* How and why did I group these /k/ words? Which group is the biggest? What do all of the **q** words have in common?

2. To get kids thinking about a strategy for spelling the /k/ sound:

📓 What's a good strategy to use if you're writing a word that starts with the /k/ sound and you don't know which letter to use? Take a minute or two to jot down some thoughts in your spelling journal. Then we'll share ideas. *(You'll work with the students to develop a multipart strategy: (1) If it starts with a /kw/ sound like* **queen***, use* **qu;** *(2) there are a lot more* **c** *words than* **k** *words that make the /k/ sound, so* **c** *is a good first guess; (3) if the second letter is an* **e, i,** *or* **y,** *the first letter has to be* **k.***)*

3. To help kids notice patterns in spelling the /k/ sound:

Did you notice that whenever the second letter is an **e, i,** or **y,** the first letter is **k?** Why do you think that is? If we write **kitten** with a **c** *(do so),* what looks funny about it? *(Students may or may not be able to tell that it looks like it says* **sitten.** *If they can, continue with a few other examples. If not, recognize that they don't have enough experience with reading for this to be obvious, and move on by saying that the /k/ rules can help them get these words right.)*

> My leaf friend Fred
>
> My name is Arielle. My friend is a leaf. He can't talk but I don't really mind. He gives me little signs with the little end of his stem. Each day after, breckfast, I would go out side and give the leaf some water, even though I knew he was dieing. I met him after school one day. I decided to pick him up. He was a leaf with a wonderfull swirl of orange, yellow, red and even a little bit of green. I thought he would be a great friend. But then I realized he would only be around this

Next Steps

›› Follow-up

Over the next couple of days:

> See if these ideas help you spell words that start with the /k/ sound better. Add words to our list if you want to. There aren't a lot of words that start with **k,** and you might find it interesting to look through the dictionary to see what some of them are.

✓ Assessment

As a journal topic, suggest a question like:

> What do you know about how to spell the /k/ sound?

Also keep an eye out for how well kids are spelling the /k/ sound in their writing.

⊕ Extension

For older students:

*The rule for words that end with the /k/ sound is that long-vowel words usually use **k,** with one of the standard long-vowel spelling patterns (**break, brake)**, and that short-vowel words typically end in **ck (pick)**.*

> Work with a partner to think of words that end with the /k/ sound, grouping them by how they're spelled, and see if you can come up with a rule.

Also:

> Here are some words that start with a /k/ sound but are spelled with **ch: chorus, chaos, chlorine.** Any ideas about what they have in common? Work with a partner to see if the dictionary can help you find out. *(The dictionary has to be one with etymology information, which will show that the words come from Greek.)*

Sample Words

The /k/ sound can be spelled:

	Easy	Medium	Harder
c	clean, cow, crash, cup, cage	castle, claw, coin, crab, cute	cactus, clue, concert, crane, cafeteria
k	kick, kiss, kid, keep	kettle, kangaroo, kite, kitchen	kernel, kindness, kayak, kingdom
qu	quack, quick, queen, quit	quarter, quilt, quiet, quiz	quality, question, quench, quotation

Lesson at a Glance: HOW TO SPELL THE /J/ SOUND

What to Do	What to Say	What Kids Need to Know
INTRODUCE		
• Distribute copies of page 275. • Have kids work in pairs to cut apart the cards and sort words.	"Here are thirty word cards. Work with a partner to cut them up and sort the words into eight groups."	There's more than one way to spell the /j/ sound.
DISCOVER		
• Spend some time discussing how pairs sorted the words. • Have kids re-sort the words according to the first two letters. • Discuss what students notice about the sort.	"What do you notice? Are there groups you thought you'd see but don't?" "Why do you think we don't have any **ga** words or **go** words in these /j/ words?"	We don't have words in English starting with the /j/ sound that use **ga, go,** or **gu;** they always start with a different sound, as in **gas** and **gosh.**
SUMMARIZE		
• Ask students to think about how they can decide which way to spell the /j/ sound at the beginning of words.	"What do these words tell you about how to spell the /j/ sound?"	If the second letter is **e** or **i,** the /j/ sound could be either **g** or **j.** If the second letter is **y,** the word must start with **g.** Otherwise, it starts with **j.**

HOW TO SPELL THE /J/ SOUND

The /j/ sound can be spelled with a **j** or a **g**. If the /j/ sound comes at the beginning of the word, and the second letter is anything except **e, i,** and **y, j** has to be used. Before those three letters, some words use **g** and some **j** (**gel, jelly**).

Who, When, and Why

Materials
▶ copies of page 275

The names of the letters **g** and **j** both include the sound /j/ at the beginning (*gee* and *jay*), so students are likely to use either letter to represent the sound, although **g** may appear more often since it's more common. This lesson would be especially valuable if you've heard kids wonder which letter to use when they're tackling unfamiliar /j/ words.

Background Knowledge

The /j/ patterns are very similar to the rules for how /s/ is spelled. Like **c, g** often represents a hard sound, like the one heard in **get**. But for the soft **g** (/j/), if the second letter is anything except **e, i,** and **y, j** has to be used (**jam, joke, jump:** none of these would work with **g**). Before those three letters, some words use **g** and some **j** (**gem, jet; giant, jig**).

Note: If the /j/ sound comes in the middle or at the end of the word, **g** is much more common; **j** rarely occurs in the middle or at the end of words, except in compounds, like **flapjack.**

Spanish doesn't have a /j/ sound. **J** and **g** are pronounced /h/ and /g/, respectively, so this lesson may be more challenging for Spanish speakers.

The Lesson

1. Distribute copies of page 275 to pairs.

    Here are thirty word cards. Work with a partner to cut them up and sort the words into eight groups.

2. Spend some time discussing how the pairs sorted the words. Next, ask pairs to sort them into groups (some probably already did so) according to the first two letters of the word (there are no words in English starting with **jy**).

   What do you notice? *(Bring out the idea that all the words start with the same sound, and the reason that there aren't any groups starting with **ga, go,** or **gu** is that we don't have words in English starting with /j/ that use those two letters.)* Are there groups you thought you'd see but don't? Why do you think we don't have any **ga** words or **go** words in these /j/ words? *(Because they always start with a different sound, as in **gas** and **gosh.**)*

3. To get kids thinking about how they can decide which way to spell the /j/ sound:

   What do these words tell you about how to spell the /j/sound? *(If the second letter is **e** or **i,** it could be either **g** or **j.** If the second letter is **y,** the word starts with **g.** Otherwise, it starts with **j.**)*

Next Steps

✓ Assessment

As a journal topic, suggest a question like:

🖎 What have you learned about spelling the /j/ sound?

You might also try a dictation a few days later, where you ask them to write half a dozen words starting with the /j/ sound (such as **Jim, gym, job, Jupiter, juice,** and **jeep**), then write a little about how they got their answers, and then discuss. I've included two words with the same pronunciation but different spellings to help kids see that sometimes you just have to know the word.

⊕ Extension

Invite students to generate a list of **ge** and **gi** words that have a /j/ sound.

   Would anybody like to use the dictionary to make a list of words in English that start with the /j/ sound and use either **ge** or **gi?** There aren't that many of them, and it could be useful to have a list of them to refer to. That way you'll know that if a /j/ sound word isn't on the list, it'll start with **j.**

Alternatively, you can provide them with a list of /j/ words that start with **ge** or **gi,** since searching through much of the **g** section of the dictionary could be tedious for kids. (See Sample Words.)

Spelling Strategies and Patterns

Sample Words

The /j/ sound is spelled **j** before:

	Easy	Medium	Harder
a	jar, jam, jab	jacket, jail, jazz	January, Japan, jaguar
e	jet, Jeep, Jess	jelly, jerk, jeans	jewelry, jersey, jester
i	jig, jive, Jim	jingle, jiggle, jitter	jinx, jigsaw, jiffy
o	jog, job, Joe	jot, jolly, joke	journal, journey, join
u	jump, jug, just	judge, July, jungle	jubilee, junior, juice

...and **g** before

	Easy	Medium	Harder
e	gee, gel, gem, germ	gene, gentle, genius, general	gesture, genuine, geography, generate
i	giant	giraffe	gibberish
other	gym		gyroscope

Lesson at a Glance: IS IT W OR WH?

What to Do	What to Say	What Kids Need to Know
INTRODUCE		
• Write the word **wing** on the board or on chart paper. • As a class, list other words that start with the same sound as **wing.** • Record the words in two columns for the **w** and **wh** spellings.	"Okay, let's make a list of words that start with the same sound as **wing.** Is it hard for you to remember which ones start with **wh?** Let's see if we can come up with a pretty good method."	Lots of words start with the /w/ sound, but sometimes they start with a **w** and sometimes they start with **wh.**
EXPLORE		
• Discuss the two groups of words. • As a class, use a dictionary to compare the number of pages of **wh** words to the rest of the **w** words.	"When you look at the two groups of /w/ words, what do you notice? Which group has more words?" "Do you notice some words in the **wh** group that seem to go together? These are the question words **what, when, where,** and **why,** and the less common ones **which, whether,** and so on." "Is there anything that the rest of the **wh** words have in common?" "Let's look at the **w** and **wh** words in the dictionary. What do you notice?"	There are more **w** words than **wh** words. Many of the **wh** words are question words. The rest of the **wh** words don't really have anything in common.
DISCOVER		
• Create a list of useful **wh** words that students can refer to. (Or see Sample Words.)	"Now let's use the dictionary to make a list of **wh** words that we might like to use in our writing, and then put that list on the word wall or in our spelling journals."	Posting a list of common **wh** words can help you get the spellings of those words right.
SUMMARIZE		
• Summarize the strategy for writing words that start with the /w/ sound.	"Let's try this out as a strategy for spelling /w/ words: (1) Is it one of the question words we listed? Then it starts with **wh.** (2) Is it on our list of common **wh** words? (3) If not, it probably starts with just plain **w.**"	If the word is one of the question words, then it starts with **wh.** If it is not a question word, and not on our list of common **wh** words, then it probably starts with just plain **w.**

IS IT W OR WH?

 There's a good method for knowing whether a word starts with **w** or **wh**: if it's one of a group of common question words or on a list of common **wh** words, then it starts with **wh**. If not, then it probably starts with just plain **w**.

Who, When, and Why

Materials
▶ dictionaries
▶ spelling journals

At first, young writers will always spell /w/ words like **with** and **where** with just **w**, since that's what they hear. But once they start seeing that some words have **wh**, this spelling will appear in their writing—though not always in the right word or the right place. This leads to some of those spellings that drive teachers crazy, like WHITH for **with** and WHERE for **were**. Children truly have no way of knowing which spelling to use unless they happen to consistently remember the spelling of a particular word. Since many of the words involved are common ones, this lesson can have quite an impact.

Background Knowledge

Over the years at spelling workshops, when I ask how we know whether a word starts with **w** or **wh**, there's often one teacher who raises her hand and goes "Wh, wh," puffing air out her lips. Many of you may not even know what she's talking about. Here's why. Words starting with **wh** were indeed once pronounced differently, having a puff of air at the beginning. (Technically, it's a /h/ sound followed by a /w/, sort of like starting the word with a whisper.) But this has largely dropped out of American English, so that even if you pronounce **wh** words differently from **w** words yourself, your students almost certainly don't.

Back in the day (way back, that is, in old English, up to around 1300), words like **whale** and **when** were spelled HWAL and HWEN, reflecting the actual sequence of sounds in the words. The spellings changed to the ones we know today, and the pronunciation stayed the same. But in more recent years, the /hw/ pronunciation started dropping out of American English. Some middle-aged and older adults still use it, but children don't. This is true in all regions of the country. Consequently, words like **which** and **witch** are homophones; kids just have to learn their spellings.

Occasionally a teacher will suggest to me that if we taught kids to pronounce the **wh** words "correctly," then they could spell them right. But language doesn't work that way; we talk the way we talk. And in order to know which words to say with a /hw/, you'd have to know they were spelled with **wh**, and if you already knew that, what's the point?

The Lesson

w	wh
wing	what
want	whale
wish	when
worry	where
wait	whisper
window	why
wet	
wood	
welcome	
water	

1. To get kids thinking about the /w/ sound, write the word **wing** on the board or on chart paper.

   Okay, let's make a list of words that start with the same sound as **wing.**

   As words are volunteered, write them in two columns, separating the **w** and **wh** spellings. Then read through the words together.

   Is it hard for you to remember which start with **wh?** Let's see if we can come up with a pretty good method.

2. Encourage students to explore and discover:

   When you look at the two groups of /w/ words, what do you notice? Which group has more words? *(There are more **w** words than **wh** ones.)* Do you notice some words in the **wh** group that seem to go together? *(Give time for students to respond.)* These are the question words **what, when, where, why,** and the less common ones **which, whether,** and so on. *(**Who** wouldn't be on your list because it starts with a different sound, but you could include it on a list of **wh** question words.)* Is there anything that the rest of the **wh** words have in common? No, you just have to know them, but there aren't that many of them.

   As a class, try using a dictionary to compare the number of pages of **wh** words to the rest of the **w** words.

   Let's look at the **w** and **wh** words in the dictionary. What do you notice? *(Confirm that **wh** words make up only a small portion of **w** words.)*

3. Create a list of **wh** words that students can use as a reference.

    Now let's use the dictionary to make a list of **wh** words that we might like to use in our writing, and then put that list on the word wall or in our spelling journals. *(Alternatively, you can invite a couple of students to compile the list, or you can provide it yourself; see Sample Words.)*

4. Help kids summarize what's been learned about the pattern:

    Let's try this out as a strategy for spelling /w/ words: (1) Is it one of the question words we listed? Then it starts with **wh.** (2) Is it on our list of common **wh** words? (3) If not, it probably starts with just plain **w.**

Next Steps

» Follow-up

A few days later, ask:

    How's it going? How do you think you're doing at *always* getting the **w** and **wh** words right?

✓ Assessment

As a journal topic, suggest a question like:

    🖊 What do you know about spelling **w** and **wh** words?

See Strategies 7 and 8 to help students have more success with particular /w/ words they're still misspelling.

Monitor students' writing to see how they spell words that start with the /w/ sound. It'll be particularly valuable to see if students are now spelling correctly the many words starting with **w** that are frequently misspelled. If a misspelled word turns up, it's a good chance to review the pattern and ask kids how they can keep from missing these any more. They can also choose these words as one-second words.

Sample Words

Words spelled with **wh:**

	Easy	Medium	Harder
Question words	what, when, where, why, which	whatever, whether	
Other **wh** words	whale, wheat, wheel, while, whip, whisper, whistle, white	whack, wharf, wheelbarrow, whether, whine, whirl, whiskers	whim, whimper, whisk, whoop

Lesson at a Glance: A FEW TRICKY CONSONANTS

What to Do	What to Say	What Kids Need to Know
EXPLORE		
• Hand out a copy of page 276 to each pair. • Have partners cut apart the cards and sort the words into four groups. • Talk about the sorts and show the words sorted according to the four patterns. • Discuss why these spellings happen.	"Work with a partner to cut out the sixteen words on this sheet of paper and then sort them into four groups." "Any ideas about why I picked these spelling patterns for you to work on today? Any ideas about why this happens?"	Some sounds are spelled with two letters.
DISCOVER		
• Talk with students about each spelling. • Write the listed word pairs on the board or on chart paper for students to see how the different **ck** spellings would look with just one letter instead of the **ck.** • Ask students to think about why those spellings don't work.	"Well, here's why. It's a little different for each of them." The **gh** spelling for /f/: "Know what? Only six common words in English spell the /f/ sound with **gh,** and you have four of them right in front of you. Any guesses about what the other two are? One you know—**rough**—and the other one you probably don't—**trough,** which is a long, narrow container for water." The **ph** spelling for /f/: "There are a lot of words /f/ that start with **ph,** but most of them are scientific and medical, like **pharmacy, photosynthesis,** and **phlebotomist.** That's someone who specializes in drawing blood!" The **sc** spelling for /s/: "When a word starts with **sc,** it usually stands for the /sk/ sound. However, in some words you only hear a /s/, but you need the two letters **sc.** There aren't very many words like this; if you can remember the **sc** in **scene, scent, science,** and **scissors,** you'll be in good shape." The **ck** spelling for /k/: "Why do you think that our four **ck** words don't have just **c** or **k?** Let's try them and see how they look." "Can you put into words why you need a **ck** in these words? Let me show you something. What if we were to write the word **puddle** with only one **d,** so it was PUDLE? That would look funny too, like it said **poodle.** A **ck** is like a double letter; we use **ck** in a lot of the same places where we'd use double letters."	The **gh** spelling for /f/: Only six common words in English spell the /f/ sound with **gh.** Remember **laugh, rough, tough,** and **cough.** The **ph** spelling for /f/: There are a lot of words that start with **ph,** but most of them are scientific and medical. The **sc** spelling for /s/: When **sc** makes the /s/ sound, the third letter is always **e, i,** or **y.** Remember the **sc** in **scene, scent, science,** and **scissors.** The **ck** spelling for /k/: A **ck** is like a double letter; we use them in a lot of the same places where we'd use double letters.

A FEW TRICKY CONSONANTS

Some consonant sounds are spelled with different letters than we'd expect.

Who, When, and Why

Materials
► copies of page 276

This is a lesson best suited for students who are a little older and have gotten pretty good at spelling most consonant sounds, although it could serve as enrichment for younger children who have wondered about "funny" spellings like **laugh.** The goal is twofold: familiarity with some specific words, which makes it more likely that kids will remember their spellings; and exploration of the principle that sounds aren't always spelled the way we'd expect them to be.

With younger children, you can skip the explanation of why these patterns exist. The explanation for the **ck** pattern is the most complicated, and can be saved for older students.

Background Knowledge

Fortunately, most consonant sounds in English are pretty easy to spell; if you know the name of the letter, it's pretty easy to remember what sound it represents (the name of the letter **b** starts with the sound /b/, and so on). Even letters like **h,** whose name doesn't include the sound, are spelled pretty consistently. The previous lessons dealt with some of the patterns that are harder and occur in a lot of words; this lesson is more of a wrap-up on some irregular but less common patterns.

Some consonant sounds are usually spelled one way, but occasionally appear another way. The ones we'll take a look at here are **gh** and **ph** for /f/, **ck** for /k/, and **sc** for /s/. Not really that many, are there? They occur for historical and etymological reasons (the language the word came from) or, in the case of **ck,** phonetic reasons (it's a special case of consonant doubling).

In Spanish, every sound is always represented by the same letter, except for a few variations like **b** and **v,** which represent the same sound. When words from other languages are imported into Spanish, they're usually assimilated into the Spanish spelling system. Therefore, not only these English spelling patterns but the underlying principles of how they work will be unfamiliar to Spanish speakers.

The Lesson

1. Hand out a copy of page 276 to each pair.

   👥 Work with a partner to cut out the sixteen words on this sheet of paper and then sort them into four groups.

2. Talk about the partners' sorts, and, if students haven't already done so, show the words sorted according to the four spelling patterns for this lesson.

Any ideas about why I picked these spelling patterns for you to work on today? *(They all use two letters to spell a sound that's usually spelled with one letter.)* Any ideas about why this happens? *(Encourage the students to speculate with as many ideas as they'd like.)*

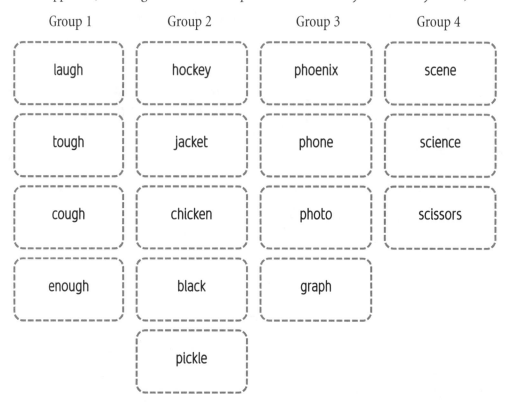

Group 1	Group 2	Group 3	Group 4
laugh	hockey	phoenix	scene
tough	jacket	phone	science
cough	chicken	photo	scissors
enough	black	graph	
	pickle		

3. Talk with students about each spelling:

Well, here's why. It's a little different for each of them.

The gh spelling for /f/:

Know what? Only six common words in English spell the /f/ sound with **gh** (plus variations on them like **laugh** and **laughter**), and you have four of them right in front of you. Any guesses about what the other two are? One you know—**rough**—and the other one you probably don't—**trough,** which is a long, narrow container for water.

The ph spelling for /f/:

There are a lot of /f/ words that start with **ph,** but most of them are scientific and medical, like **pharmacy, photosynthesis,** and **phlebotomist.** That's someone who specializes in drawing blood!

The sc spelling for /s/:

When a word starts with **sc,** it usually stands for the /sk/ sound. However, in some words you only hear /s/, but you need the two letters **sc.** (In these words, the third letter is always **e, i,** or **y.**) There aren't very many words like this; if you can remember the **sc** in **scene, scent, science,** and **scissors,** you'll be in good shape.

The ck spelling for /k/:

Why do you think that our four **ck** words don't have just **c** or **k?** Let's try them and see how they look.

Spelling Strategies and Patterns

blac/blak
hocey/hokey
jacet/jaket
picle/pikle

4. Write the following words on the board or on chart paper for students to see how the **ck** spellings would look if they were spelled differently: **blac/blak, hocey/hokey, jacet/jaket, picle/pikle.**

Encourage students to respond, and look for answers like "they just don't look right" or "they look like they say something else, like JASSET or HOKE-EY."

Can you put into words why you need a **ck** in these words? *(Any reasonable responses are good here.)* Let me show you something. What if we were to write the word **puddle** with only one **d,** so it was PUDLE? *(Write it so the kids can see it.)* That would look funny, too, like it said **poodle.** A **ck** is like a double letter; we use the **ck** in a lot of the same places where we'd use double letters.

Next Steps

 ### Follow-up

You might want to ask kids to look over some of their writing to see if they can find places they used these spellings. Invite volunteers to share their words with the class.

 ### Assessment

As a journal topic, suggest a question like:

📓 What did you learn about consonants today, and what about it was interesting to you?

Sample Words

Some tricky consonant spellings:

gh for /f/	**ph** for /f/	**sc** for /s/	**ck** for /k/
rough	phase	science	pack
tough	pheasant	scientist	sack
enough	pharmacy	scientific	tackle
cough	phrase	scene	check
laugh	Philip	scent	black
trough	phone	scenery	peck
slough	phonics	scissors	heckle
	photo		tickle
	phoenix		sick
			pickle
			locket
			clock
			sock
			duck
			truck
			chicken
			hockey
			jacket
			racket

Lesson at a Glance: LONG A

What to Do	What to Say	What Kids Need to Know
DAY 1: EXPLORE		
• Hand out a copy of page 277 to each student. • As a class, generate word families for **-aid** and **-ade.** • Discuss how to know whether the long **a** sound is spelled with **ai** or **a** with a silent **e.** • Ask students to volunteer other words that belong in each family. If a student suggests the wrong category for a word, just put it in the correct one.	"Let's work with some word families. How many words can we think of that rhyme with **maid** and are spelled with the same pattern? **(laid, paid, raid, braid)** Now let's do a word family for **made. (fade, blade, spade)** For any of those words, is there a rule that tells you whether to use **ai** or **a** with a silent **e** at the end?" "Let's think of some other words that use either of these patterns to spell this long **a** sound."	The long **a** sound can be spelled many different ways. There isn't really a rule to help you know how to spell the long **a** sound.
DAY 1: DISCOVER		
• Discuss with students any strategies they could use to help them spell the long **a** sound.	"If you were going to write one of these long **a** words but didn't already know how to spell it, what would be a good idea for how to come up with a spelling?"	Younger children may not be able to use a helpful strategy. More mature students will use strategies such as trying it both ways or checking a dictionary.
DAY 2: EXPLORE		
If students are ready for another long **a** pattern: • Using the same chart, continue the discussion by generating a word family list for **-ay** and talking about the pattern.	"Let's find words for another word family, words that rhyme with **play** and have the same spelling pattern." "Do you notice anything that would help you know when to use the **ay** spelling?"	The pattern for **-ay** words is more predictable than other long **a** patterns. The **-ay** words all have the long **a** sound at the end.
DAY 2: DISCOVER		
• Talk about other ways to spell the long **a** sound. (See Sample Words for words with other spellings of long **a.**) • Discuss strategies to help with spelling long **a.**	"Most words with the long **a** sound use one of these three spelling patterns. But can you think of any words that spell it differently? These spellings are uncommon. The only way to get these less common words right is to remember them, but the good part is that there aren't too many of them."	Most long **a** words are spelled with **ai, a_e,** or **ay.** Other spellings of long **a** are uncommon. You just have to know the words to get them right.

LONG A

✳ You can make a good first guess for a word that's spelled with long **a,** and then have a strategy for what to do after writing your first attempt at the word.

Who, When, and Why

By second grade, kids have figured out the easy CVC (consonant-vowel-consonant) pattern for short-vowel spellings **(bat, bed, bit, Bob, bug)**, but the long vowels are harder because each one has more than one possible spelling, and there's no easy way to know which one to use for a particular word.

This long **a** lesson can be done initially with children who have begun to explore different spellings for long **a** in their writing; they may sometimes get them right, but other times have invented spellings like MAEK or SAIF. Step 1, in which children explore common patterns for spelling long **a,** is enough for one day. Older students may still be able to make use of some fine-tuning with this spelling pattern, particularly in longer words.

Background Knowledge

Like all the long vowels, long **a** is usually spelled with more than one letter, particularly in one-syllable words. The most common spellings are **ai, a** with a silent **e** at the end of the word, and **ay.** The pattern **ay** is typically found at the end of a word, syllable, or root word **(played).** The ideas in the lesson will be clearest if you stick to one-syllable words, but I'll conclude with a section on longer words, where the most common spelling is just the letter **a.**

The Lesson

1. Hand out copies of page 277. To get kids thinking about long **a** words:

Let's work with some word families. How many words can we think of that rhyme with **maid** and are spelled with the same pattern? **(laid, paid, raid, braid)** Now let's do a word family for **made. (fade, blade, spade)** For any of those words, is there a rule that tells you whether to use **ai** or **a** with a silent **e** at the end? *(No, you just have to know the word.)* Let's think of some other words that use either of these patterns to spell this long **a** sound, like **cape** and **rain.** *(There will be quite a few; record thirty or more on chart paper, leaving room to add more groups of words. Encourage students to record the words on their own charts. If a student suggests the wrong category for a word, just put it in the correct one.)*

If you were going to write one of these long **a** words but didn't already know how to spell it, what would be a good idea for how to come up with a spelling? *(Younger children might not be able to say more than a general strategy, such as "I'd sound it out."*

Somewhat older students, who will get more out of the lesson, will be able to respond with comments like "I'd try both ways and then see which one looked better, or check it in the dictionary." You might choose to stop the lesson at this point, since this is enough to absorb at one sitting, particularly for younger students. You could continue on another day with the rest of the lesson if the students seem developmentally ready for it.)

2. If students are ready for another long **a** pattern, have them pull out the chart they began for Step 1.

> You may want to save Steps 2 and 3 for another day.

Let's find words for another word family, words that rhyme with **play** and have the same spelling pattern.

List the words they suggest on the board or on chart paper. Have students record them on their charts.

Do you notice anything that would help you know when to use this **ay** spelling? *(The words all have the long **a** sound at the end.)*

3. Invite students to list words with other long **a** patterns.

Most words with the long **a** sound use one of these three spelling patterns. But can you think of any words that spell it differently? *(See Sample Words.)* These spellings are uncommon. The only way to get these less common words right is to remember them, but the good part is that there aren't too many of them.

Next Steps

Follow-up

Right away:

You might want to suggest that students keep their charts in their spelling journals for later reference.

Over the next few days:

Keep an eye out for long **a** words in your reading, and think about how you spell them when you write them. You can add more words to your chart if you like.

Assessment

As a journal topic, suggest a question like:

What advice would you give someone about how to spell long **a?**

Also, look for invented spellings of long **a** words in students' writing. Are they logical? That is, do they most often use the two most common spellings, or **ay** at the ends of words? You might also see some overgeneralizations, such as misspelling the past tense of **ay** words—as in PLAID for **played.** (Of course, **paid** would be correct!) This could be followed with a brief lesson on how these root words don't change when you add a suffix.

Extension

With older students, you might want to explore how long **a** is spelled in longer words. Hand out copies of page 278 to kids who are doing the activity.

With a partner, see if you can think of a long **a** word that's two syllables or longer for every letter of the alphabet. For instance, you might have **baby** for **b** and **complain** for **c.** Use a paper word wall (Routman, 1999). When you've filled in as many boxes as you can, see if you can come up with a rule for how to spell long **a** in longer words. *(It's usually just the letter **a,** except if it's in the last syllable, when it works like one-syllable words.)*

Sample Words

Long *a* words:

	Easy	Medium	Harder
ai	aid, bait, gain, jail, pain, rail,wail, aim, fail, nail, paid, rain	braid, brain, claim, strain, waist, chair, faint, grain, paint, trail, train	drain, faith, flail, frail, gait, quaint, raid, snail, stain, taint, traipse, trait, vain
a_e	age, face, gave, late, make, name, safe, rake, tape, vase	blame, blaze, glaze, grade, grape, scale, daze, brave, trade, whale	bathe, crave, drape, grace, grave, phase, phrase, quake, scrape, trace
ay	day, hay, lay, may, pay, say, stay, way	gray, play, clay, pray, tray, spray	fray, sway, X-ray
eigh		eight, sleigh, weigh	freight, weight
ey	they	obey	prey
ea	bear, break, great	steak	
ei		reins	reign, veil, vein

Extension word list: multisyllable long *a* words

a	bacon, basic, danger, fable, favor, navy, radio, temptation
ai	complain, contain, daily, daisy, maintain, pertain, reclaim, remain
a_e	elevate, escape, illustrate, lemonade, persuade, rebate, rotate
ay	betray, decay, display, portray, relay, subway, Sunday, today
ei	neighbor, reindeer
Oddballs	gauge, matinee, café

Lesson at a Glance: LONG E

What to Do	What to Say	What Kids Need to Know
DISCOVER		
• Hand out copies of page 279 to pairs. • Have kids cut apart the cards and sort them. • After kids have sorted, discuss the results as a class. • Ask kids to think of other words in each group.	"Here are some word cards with long **e** words. Work with a partner to cut them up and sort the words into six groups. Think about the long **e** sound when you do this word sort." "What did you notice?" "Take some blank cards and see how many other words you can think of for each group."	There are many ways to spell the long **e** sound.
SUMMARIZE		
• Invite kids to share what they discovered and summarize what they've learned.	"What did you discover? Which spelling patterns could you find more words for? Does this give you some ideas about how to spell words with long **e** words that you don't even know?"	To spell the long **e** sound, **ea** and **ee** are good first guesses, but you can't really be sure unless you know the word or look it up.

LONG E

 There are a few common ways to spell the long **e** sound (**ea, ee**), and several less common ones (**e, y, ie, ei**) that are a matter of just knowing the word.

Materials
► copies of page 279 and 280

Who, When, and Why

Students who are usually using two letters to spell long **e,** even if they don't always get it right, are ready for this lesson. For instance, you may see BEAF and MEEL. Younger students may overgeneralize the use of **ee** and **ea,** leading to their missing words with other spellings that they may have known before; **chief** may become CHEEF. This is normal and will work itself out over time. With older students, you can move on to looking more at two-syllable words, where **e** is a frequent spelling within the word, or where **y** and **ey** appear at the end.

Background Knowledge

As with the other long vowels, the trick with long **e** is to realize that there aren't rules for spelling it that work consistently, but there are some regularities:

- The most common spellings of long **e** are **ee** and **ea,** and there are a lot of homophone pairs with these two spellings (**read/reed, meat/meet, steal/steel**).

- Some words have one of the first two spellings plus an **e** at the end (**please, freeze**).

*For more on **ie** and **ei** see Pattern 12 on the **i** before **e** rule.*

- There are also words with **ei** (**seize**), the special case of **cei** words (**ceiling, receive**), and some **i** before **e** words (**chief, niece**).

- There are some rare long **e** spellings, like **eo** (**people**) and, would you believe, **agh** (**shillelagh**).

- At the ends of words, **ee, y,** and **ey** appear (**flee, silly, monkey**).

- One-syllable words mostly use **ee,** except for **key.**

- Also, there are a few short function words that are just a consonant or two plus long **e** (**be, he, me, she, we**).

These varied spellings of the sound at the end of the word make long **e** a little more challenging to spell correctly than long **a.**

In Spanish, long **e** is always spelled with the letter **i** (**niño, listo**), so these English spellings will seem pretty complicated to Spanish speakers.

The Lesson

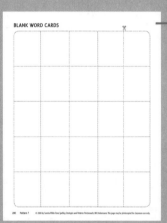

1. Hand out copies of page 279 to pairs. To get kids thinking about long **e** words:

   Here are some word cards with long **e** words. Work with a partner to cut them up and sort the words into six groups. Think about the long **e** sound when you do this word sort. *(I've avoided putting any pairs of homophones in the word sort even though there are many with long **e**, such as **meet** and **meat**; see Pattern 20 on homophones.)*

2. After kids have sorted, talk about what they discovered.

   What did you notice?

   Once you've ensured that they have the cards sorted by the way each word spells long **e,** you may want to distribute blank copies of page 280 so kids can use them to write more words:

   Take some blank cards, and see how many other words you can think of for each group.

3. Invite kids to share what they noticed while thinking up words.

   What did you discover? Which spelling patterns could you find more words for? Does this give you some ideas about how to spell long **e** words that you don't even know? (**Ea** and **ee** are good first guesses, but you can't really be sure unless you know the word or look it up.)

Next Steps

» Follow-up

Kids might want to jot down the words they sorted in their spelling journals, or at least record the words they don't already know how to spell. By keeping running lists of long **e** words, they'll have a handy resource to use for their writing.

✓ Assessment

As a journal topic, suggest a question like:

   What do you know about good strategies for spelling words with the long **e** sound?

If you've done this lesson after another vowel lesson, have kids discuss or freewrite about the following:

   What do you think and know about how to spell long vowels? Even though there can be a lot of different ways to spell them, how good do you think your chances are of getting them right?

Sample Words

Ways to spell long *e*:

	Easy	Medium	Harder
ee	need, keep, feel, week, seen	street, cheek, queen, wheel, bleed	greedy, indeed, needle, feeble, sleeping
ea	mean, real, seat, pea	clean, teach, dream, squeak	defeat, eagle, reason, feature
ea_e	leave, tease, peace	please, grease, leave	disease
ee_e	geese, freeze, breeze,	cheese, squeeze, sleeve, sneeze	
ei	seize	Keith	either, caffeine
cei			ceiling, receive, deceive
ie	field, piece, chief, thief	grief	believe, brownies
-ee	bee, tree, free	agree, flee	coffee, committee, degree
-y	city, any, busy, lady	study, crazy, angry, misty	biology, bravery, stingy, springy
-ey	key, money	donkey, monkey, honey	valley, chimney
e	be, we, she, he, me	even, equal	coyote
Oddballs		people	phoenix, algae

Lesson at a Glance: LONG I

What to Do	What to Say	What Kids Need to Know
DISCOVER		
• Distribute copies of page 281. • Ask kids to think of words for each category.	"Work with a partner to write as many long **i** words as you can in each of these word families. The words should end with the pattern at the top of the box, and should rhyme with the first word there. If you can think of another word family with the long **i** sound, put it on the back of the page."	The long **i** sound can be spelled many different ways.
SUMMARIZE		
• Discuss what kids have noticed. • Ask them to summarize what they learned.	"What did you discover? What have you learned about long **i** words?"	Many long **i** words are spelled with an **i** and then a silent **e** at the end. If the long **i** is at the end of the word, the **i** and **e** are together. Some words end in **y;** you know which ones because there are two consonant letters before the **y** (except **by** and **my**). Eight words (plus a few more uncommon ones) use **igh** to spell long **i.**

LONG I

 Your best bet for spelling long **i** is **i** with a silent **e** at the end, except for some words that have the long **i** sound at the end, and eight **igh** words.

Who, When, and Why

Materials
▶ copies of page 281

Students may be more likely to get long **i** words right than other long-vowel words, since the sound is spelled more regularly. But it wouldn't hurt to bring the pattern into more conscious awareness. As with the other long vowels, older students might want to look for how the sound is spelled in longer words.

Background Knowledge

Your Best Bets:
- *Try **ie** or **y** if the long i sound comes at the end of the word.*
- *Learn the few **igh** words that have a long i sound.*
- *Try just **i** if the long i sound is in a multisyllable word.*
- *The rest of the time **i** with a silent final **e** is your best bet.*

Long **i** is pretty easy to spell in one-syllable words, since it's usually spelled with **i** and then a silent final **e** (**fine, bike, ride**). At the ends of words, the **i** and **e** appear together in a few words (**pie, die, lie, tie**), while others end with **y** (**try, fly, shy,** usually if there are two consonant letters before the vowel sound). Some words spell **i** with **igh,** but there are only a very few of them (**thigh, high, sigh, fight, might, sight, right, tight**). In words of more than one syllable, as with other long vowels, the long **i** is most often spelled with just **i** (**driver, license**).

In Spanish, the closest sound to long **i** is spelled with the letters **ay** and **ai** (**cayó, bailar**), but each letter's sound is pronounced, so the sound is more like ah-ee than long **i.** Spanish-speaking students will therefore be trying to spell a sound that doesn't quite exist in their first language.

LONG I PATTERNS

ide	ime
bride	time

ine	ipe
pine	wipe

ite	ie
white	pie

y	igh
fly	high

408 Pattern 8 © 2008 by Sandra Wilde from Spelling Strategies and Patterns. Portsmouth, NH: Heinemann. This page may be photocopied for classroom use only.

The Lesson

1. Hand out copies of page 281 to pairs. To get kids thinking about long **i** words:

   Work with a partner to write as many long **i** words as you can in each of these word families. The words should end with the pattern at the top of the box, and should rhyme with the first word there. If you can think of another word family with the long **i** sound, put it on the back of the page.

2. Invite kids to share their work:

   What did you discover? *(I've picked the patterns for **i_e** that include the most words, but you can help kids discover these larger generalizations.)* What have you learned about long **i** words?

   - A lot of long **i** words are spelled with an **i** and then a silent **e** at the end **(wipe)**; if the long **i** is at the end of the word, the **i** and **e** are together **(pie)**.
   - Some words end in **y;** you know which ones because there are two consonant letters before the **y (fly)**, with the two exceptions of **by** and **my**.
   - Eight words (plus a few more uncommon ones) use **igh** to spell long **i**.

   That's it!

Next Steps

✓ Assessment

A week or so later, as a journal topic, suggest a question like:

   What do you know that helps you spell long **i** words?

This will give you a sense of how well kids have remembered these fairly simple patterns.

＋ Extension

Kids are welcome to think of more long **i** words to add to their lists; it's only rarely that they'll find any that don't follow these patterns.

Sample Words

Ways to spell long *i*:

ide	bride, ride, tide, wide, pride, glide, side, hide
ime	dime, time, grime, lime, mime, prime, crime
ine	dine, fine, line, mine, nine, pine, vine
ipe	wipe, gripe, pipe, ripe
ite	kite, bite, white, quite
ie	pie, die, lie, tie
y	by, cry, dry, fly, my, sty, try, pry, sly
igh	thigh, high, sigh, fight, might, sight, right, tight, light, night, right
oddballs	height, feisty, aisle, bayou, eye, buy, coyote, dye, rye

Lesson at a Glance: LONG O

What to Do	What to Say	What Kids Need to Know
EXPLORE		
• Have kids work with a partner to make a list of long **o** words in their spelling journals. • Ask them to group their lists by spellings.	"Work with a partner to do two things: think of as many one-syllable words with the long **o** sound in them as you can, and write them down in you spelling journal in different groups, depending on how the sound is spelled."	There are a few different ways to spell the long **o** sound.
DISCOVER		
• Discuss what kids notice about their lists.	"How did that go? Let's combine what everybody came up with and see if we can make some generalizations."	The **oa** and **o_e** spellings are most common. The **ow** spelling is usually at the end of words (with exceptions like **toe** and **go**).
SUMMARIZE		
• Help kids think of strategies for spelling long **o.**	"So what's your best rule of thumb when you're spelling one of these words? Would it make sense to go with: Try **oa** and **o** plus silent **e,** and see if you can tell which one is right; or if it's at the end of the word try **ow** first."	Try **o** with silent **e** or **oa** first. If it's at the end of the word, try **ow.**

LONG O

 There are three main ways to spell long **o**: **oa**, **o** with a final silent **e**, and **ow**.

Who, When, and Why

If your students have been exploring other long-vowel spelling patterns, they'll find long **o** pretty easy. As with the other long-vowel spelling patterns, children are ready for this one when they're exploring how to spell the sound in their writing but not consistently getting it right. As always, older students might want to think about spelling long **o** in longer words: what would be your hunch about spelling long **o** if the word is longer than one syllable? How could you check it out? (A single **o** is the most common, except in a stressed final syllable, when it's usually **o_e,** as in **notion** and **explode.**)

Background Knowledge

The two most common spellings of long **o** are **oa** and **o** with a final silent **e** (**coat, rope**). At the ends of words **ow** is most common (**low, crow, know**), with a few exceptions (**go, so, bro; doe, toe, Joe**). The rare spelling **ough** occurs in **though** and **dough** (and also, but with a different pronunciation in each, in **cough, tough, slough, ought,** and a few other words). As with other long-vowel words, the letter **o** by itself is most common in the first or middle syllable of longer words (**ocean, devotion**).

In Spanish, long **o** is always spelled with just the letter **o,** regardless of the length of the word (**dos, loco**), so the English spellings of this sound will seem more complicated to Spanish speakers.

The Lesson

Note that this activity
combines thinking of
words and word sorting;
it's a little more
challenging than some of
the tasks in the other
long-vowel lessons, but
those lessons should have
helped prepare the
students for this more
difficult activity. If you
think it will be too
challenging, or are
teaching this lesson
before the other long-
vowel lessons, you may
want to substitute one of
the activities from those
lessons. See Patterns 6–8.

1. To get kids thinking about long **o** words:

   Work with a partner to do two things: think of as many one-syllable words with the long **o** sound in them as you can, and write them down in your spelling journal in different groups, depending on how the sound is spelled.

2. After kids have had a chance to create lists:

   How did that go? Let's combine what everybody came up with and see if we can make some generalizations.

   Help kids realize that the spellings **oa** and **o_e** are most common and occur equally often, and that **ow** is usually found at the end of words. They are also likely to have found a few exception words like **toe** and **go.**

3. Ask kids to think of some strategies for spelling long **o:**

   So what's the best rule of thumb when you're spelling one of these words? *(Leave time for discussion.)* Would it make sense to go with: Try **oa** and **o** plus silent **e,** and see if you can tell which one is right; or if it's at the end of the word try **ow** first.

Next Steps

» Follow-up

Since there aren't many words that end with long **o**, it might be worthwhile to post a chart of them.

✓ Assessment

As a journal topic, suggest a question like:

   How much did you already know about spelling long **o** words, and what did you learn today that was new?

Sample Words

Ways to spell long *o*:

oa	o_e	ow	oe	o	oddballs
soap	home	bow	doe	bro	dough
boat	mole	blow	foe	fro	oh
throat	rose	flow	hoe	go	sew
road	robe	low	Joe	lo	shoulder
toad	joke	mow	toe	no	
oak	hope	know	woe	so	
coal	more	row			
goal	smoke	sow			
loan	whole	show			
	close	snow			
	lone	stow			
	nose	tow			

Lesson at a Glance: LONG U AND THE TWO OO'S

What to Do	What to Say	What Kids Need to Know
INTRODUCE—Long and Short oo (oo spelling)		
• Have pairs work together to list words with double **o.** • Have pairs sort their words into two groups.	"Work with a partner to think of as many words you can that have double **o** in them, and then split the words into two groups."	Double **o** can have more than one sound.
EXPLORE—Long and Short oo (oo spelling)		
• After pairs have sorted their words, discuss what they found.	"What did you find out? What do you think about spelling these words?"	Even though the words sound different, they are all spelled with **oo.**
INTRODUCE—Long u and Long oo (u_e spelling)		
• Write (C)_**u**_**e** on the board and read it aloud, explaining the meaning. • Hand out a copy of page 282 to each student. • Have kids generate words for each word family and then sort the words in each family by sound.	"Work with your partner again to find words that fit into this pattern: **u_e.** Examples include words that start with either one or two consonants, then have a **u,** another consonant, and end with an **e.** There aren't that many, so I'm going to give you a sheet that breaks them into word families; all you have to do is think of the first one or two letters." "When you've come up with as many as you can, see if you can put them into two groups. Use different symbols or colors of highlighter to mark them. This is a little trickier than the last ones we did."	Words spelled with **uCe** can have more than one sound.
DISCOVER—Long u and Long oo (u_e spelling)		
• After kids have had a chance to sort their lists, talk about what they've found.	"I bet you never realized before that these words have two different vowels sounds in them: either long **u** like in **use** or **oo** like in **rude.** But what makes them still pretty easy to spell?"	Even though the words sound different, they are all spelled with **uCe.**

LONG U AND THE TWO OO'S

 Two sounds are spelled with a double o: the one we hear in **food** and the one we hear in **book**. The vowel sound in **food** is also spelled **u_e**, as in **dude**. Words like **fuse** have the same spelling with a different sound.

Who, When, and Why

As with the other vowel lessons in this program, students can most benefit from this lesson if they're exploring the spelling patterns but haven't yet mastered them. Thus you might see FUDE and DOOD for **food** and **dude.**

Spanish speakers won't be familiar with most of these spelling patterns. In Spanish, long **oo** is the only one of these three sounds that's treated as a single sound, and it's spelled consistently with **u** (**mucho, sucio**); when a long **u** sound appears, it's spelled as the two sounds that it is—with a **yu** (**Yuma**).

Background Knowledge

Oh, these are tricky ones! I've grouped them together, since the sounds are closely related.

Long u: Let's start with long **u,** by which I refer to the name of the letter. We see this spelled most often with a **u** followed by a consonant and **e,** as in **fuse.** We also find it spelled with **ew,** as in **few,** which happens particularly at the ends of words and syllables.

Long oo: But these same spellings are also used to spell the long **oo** sound, as in **lute** and **chew.** (The difference phonetically is that long **u** is actually a diphthong, two sounds in a row: /y/ followed by long **oo;** it's the difference between **ooh** and **you.**) But the long **oo** sound is also, and more often, spelled with two o's, as in **loot** and **loo.** There are a few other patterns, as in **blue, suit,** and **soup,** and in exception words, like **move.**

Short oo: And to add one more level of confusion, the double **o** spelling is also used for what we can call the short **oo** sound, as heard in **book.** (This sound is also occasionally spelled with **u,** as in **put** and **pull**—not to be confused with **putt,** which has a short **u.**)

	Short oo	Long oo	Long u
oo	look	soon	
u_e		rude	cute

Whew! It's a miracle that we—and children—spell words with these sounds as well as we do. But that, actually, is an indication that, although the patterns involved are complex, they're not really so difficult in practice. Many people don't even realize there's a difference between the long **u** and the long **oo,** probably because of their close phonetic relationship. So I've deliberately kept this lesson on the simple side, to avoid confusion for kids on a spelling pattern that's probably not too hard for them already.

The Lesson

Long and Short **oo** (**oo** spelling):

1. To get kids thinking about words with double o:

   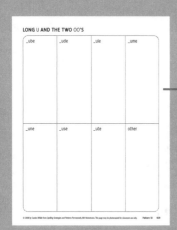 Work with a partner to think of as many words you can that have double **o** in them, and then split the words into two groups.

2. After pairs have sorted their words:

   What did you find out? What do you think about spelling these words? (*Get across the idea that it's easy because they all have* **oo**, *even though they don't all have the same vowel sound.*)

   Long **u** and Long **oo** (**u_e** spelling):

3. Hand out a copy of page 282 to each student.

   Work with your partner again to find words that fit into this pattern: u_e (cute, flute). Examples include words that start with either one or two consonants, then have a **u**, another consonant, and end with an **e**. There aren't that many, so I'm going to give you a sheet that breaks them into word families; all you have to do is think of the first one or two letters.

   When you've come up with as many as you can, see if you can put them into two groups. Use different symbols or colors of highlighter to mark them. This is a little trickier than the last ones we did. (*See Sample Words for lists.*)

   After kids have had a chance to sort their lists:

4. I bet you never realized before that these words have two different vowel sounds in them: either long **u** like in **use** or **oo** like in **rude**. But what makes them still pretty easy to spell? (*They're all spelled the same way, so if you know that, you don't even have to think about which sound it is. Note: a case could be made for not doing this part of the lesson, since it creates awareness of a distinction that's not needed in order to spell the words correctly. However, it does have the advantage of making kids aware of the spelling of all the one-syllable words that follow this pattern.*)

5. If you like, you could mention to students that there's no way to know whether to use **u_e** or **oo** in spelling a long **oo** word; you just have to know the word. However, since they will have had separate exposure to many words with each spelling in the course of the lesson, they may do pretty well anyway at keeping each word in its own category.

Next Steps

 Follow-up

In some ways, trying to get students to make generalizations about these patterns could create some confusion—because once you start thinking about the pattern, you see how complex it is. So let's take a day off from writing in the spelling journal. Instead, in this case, I'd just keep an eye out for any misspellings of these words in their writing and, if you feel you need to work on it at all, do so in individual conferences, probably as a part of support for editing.

Sample Words

The long *u* sound can be spelled:

	Easy	Medium	Harder
u_e	use, fuse, mule, cute, fume, mute	huge	excuse, refuse, refuge
ew	few	ewe	view
	pew	skew	
u	unit	union	unique
	unite	unicorn	uranium

Oddballs: venue, hue

The long *oo* sound can be spelled:

	Easy	Medium	Harder
oo	moon, soon, too, zoo, loop, hoop, tool, pool, boot	bloom, stool, moose, broom	raccoon, cartoon, mushroom
u_e	rude, rule ,tube	crude, flute	exclude, prelude, luge
ew	dew, new	chew, stew, knew, crew, screw, grew	shrew
ue	blue, clue, sue, due	true, glue	issue, cruel
ui	suit	juice	recruit, pursuit
oe	shoe	canoe	

Oddballs: lieu, to, two, you, caribou, move, route, lose

The short *oo* sound can be spelled:

	Easy	Medium	Harder
oo	foot, good, wood	hoof, brook	neighborhood
u	put, pull, push	bush	sugar
ou	should, would, could		

Lesson at a Glance: R-CONTROLLED VOWELS

What to Do	What to Say	What Kids Need to Know
EXPLORE		
• Hand out copies of page 283. • Have kids work with partners to cut apart the cards and sort the words by sound.	"Go ahead and work with your partner on sorting these words into groups. See if you can figure out what all of the words have in common. Use sounds rather then spellings to make your groups. Don't be surprised if this task is somewhat hard!"	The vowels are followed by an **r**.
DISCOVER		
• Ask kids to share what they discover. • Invite them to suggest ideas about how to spell the words correctly.	"What do all these words have in common? What do you notice about the way the vowels sound? Do you have any ideas about how you can remember to spell these words right?"	When a vowel sound is followed by an **r**, the **r** can make the vowel sound different. Sometimes you can sort of hear what vowel letters to use, but often you just have to know the word.

R-CONTROLLED VOWELS

 When a vowel sound has an **r** after it, the **r** makes the vowel sound a little different. Sometimes you can hear which vowel it should be, and sometimes you just have to know the word.

Who, When, and Why

Materials
▶ copies of page 283

Because the principle of this lesson is simple, it can be done at any developmental level, but it might make more sense with students who are already spelling the other vowel sounds pretty well (for instance, even their invented spellings are high-level, such as GEAN for **gene**), rather than overwhelming kids who are still figuring out long **a.**

Background Knowledge

R-controlled vowels (that is, vowels followed by an **r**) are way too complicated to talk about rules for; despite this, they appear in some state standards for reading, so I'm going to tell you what we know about them for spelling and you can decide whether the topic is worth exploring with kids. But I promise you, it's not going to be a set of rules!

Many vowel sounds can be followed by an **r**. Here they are:	
carry	(short **a**; for many speakers these words are pronounced with the long **a** of **hairy**)
hair, bear	(long **a**)
hear, deer	(long **e**)
hire	(long **i**)
cart, heart	(short **o**)
boar, sore	(long **o**)
sure, moor	(long **oo**; for some speakers these may be pronounced to rhyme with **her** and **bore** respectively)
fir, fur, her, work	(short **u**)
hour	(**ow**)
mother	(schwa in second syllable)

As you can see, some of these vowel sounds followed by **r** have more than one spelling. You may also have realized that it's not always obvious which vowel is there, which is exactly the problem; the **r** distorts the vowel sound. One more complicating factor is that some of the combinations with the long vowel sounds are pronounced as two syllables, so that **fire** comes out similar to **flyer.**

Spanish only has five vowel sounds; three of them are followed by **r** in the infinitive (base) form of verbs **(hablar, comer, decir)**. Students who speak Spanish as a first language may or may not have trouble with the great number of **r**-controlled vowels in English, but there's no reason to think it would be of any special concern. For all these reasons, it would be nuts to try to teach these patterns in specific detail.

The Lesson

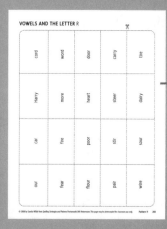

VOWELS AND THE LETTER r

cord	word	door	carry	tire
Harry	more	heart	steer	dairy
car	fire	poor	stir	sour
our	fear	flour	pair	wire

1. A word sort is especially good for this topic, since it gives you information about whether students can categorize the fine distinctions between these sounds, as well as which distinctions they make in their own speech. *(For instance, I pronounce **Harry, Moore,** and **sure** as **hairy, more,** and **sher** respectively, and I imagine that many of you and your students do as well. You may not even realize that other people pronounce them differently.)* Hand out copies of page 283. Or, if your students need more of a challenge, see the Sample Words.

   Cut apart the word cards on this sheet. Then, go ahead and work with your partner on sorting the words into groups. See if you can figure out what all of the words have in common. Use sounds rather then spellings to make your groups. *(I've included two words for each sound, but if the kids group **Harry** and **carry** with **dairy** and **pair,** and **poor** and **door** with **cord** and **more,** you'll know that their version of English doesn't make all the fine distinctions that are possible between these vowel sounds.)* Don't be surprised if this task is somewhat hard!

2. After kids have had a chance to sort with their partner:

   What do all these words have in common? *(They all have vowels with an **r** after them.)* What do you notice about the way the vowels sound? *(The **r** can make the vowels have a different sound.)* Do you have any ideas about how you can remember to spell these words right? *(Sometimes you can sort of hear what vowel letters to use, but often you just have to know the word.)*

   This may seem like a bit of a dead end, but it's just too confusing to teach any more about it.

Spelling Strategies and Patterns

Next Steps

Follow-up

I wouldn't bother with any follow-up or assessment here! **R**-controlled vowels are complicated, but most people end up spelling them pretty well without much—if any—conscious knowledge or thinking about how they work. If you were to ask an adult what she knows about how to spell **r**-controlled vowels, you probably wouldn't get much beyond a blank stare, yet she'd probably do just fine on a spelling test on them.

Sample Words

If you'd like to teach the lesson with harder words, you can use the blank word card sheet on page 280 and add words from the Medium or Harder list.

Words with **r**-controlled vowels:

Easy	Medium	Harder
our	earth	scour
car	sour	polar
Harry	square	barbed
cord	starve	repair
fear	over	worthy
fire	storm	fortune
more	mature	tier
word	hourglass	require
flour	parent	furnace
poor	sphere	heir
heart	purr	rigorous
door	where	guitar
pair	entire	allure
stir	first	before
steer	where	embarrass
carry	party	insure
wire	sailor	sincere
sour	wiring	admire
dairy	thorn	journey
tire	career	research
	cure	apparent
	marriage	

Lesson at a Glance: I BEFORE E (IT STILL WORKS!)

What to Do	What to Say	What Kids Need to Know
INTRODUCE		
• Ask kids to list words with **ie** or **ei**. • On the board or on chart paper, group the words they provide in **ie** and **ei** columns.	"Let's think of some words that have either **ie** or **ei** in them and write them on the board. When you tell me the words, I'll put them in two groups."	There are many words spelled with **ie** and **ei**.
EXPLORE		
• Discuss ways students can remember which words have which spellings. If necessary, introduce the **i** before **e** rule. • Ask kids to check off each word on the list that follows the rule.	"There are a lot of words with each spelling, aren't there? Does anyone have an idea of how to know or remember which words use which spellings?" "Okay, so let's see if the rule **i** before **e**, except after **c** works. Put a check mark by all the words that it works for."	The rule "**i** before **e** except after **c**" is a helpful place to start.
DISCOVER		
• Talk about the exceptions to the rule.	"There are some other rules in life, not just in spelling that sound like this: do this, except in these other cases, you should do that. Like walk to school unless the weather's bad, then take the bus. So we can say, as a general rule, use **i** before **e**, except in these special cases, like when the vowel sounds are found after **c**." "But what about the words **either, weight, weird,** and **being?** They all have **ei.** How can we know or remember them? Well, first of all, there's another part to the rule: **i** before **e**, except after **c**, or when sounded like **a**, as in **neighbor** and **weigh.**" "So if it sounds like a long **a**, you use **ei.** That takes care of **weight.** Does anybody have a hunch about why **being** is spelled the way it is? And the last two? I guess you could always say that **weird** is spelled weird!"	Use "**i** before **e**, except after **c**, or when sounded like **a**, as in **neighbor** and **weigh**" in most cases. If you can hear two separate vowel sounds, and you use a letter to spell each one, then the rule doesn't apply. A few words are just exceptions. You just have to remember them.

I BEFORE E (IT STILL WORKS!)

Okay, you know the rule, but do you know the whole rule? Here it is: **i** before **e**, except after **c**, or when sounded like **a**, as in **neighbor** and **weigh**. And it works, with a few exceptions.

Who, When, and Why

Materials
▶ copies of page 284

This rule is useful when you know that a word is spelled with either **ie** or **ei**, but you aren't sure which. A younger, more phonetic speller who's still spelling **friend** as FREND, isn't ready for this lesson; the kid who spells it as FREIND is.

Background Knowledge

Leonard Wheat, in 1932, wrote about the four spelling rules that work well enough to be worth teaching. He's still right (the language has changed a little since then, but not the spelling system), and this rule is one of the four. (The other three have to do with changes in root words before suffixes; we'll get to them in Pattern 13.) There are a few exceptions, but not many. By the way, the rule only works if the two letters are in the same syllable, representing a single sound. In a word like **science** or **being,** each vowel carries its own sound.

In Spanish, each vowel usually represents a single sound, so that **ie** represents two sounds **(Diego)**. Therefore, students who speak Spanish as their native language may not think of using these spellings for a single sound.

The Lesson

Word list (top box)

either	friend
receive	believe
weight	candies
ceiling	piece
weird	science
being	

1. To get kids thinking about words spelled with **ei** or **ie:**

   Let's think of some words that have either **ie** or **ei** in them and write them on the board. When you tell me the words, I'll put them in two groups. *(Possible list, adding words of your own if you like:* **either, receive, weight, ceiling, weird, being; friend, believe, candies, piece, science.***)*

2. Get kids thinking about how to remember the spellings.

   There are a lot of words with each spelling, aren't there? Does anyone have an idea of how to know or remember which words use which spellings? *(At this point, you may discover that some of the students already know at least the shorter form of the rule. If so, go ahead as follows. If not, introduce the rule after the students have shared other ideas.)* Okay, so let's see if the rule **i** before **e,** except after **c** works. Put a check mark by all the words that it works for.

Word list (bottom box, with check marks)

either	friend ✓
receive ✓	believe ✓
weight	candies ✓
ceiling ✓	piece ✓
weird	science
being	

3. To help kids think about the words that don't fit the rule:

   There are some other rules in life, not just in spelling that sound like this: do this, except in these other cases, you should do that. Like walk to school unless the weather's bad, then take the bus. So we can say, as a general rule, use **i** before **e,** except in these special cases, like when the two vowels are found after **c.**

   But what about the words **either, weight, weird,** and **being?** They all have **ei.** How can we know or remember them? Well, first of all, there's another part to the rule. *(Recite the whole rule.)* So if it sounds like a long **a,** you use **ei.** That takes care of **weight.** Does anybody have a hunch about why **being** is spelled the way it is? *(It's because you can hear two separate sounds, and you use a letter to spell each one. The rule doesn't apply here.)* And the last two? *(They're just exceptions. You just have to remember them.)* I guess you could always say that **weird** is spelled weird!

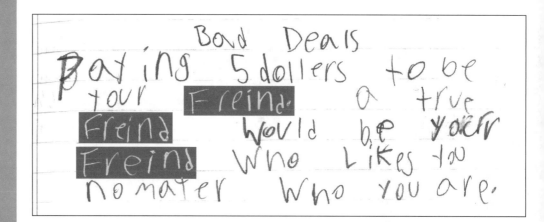

Bad Deals
Paying 5 dollers to be your Freind. a true Freind would be yourr Freind who Likes you no mater who you are.

Next Steps

» Follow-up

You can invite kids to keep an eye out for these words in their reading and see if the words they see follow the rule or not. You might want to consider handing out copies of page 284 so kids can record any **ei** and **ie** words they learn and can refer to the list in the future.

✓ Assessment

As a journal topic, suggest a question like:

📝 What do you know about whether to use **ei** or **ie?**

I'd especially look for whether kids realize that **ie** is the default spelling.

Sample Words

Words with **ei** and **ie:**

	Easy	Medium	Harder
ie	friend, believe, thief, field, piece, candies	pier, shield, niece, fiend, brief, chief	achieve, siege, grief, shriek, pierce
cei	receive, ceiling	receipt, deceit	conceited
ei (long **a** sound)	weight, neighbor, eight	vein, sleigh	rein, reign, heir
two sounds	being, science	happiest, carrier	variety, reinvent

Oddballs: either, weird, height, foreign, seize, protein, ancient

Lesson at a Glance: ADDING SUFFIXES: CHANGING Y TO I

What to Do	What to Say	What Kids Need to Know
EXPLORE		
• Write **cry/cried, happy/happiness, lily/lilies, lazy/ laziness** on the board or on chart paper. • Have students talk with a partner about the spelling changes. • Repeat with **monkey/ monkeys, play/ played, fry/frying, fly/flying.**	"Take a look at these pairs of words. What do you notice? Talk with a partner about what kind of pattern you see. Any ideas about why this happens?" "Now look at these pairs of words. We said that we saw **y** changing to **i** before suffixes, but that doesn't happen in these. There are two different rules for how we know when the change from **y** to **i** doesn't happen. Work with a partner to see if you can figure them out."	Sometimes a **y** changes to an **i** before a suffix.
DISCOVER		
• Ask students to share ideas why the spelling changes in some cases, but not in others.	"What do you think?" "Any ideas as to why we don't make the change in these two cases? Take a look at what we'd end up if we did: **monkeis, plaied, friing, fliing.** Those all look pretty weird, don't they?"	Changing **y** to **i** only happens if the word ends with a consonant before the **y,** and we don't do it before the suffix **-ing.**
SUMMARIZE		
• Ask students to consider a strategy to get spelling correct.	"So what are things you might do to help you get the spelling of these kinds of words right? It might work okay to try to remember the rules, but it can also work to just remember to change **y** to **i** before a suffix unless it looks weird if you do."	Use the rule: many words ending in **y** change **y** to **i** before an added suffix, except words that end with a vowel and **y** and when the suffix is **-ing.** Or: think about whether or not the word looks weird.

ADDING SUFFIXES: CHANGING Y TO I

 Many words ending in **y** change the **y** to **i** after a consonant and before an added suffix, except when the suffix is **-ing**.

Who, When, and Why

Materials
► **none**

As students get older and many words are spelled correctly, we often see kids produce a fair number of invented spellings that show they don't yet know or don't consistently apply rules for spelling changes before suffixes. Most words don't change before suffixes, but in three cases they do: in many (but not all) words ending in **y**, in many words ending in **e**, and in words ending in a CVC pattern. These are the other three rules mentioned by Wheat (1932), along with the **i** before **e** rule, as being consistent enough to be worth teaching. (See Pattern 12.)

This is one of three lessons on changes before suffixes (see Patterns 14 and 15); if the students are far enough along that they just need a review, I might combine the three lessons into one. Otherwise, the rules are complicated enough that each deserves its own lesson.

The three lessons are meant for students who spell suffixes consistently but don't—ever or sometimes—use the rules that change some root words before suffixes. A young speller focusing largely on phonetics is likely to spell **walked** as WOKT and **dreaming** as DREMEN (since we often pronounce the **-ing** suffix as a long **e** plus an /n/ rather than with a clear /ng/ sound). More sophisticated invented spellings of these words are WOKED and DREEMING; even though they're not correct, the writer has generalized that the suffixes are spelled consistently rather than phonetically. This lesson is especially apt when you see spellings like TRYED and LOVEING; you can indeed often see a child write the root word and then the suffix, maybe even with a brief pause showing that he's thinking of them as separate units. The next step is to learn the special rules for joining those units in some cases.

Background Knowledge

*If the word ends with a consonant and **y,** change the **y** to **i.** Don't change the **y** to **i** before the suffix **–ing.***

When a word ends in a consonant and a **y,** the **y** changes to an **i** before all suffixes except -ing (**cries, tried, happiness, merriment; crying, trying**). With an **s** suffix, an **e** is inserted between the **i** and the **s** (**tries**). If the **y** is preceded by a vowel, it doesn't change (**says, monkeys, played**).

In Spanish, suffixes work a little differently than in English; except for plurals, which are created by adding either **s** or **es** (**pesos, ciudades**), where English often simply adds a suffix (that is, in verbs: **talk/talked**), Spanish typically keeps the base of the word and changes the ending, so that the suffix is added to the base, not the whole word. (**hablo/hablé**). Also, in Spanish, when a spelling changes, the pronunciation changes, whereas the **y** to **i** pattern in English is a spelling change only; you can't hear it.

The Lesson

**cry/cried
happy/happiness
lily/lilies
lazy/laziness**

1. To get kids thinking about changing word endings, write the following words on the board or on chart paper: **cry/cried; happy/happiness; lily/lilies; lazy/laziness.**

   👥 Take a look at these pairs of words. What do you notice? Talk with a partner about what kind of pattern you see. *(As a whole group, work to develop the idea that they're seeing, in each of these pairs, a **y** changing to an **i** before a suffix.)* Any ideas about why this happens? *(There isn't a real reason; somebody back in the day probably just thought it looked better not to have a **y** there.)*

**monkey/monkeys
play/played
fry/frying
fly/flying**

2. To extend the conversation, write **monkey/monkeys; play/played; fry/frying; fly/flying** on the board or on chart paper.

   👥 Now look at these pairs of words. We said that we saw **y** changing to **i** before suffixes, but that doesn't happen in these. There are two different rules for how we know when the change from **y** to **i** doesn't happen. Work with a partner to see if you can figure them out.

3. Invite students to share their ideas:

   What do you think? *(Lead them toward the understanding that changing **y** to **i** only happens if the word ends with a consonant before the **y**, and we don't do it before the suffix -**ing**.)*

If students can't recognize the patterns or the oddities, revisit this lesson when more of them are able to. You can be on the lookout for examples of invented spellings that experiment with the pattern in their writing.

4. See if students can come up with theories about why the exceptions to the rule exist.

   Any ideas as to why we don't make the change in these two cases? Take a look at what we'd end up if we did: **monkeis, plaied, friing, fliing.** Those all look pretty weird, don't they? *(Note: If they don't look weird to students, then they haven't had enough experience with written English to recognize unlikely patterns and are more likely to get words like these wrong.)*

5. Invite students to summarize what they've discovered.

   So what are things you might do to help you get the spelling of these kinds of words right? It might work okay to try to remember the rules, but it can also work to just remember to change **y** to **i** before a suffix unless it looks weird if you do.

Spelling Strategies and Patterns

Next Steps

» Follow-up

You should expect to see some improvement in kids' spellings of these words; keep an eye out to see whether they appear to have mastered the pattern or still need some work on it.

✓ Assessment

As a journal topic, suggest a question like:

📝 What's your version of the rule about changing **y** to **i?**

Sample Words

Changing **y** to **i:**

y + suffix	vowel + y + suffix	y + ing
hurry/hurried	monkey/monkeys	buy/buying
happy/happily	journey/journeyed	hurry/hurrying
grocery/groceries	alley/alleys	cry/crying
city/cities	say/says	apply/applying
cherry/cherries	buoy/buoyed	rely/relying
pretty/prettiest	buy/buys	say/saying

Lesson at a Glance: ADDING SUFFIXES: DROPPING THE FINAL E

What to Do	What to Say	What Kids Need to Know
EXPLORE		
• Write the words **come/coming; take/taking; hope/hoping; bike/biking** on the board or on chart paper. • Ask partners to discuss what is going on. • Have pairs share what they came up with. • Write more word pairs for partners to think about: **face/faced; love/loved; live/lived; pause/paused.** • Discuss what they came up with.	"Take a look at these pairs of words and discuss with a partner what you think is going on, and if you can come up with a rule." "What did you come up with? Pretty easy, isn't it? Now try these words." "Usually we add on **-ed** for words like this, don't we, like **walk/walked**? But here it's like we're just adding a **d.** Can anyone explain what you think is going on?" "I think these are especially easy to get right, don't you? Because it would just look funny to write LOVEED for **loved.**"	You drop the **e** at the end of a word when you're adding **-ing** or **-ed.**
DISCOVER: Optional		
• Write the following words on the board or on chart paper: **tie/tied/tying; lie/lied/lying; agree/agreed/agreeing; cue/cued/cueing; shoe/shoed/shoeing rescue/rescued/rescuing; argue/argued/arguing.** • Help kids understand exceptions to the rule.	"Should you follow this rule every time a word ends with **e?** Take a look at these. These root words all end with a vowel before the **e.** Let's take a look first at all the **-ed** words. What do you notice? What about **-ing?**"	With words that end in a vowel and **e,** the **e** is always dropped before **-ed** (or we could say we just add a **d** to the root word). Before adding **-ing, ie** gets changed to **y;** other words sometimes drop the **e** and sometimes don't.

ADDING SUFFIXES: DROPPING THE FINAL E

 Many words drop the final **e** before **-ing** and **-ed.**

Who, When, and Why

Materials
▸ none

This is one of three lessons on changes before suffixes: Pattern 13, Changing **y** to **i**; Pattern 14, Dropping Final **e**; and Pattern 15, Doubling the Final Consonant. The lessons may be taught as a block or as needed, and are most appropriate for students who spell suffixes consistently but may make spelling mistakes when joining them to root words.

This is a pretty simple pattern that children are likely to already be following before **-ed.** If the lesson is carried out with kids who are at the right point to learn it, it's likely to be very successful. For instance, spellings like HATEING and FILEING show that students have a strong sense of the suffix. (You're very unlikely to see HATEED or FILEED.)

Background Knowledge

When a word ends in a consonant and an **e**, the **e** is dropped before suffixes starting with a vowel, basically **-ing** and **-ed (taking, placed).** Note that it doesn't look like the **e** has been dropped from **place,** but the **e** in **placed** is technically the **e** of the suffix. The main reason for this rule is that words would look strange otherwise!

If **coming** were spelled COMEING, the **ei** would look like a digraph, making its pronunciation unclear. If the word ends in another vowel and an **e**, the **e** is always dropped before **-ed,** but is sometimes retained and sometimes dropped before **-ing (toeing, cueing; issuing, gluing);** when it's left in, it's to make the pronunciation clearer; TOING would seem to rhyme with **boing.** Words ending in **ie** are an exception, so that we have **lying** and **tying.** There aren't many words in either of these last two categories, so I wouldn't spend much if any time on them.

*Note: There are also a very few words in English that end with a pronounced, rather than slient, **e (acne, cafe),** but they tend to be nouns that don't take on suffixes starting with a vowel anyway, so there's no need to bring them up at all.*

Rule	Word	+ Suffix	=	What to do
Ce + ed	place	ed	placed	drop e
Ce + ing	take	ing	taking	drop e
VCe + ed	glue	ed	glued	drop e
VCe + ing	cue	ing	cueing	depends on word
VCe + ing	issue	ing	issuing	
Cie + ying	lie	ing	lying	change ie to y

Nothing like this pattern occurs in Spanish, but it's easy enough that it shouldn't give Spanish speakers any particular problems.

**come/coming
take/taking
hope/hoping
bike/biking**

1. The words **come/coming; take/taking; hope/hoping; bike/biking** on the board or on chart paper help introduce the idea to children.

   👥 Take a look at these pairs of words and discuss with a partner what you think is going on, and if you can come up with a rule.

   After they've had a chance to discuss:

   What did you come up with? *(You drop the **e** at the end of a word when you're adding -**ing**.)* Pretty easy, isn't it?

**face/faced
love/loved
live/lived
pause/paused**

2. Write more word pairs for kids to think about: **face /faced; love/loved; live/lived; pause/paused.**

   Now try these words. Usually we add on -**ed** for words like this, don't we, like **walk/walked?** But here it's like we're just adding a **d.** Can anyone explain what you think is going on? *(You actually drop the **e** from the word, then add the -**ed**.)* I think these are especially easy to get right, don't you? Because it would just look funny to write LOVEED for **loved.**

**tie/tied/tying
lie/lied/lying
agree/agreed/agreeing
cue/cued/cueing
shoe/shoed/shoeing
rescue/rescued/rescuing
argue/argued/arguing**

3. Give kids some words that don't fit the rule to get them thinking: **tie/tied/tying; lie/lied/lying; agree/agreed/agreeing; cue/cued/cueing; shoe/shoed/shoeing; rescue/rescued/rescuing; argue/argued/arguing.** *(This step is optional. These patterns make things so complicated, and affect so few words, that it might be better to skip them. You could also just cover **lying** and **tying** as exceptions to the main rule.)*

   Should you follow this rule every time a word ends with **e?** Take a look at these words. These root words all end with a vowel before the **e.** Let's take a look first at all the -**ed** words. What do you notice? *(The **e** is always dropped. Or we could say we just add a **d** to the root word.)* What about -**ing?** *(Bring out: **ie** gets changed to **y**; other words sometimes drop the **e** and sometimes don't.)*

Next Steps

✓ Assessment

As a journal topic, suggest a question like:

 What have you learned today about dropping the final **e** before suffixes?

this weekend I might go to this Gancin place.

Lesson at a Glance: ADDING SUFFIXES: DOUBLING THE FINAL CONSONANT

What to Do	What to Say	What Kids Need to Know
INTRODUCE		
• Write the following word pairs on the board or on chart paper: **hit/hitting, dip/dipped, plan/planning, big/bigger.** • Discuss what kids know about the pattern.	"Take a look at these pairs of words. Talk with a partner about this pattern and what you know about it. As a whole group: let's hear what you know already, plus anything you aren't sure about."	Sometimes consonants get doubled before suffixes.
EXPLORE		
• Work as a group to list words that do and don't double a consonant. • As an alternative to students generating a list, you can provide one (see Step 2 on page 190).	"Let's make a list of words where there's a double consonant before a suffix and words where there isn't. I'll give you one piece of information before we start: we only double consonants before suffixes beginning with vowels (**-ed** or **-ing**), which is why we don't write CATTS or SADDLY."	We only double consonants before suffixes beginning with vowels.
DISCOVER		
• Encourage the children to come up with hypotheses about how to know if the consonant doubles or not. • If they come up with an incorrect hypothesis, provide a counterexample.	"So how do you know when to double a consonant?" Examples: If someone says, "It doesn't double if the last letter is **d,**" mention **sadder.** However, if someone says, "It doesn't double if the last letter is **x,**" they're correct, but you can still say, "Hmmm, maybe so; can anyone think of an exception?" "So what kind of a guideline can we use to know when to double a consonant?"	If a word ends with a consonant, vowel, and consonant (or CVC), double the final consonant before **-ed** and **-ing,** unless the final consonant is **x.**

ADDING SUFFIXES: DOUBLING THE FINAL CONSONANT

 Many words double a final consonant before the suffixes -**ed** and -**ing**. If a word ends with a consonant, vowel, and consonant (CVC), double the final consonant before -**ed** and -**ing**, unless the final consonant is **x**.

Who, When, and Why

Materials
▸ spelling journals

This is one of three lessons on changes before suffixes: Pattern 13, Changing **y** to **i**; Pattern 14, Dropping Final **e**; and Pattern 15, Doubling the Final Consonant. The lessons may be taught as a block or as needed and are most appropriate for students who spell suffixes consistently but may make spelling mistakes when joining them to root words. In the case of this pattern, you may see spellings like HITING and POPED.

Background Knowledge

In one-syllable words ending in CVC, the final consonant doubles before a suffix starting with a vowel, typically -**ed** or -**ing** (**hopped, skipping**). Sometimes teachers have done lessons saying that the consonant doubles when there's a short vowel, and most of these words do indeed have short vowels, but it's the spelling pattern, not the sound, that matters, as we can see from the lack of doubling in **heading** and **bending**. The main reason for this doubling is that otherwise the word would appear to have a long vowel: **pinning** would appear to say **pining**.

There are a few exceptions: a **c** at the end of a word doubles to **ck** (not many simple words end in **c**, but we see this doubling in **picnicking**, for instance). The letter **x** never doubles (**fixing**), probably because it's already a blend (/ks/). For longer words, the final consonant is likely to be doubled if it has the CVC pattern and if that syllable is stressed (**regretting** vs. **metering**), though not in British spelling (**travelled** vs. **traveled** for Americans). For most students, I'd recommend sticking to one-syllable words.

The Lesson

hit dip
hitting dipped

plan big
planning bigger

1. To get kids thinking about consonant doubling, write the following word pairs on the board or on chart paper: **hit/hitting, dip/dipped, plan/planning, big/bigger.**

   Take a look at these pairs of words. Talk with a partner about this pattern and what you know about it. As a whole group: let's hear what you know already, plus anything you aren't sure about. *(It's likely that students will know that consonants sometimes get doubled before suffixes, but not really be sure exactly when.)*

2. To help kids think about when to double a consonant:

   Let's make a list of words where there's a double consonant before a suffix and words where there isn't. I'll give you one piece of information before we start: we only double consonants before suffixes beginning with vowels (**-ed** or **-ing**), which is why we don't write CATTS or SADDLY. *(As an alternative to students generating a list, you can provide the one below; if the kids make the list, make sure it includes examples like the ones I've provided in the "Doesn't double" column. Or if you think kids need more of a challenge, see Sample Words.)*

   > *Indeed, most adults couldn't say when to double the consonant; we just know if it looks right or not. This, of course, suggests that this lesson, like many of the other pattern lessons, is more about reinforcing kids' implicit knowledge about spelling rather than starting from a blank slate.*

Doubles	Doesn't double
zapped, getting, tripper, hopped, sunning	tracked, fixing, sleeping, header, colder

   Students may want to record the list in their spelling journal for later reference.

   You might want to jot these lists down in your spelling journal and keep a running list that you can refer to when you are writing.

3. Encourage the children to come up with hypotheses about how to know if the consonant doubles or not. They may come up with an incorrect hypothesis based on the limited data they have; if so, find a counterexample.

   So how do you know when to double a consonant? *(Example: if someone says, "It doesn't double if the last letter is **d**," mention **sadder.** However, if someone says, "It doesn't double if the last letter is **x**," they're correct, but you can still say, "Hmmm, maybe so; can anyone think of an exception? No, there aren't any exceptions; you're right about that.")*

4. If you allow enough time, students are likely to be able to come up with the rule.

   > *I would probably also show them **picnicking,** but this pattern is too rare to bother including in the rule.*

   So what kind of a guideline can we use to know when to double a consonant? *(If a word ends with a consonant, vowel, and consonant (CVC), double the final consonant before **-ed** and **-ing,** unless the final consonant is **x.**)*

Spelling Strategies and Patterns

Next Steps

» Follow-up

As a follow-up, I'd invite students to discuss how well they think they do at remembering when to double the consonant before a suffix, and how much they think they're spelling the words correctly because of knowing the rule and how much because they can just tell if it looks right. This pattern, like the other two suffix-related spelling patterns, can be monitored in proofreading even if the words aren't spelled correctly in a first draft.

✓ Assessment

As a journal topic, suggest a question like:

What have you learned about doubling consonants?

+ Extension

For older students: this is a fairly challenging activity, but students who are ready to learn about consonant doubling in longer words should be able to handle it. I would, however, consider it completely optional, since even most adults don't know the pattern.

With a partner, look in the dictionary for verbs longer than one syllable that end with a consonant, and see if they double the consonant before **-ed** and **-ing.** You might think of words first and then look them up, or you might just browse until you find some. *(You'll of course need to make sure that you have dictionaries that provide this suffix information.)* You may have been a little surprised to discover that even with the CVC pattern, the consonant doesn't always double. Can you come up with a theory that explains when you do? *(CVC pattern, plus stress on the last syllable.)* Any idea as to why this pattern exists? *(Actually, the double consonant gives you a signal as to where the stress falls; you could say it makes that syllable a little "heavier." But we get by without it in the root word—**expel/expelling**—so go figure!)*

Sample Words

Doubling the final consonant:

Easy	Medium	Harder
zapped	knocked	suspended
getting	wrapping	regretted
tripper	quilting	repeating
hopped	rainy	filtering
sunning	plusses	tonnage
tracked	smoothly	transmitter
fixing	thankful	muttered
sleeping	plotted	occurred
header	sadness	piloted
colder	knitting	maddening

Lesson at a Glance: DOUBLE CONSONANTS

What to Do	What to Say	What Kids Need to Know
INTRODUCE		
• Invite kids to tell what they know about double consonants.	Let's talk about double consonants, when you have two of one letter together in a word, like the two **t**'s in the word **letter.** What do you know about which words have double letters and why? What do you not know or wonder?	Some words have double consonants and some don't.
EXPLORE		
• Give partners a dictionary, and assign each pair a different letter of the alphabet. • Have pairs list the first 25 familiar, double-consonant words that they can find, and have them record the list in their spelling journal. (You may want to write the instructions on the board or on chart paper.) • Invite students to discuss what they've found.	"I'd like to invite you and your partner to make a list of the first 25 words you find in your section of the dictionary that have double consonants in them and that you know. Record the list in your spelling journal." "After you've listed the words, talk with your partner about whether there's any way to know ahead of time if a word has a double consonant." "Let's come back together and talk about what we've discovered. Since you listed only words that you know, did you already know that they have double consonants in them? How good are you at remembering the double consonants if you write these words?" "Is there any way to know if a word has a double consonant in it if you haven't seen it before? Are there any patterns you noticed in the words you found?"	It's tricky to predict which words do and don't have double consonants. At most, students might have noticed that we often see **ff, ll, ss,** and **zz** at the ends of (usually one-syllable) words, and they may be able to say that a word like **better** just wouldn't look right or would look like it had a long vowel if it didn't have the double consonant. But remember that these rules aren't particularly consistent.
SUMMARIZE		
• Help students develop a strategy they can use when they are writing.	"So what do you think about double consonants in your writing?"	Most of the time, you just have to know if the word has a double consonant; sometimes there's a pattern or rule that can help you; sometimes you can just tell if it looks right; but the rest of the time you'll just have to check when you're editing.

DOUBLE CONSONANTS

 Sometimes you can tell if a word needs a double letter by whether it looks right or not. Other times, you just have to check.

Who, When, and Why

Materials
▶ dictionaries
▶ spelling journals

There's a definite developmental component to this topic, since getting double letters right depends so much on both knowing a lot of words and knowing whether a spelling looks better with or without a double consonant. With younger students, this exploration is primarily about awareness, whereas you can push the expectations a little higher with upper-grade kids.

Once students have discovered double letters and use them in their invented spelling, they're ready to start thinking about how we know when to use them. This lesson will be most effective if they have enough experience reading to know that **diner** says **diner,** not **dinner.** Older students are likely to do pretty well with double letters in short words, but with no rules of thumb for deciding about double letters in longer words. Failing to make the right decision about whether a word has a double letter or not is one of the most common patterns seen in adult invented spelling.

Background Knowledge

Man, double consonants are hard! Why does **crevasse** have double letters when **carafe** doesn't? **Happen** needs a double letter to show that the preceding vowel is short, but what if you're eight years old and HAPEN looks like just as good a way to spell **happen?** Why do **will, kiss,** and **puff** end with double letters when **did, big,** and **sub** don't? Why do we have both **canon** and **cannon,** pronounced the same? And with long words, it gets really hard. Shouldn't **melancholy** have double **l**'s with those short vowels in there? **Hillbillies** does! Yikes.

It's really complicated, but I'll give you an overview. None of these patterns work consistently enough to be considered a hard-and-fast rule. Double consonants show that the preceding vowel is short; show that stress falls on the last syllable; are used with words ending in /f/, /l/, /s/, or /z/; or reflect a word's origin or etymology. You will of course be able to think of exceptions to all of these, and the exceptions increase as words get longer.

Spanish doesn't have double consonants other than **ll** and **rr,** which are considered separate letters because they have their own sounds, so this lesson could be more challenging for students who speak Spanish as a first language.

The Lesson

Find 25 words:
- **in your section,**
- **that have double consonants,**
- **and that you know.**

List them in your spelling journal.

1. To get kids thinking about words with double consonants:

   Let's talk about double consonants, when you have two of one letter together in a word, like the two **t**'s in the word **letter.** What do you know about which words have double letters and why? What do you not know or wonder? *(The idea here is to accept all answers; you're trying to get a sense of what the kids know, and get them thinking about whether there's any rhyme or reason to double letters.)*

2. Next, have the students work with partners. Give each pair a dictionary, and assign each pair a different letter of the alphabet. You may want to write the instructions on the board or on chart paper.

   I'd like to invite you to make a list of the first 25 words you find in your section of the dictionary that have double consonants in them and that you know.

   Record the list in your spelling journal. After you've listed the words, talk with your partner about whether there's any way to know ahead of time if a word has a double consonant.

3. Invite students to discuss what they've found:

   Let's come back together and talk about what we've discovered. Since you listed only words that you know, did you already know that they have double consonants in them? How good are you at remembering the double consonants if you write these words?

4. To get kids thinking about how to know when to double a consonant:

   Is there any way to know if a word has a double consonant in it if you haven't seen it before? Are there any patterns you noticed in the words you found? *(At most, students might have noticed that we often see **ff, ll, ss,** and **zz** at the ends of [usually one-syllable] words, and they may be able to say that a word like **better** just wouldn't look right or would look like it had a long vowel if it didn't have the double consonant. But remember that these rules aren't particularly consistent.)*

5. Help students develop a strategy they can use when they're writing.

   So what do you think about double consonants in your writing? *(Any thoughts from the students are good at this point.)* Let me suggest an idea: double consonants are tricky. Most of the time, you just have to know if the word has a double consonant; sometimes there's a pattern or rule that can help you; sometimes you can just tell if it looks right; but the rest of the time you'll just have to check when you're editing.

Next Steps

 ## Follow-up

The next time kids edit their writing:

> Knowing when to double consonants (both doubling when you should and not doubling when you shouldn't) is something that being a good proofreader really helps with, since there aren't any rules that really work. So think especially about doubling consonants when you edit.

A few days later:

> Have you been any more aware of double consonants since we talked about them? How do you think you're doing with them?

Assessment

As a journal topic, suggest a question like:

> What are your thoughts about double consonants? What's your best strategy for always getting them right?

Sample Words

Doubling consonants:

Easy	Medium	Harder
happy	jolly	cottage
messy	simmer	fillet
silly	pillow	grasshopper
rabbit	batter	buttercup
kitten	mattress	muffler
grabbed	burrow	buffalo
hugged	carrot	lemming
apple	mittens	cellar

Lesson at a Glance: SCHWA: WHAT IS IT AND HOW DO I SPELL IT?

What to Do	What to Say	What Kids Need to Know
EXPLORE		
• If possible, ask the students beforehand to make a list of words they've misspelled in their writing recently. • Discuss which is more difficult: spelling consonant sounds or vowel sounds. • Ask kids to try to write **regicide.** Make sure you pronounce it with a schwa in the middle: REJ-uh-side, not REJ-IH-SIDE. Then show them how it's spelled and discuss the schwa in the second syllable. • Ask kids to consider why spelling the /ə/ sound is so difficult.	"Which is harder when you're spelling, vowels or consonants?" "Do you ever spell a word wrong because you can't even tell what one of the vowel sounds is? Here's an example: try writing this word that I'm pretty sure you don't know: **regicide.** It means 'killing a king.'" "Here's how it's spelled. Let me see if I guessed right: most of you got the **e** at the beginning right, not very many of you got the **i** in the middle right, and a lot of you got the **i** and silent **e** at the end right? How did I know that? What was hard about the **i** in the middle? So why is it that you sometimes can't tell what vowel letter to use?"	There are arguments for both, but vowel sounds are usually harder to spell for a number of reasons: most of them can be spelled in more than one way, we have only five vowel letters but a lot of vowel sounds, and so on. Some vowel sounds are hard to spell because you can't clearly hear what letter to use.
DISCOVER		
• Introduce the word **schwa** and the symbol for it; write both on the board or on chart paper. • As a class, discuss some strategies students can use to spell the schwa sound.	"Have you ever seen this symbol—/ə/— maybe in a dictionary? It's the symbol for that little "unh" sound, and it's called a **schwa.**" "So how can you get these vowels right if you can't even hear what letter to use? The good thing is that most of them you'll just pick up through reading (adults get most of them right without trying). But I'm going to show you two good strategies. ***Strategy 1:*** The first strategy is to think if you know a related word where you can hear the sound. The word **economy** has a schwa after the **n,** but if you know **economical,** you can hear a short **o** there and know to spell **economy** with an **o.** But this doesn't work very often, and it works mostly with bigger words. ***Strategy 2:*** Your best strategy is going to be the spellchecker. Type in your best guess for the word, and hopefully the spellchecker will find it. You can try the dictionary too, but if the schwa is near the beginning of the word, you may have trouble finding it at all. Let's try it with a few words. Try writing **esophagus** and **rhinoceros.** Underline the sounds you think are schwas. Then find the words in the dictionary and see how well you did.	To correctly spell the schwa sound for a word you don't know, you can either think if you know a related word where you can hear the sound or use a spellchecker.

SCHWA: WHAT IS IT AND HOW DO I SPELL IT?

 Most of the time the sound of a vowel helps you figure out how to spell it, but not always. For the words where it doesn't, you can spellcheck or think of a related word.

Who, When, and Why

Materials
▶ none

This lesson is best for students who already have a good handle on spelling most vowel sounds, even if they don't always get them right. By the way, even spelling bee contestants often make mistakes on schwa vowels. If you don't know the word and can't think of a related one, your remaining strategy is to make a guess. Only older students will find using the spelling of related words to spell schwa very helpful, since these are mostly longer words that take on suffixes and become even longer (**compute/computational**), and often the related word keeps the schwa anyway (**connect/connection**).

Background Knowledge

A main character of the young adult novel *The Schwa Was Here* (Shusterman, 2004) calls himself The Schwa because he's so unnoticed by the world. The schwa sound, which is the unaccented vowel we hear in the first syllable of **about,** is almost certainly the sound most often misspelled, precisely because it's so weak phonetically; we can't tell from hearing the word what letter to use.

The schwa vowel, represented with the symbol /ə/, is defined linguistically as an unstressed reduced vowel, and always occurs in unstressed syllables. It's spelled in a way that's logical, but if you don't know the origin of the word, that may not help. Here's an example that you may find useful: in the word **medical,** we can clearly hear that there's a short **e** in the first syllable. But in **medicinal,** the stress shifts to the second syllable and the short **e** is reduced (that is, weakened) to a schwa. But here's the good part: in **medicinal,** the short **i** we can now hear in the second syllable tells us that the second (schwa) vowel in **medical** is spelled with an **i.**

One more piece of information: schwa can be spelled with any vowel letter, or sometimes more than one letter, depending on the word, since any vowel sound can be reduced to schwa in an unaccented syllable. You can see this in the following words, where I've highlighted the spelling of schwa: **about, target, pencil, apron, circus, luscious.**

The spelling of the schwa sound will be particularly challenging for Spanish-literate students, because Spanish doesn't have a schwa; all vowels retain their full sound. Thus, even though English speakers typically say **enchilada** with a schwa after the **ch,** Spanish speakers will retain each vowel sound (ayn-chee-la-da).

The Lesson

1. If possible, ask the students beforehand to make a list of words they've misspelled in their writing recently.

   Which is harder when you're spelling, vowels or consonants? (Students may have arguments for both, but work to eventually bring out the idea that vowel sounds are hard to spell for a number of reasons: most of them can be spelled in more than one way, we have only five vowel letters but a lot of vowel sounds, and so on.)

2. To get kids thinking about words with the schwa sound:

   Do you ever spell a word wrong because you can't even tell what one of the vowel sounds is? Here's an example: try writing this word that I'm pretty sure you don't know: **regicide.** *It means "killing a king." (Make sure you pronounce it with a schwa in the middle—REJ-uh-SIDE, not REJ-IH-SIDE.) Here's how it's spelled (write on board). Let me see if I guessed right: most of you got the* **e** *at the beginning right (have students raise hands), not very many of you got the* **i** *in the middle right (have students raise hands), and a lot of you got the* **i** *and silent* **e** *at the end right (have students raise hands). How did I know that? What was hard about the* **i** *in the middle? (Bring out the idea that you can't really hear what letter to use.)*

3. Ask kids to consider why spelling the /ə/ sound is so difficult:

   > *By the way, it's not that we're "lazy" in the way we say words; these are just the way they're said.* **Medical** *isn't "properly" pronounced MED-IH-KAL; it's MED-uh-kul.*

   So why is it that you sometimes can't tell what vowel letter to use? (See what they have to say; work towards the idea that it's the way the words are pronounced, for some vowels there's just sort of an "unh" sound.)

4. At this point, I'd tell the kids about the name and symbol schwa, since it will be the most direct way to talk about these words; I'd keep it brief, however.

   > *I'm reminded of a Simpsons episode where Lisa's teacher is abruptly called away and the principal has to fill in briefly; in what was surely chosen as the most boring topic the writers could think of, he writes a schwa on the blackboard and starts droning on about it.*

   Have you ever seen this symbol—/ə/—maybe in a dictionary (write the symbol on the board)? It's the symbol for that little "unh" sound, and it's called a **schwa** *(write the word on the board).*

5. As a class, discuss some strategies students can use to spell the schwa sound.

   So how can you get these vowels right if you can't even hear what letter to use? The good thing is that most of them you'll just pick up through reading (adults get most of them right without trying). But I'm going to show you two good strategies.

   Strategy 1: The first strategy is to think if you know a related word where you can hear the correct sound. The word **economy** *has a schwa after the* **n,** *but if you know* **economical,** *you can hear a short* **o** *there and know to spell* **economy** *with an* **o.** *But this doesn't work very often, and it works mostly with bigger words.*

Spelling Strategies and Patterns

Strategy 2: Your best strategy is going to be the spellchecker. Type in your best guess for the word, and hopefully the spellchecker will find it. You can try the dictionary too, but if the schwa is near the beginning of the word, you may have trouble finding it at all. Let's try it with a few words. Try writing **esophagus** and **rhinoceros.** Underline the sounds you think are schwas *(the first, third, and fourth vowels in the first word and the last two vowels in the second).* Then find the words in the dictionary and see how well you did.

Next Steps

 ### Follow-up

Point out that kids should pay special attention to words with a schwa sound when they're editing.

It's important to be aware when a word has a schwa in it, because there's a reasonable chance that you've gotten it wrong if you don't already know the word. If you hear a schwa, you should check your spelling.

 ### Assessment

As a journal topic, suggest a question like:

 Did you realize that even adults and spelling bee champions have trouble spelling schwa sounds? What are your ideas about how you can get them right most of the time?

Sample Words

Spelling with schwa:

Easy	Medium	Harder
carpet	atom	observe
pedal	rebel	cadet
pencil	again	modify
ago	orphan	patience
parrot	connect	spectrum
oven	census	tenant

Lesson at a Glance: SILENT LETTERS: HOW DO I KNOW THEY'RE THERE?

What to Do	What to Say	What Kids Need to Know
EXPLORE		
• Talk about silent letters that children are familiar with. As they name words, write them in groups. • You can start with the words that occur to kids, and then suggest other groups (see Sample Words). • Have one child look up **kn** words and count how many there are. Have another child look up **n** words and count how many pages there are.	"Let's talk a little about silent consonants. What are they, and can you give some examples? Think especially about the ones at the beginnings of words." "So think about if you're going to write a word that starts with an **n** sound, like **nice** or **knife.** Some of the time, it's going to start with the letters **kn.** How do you know which words use **kn?**"	Some words have letters that you can't hear. There aren't many words with silent letters and that they're often two-letter pairs.
DISCOVER		
• Discuss the findings. • Hand out copies of page 285 for kids to record **kn, wr,** and **gn** words they think they might want to use in their writing. (Older kids might also want to do **ps** and **pt** words, although there are very few of either.) • Briefly discuss the **gh** spelling.	"What does this tell us, and what strategy does it suggest? And you know what? Some of them you probably won't ever use, like **knickerbocker** and **knavishness,** and others are related, so if you can spell **knee,** you can spell **kneel** and **kneecap.**" "Would anybody like to make a list of the top ten **kn** words, maybe to add to our word wall? We could do the same for **wr** and **gn** words, and keep them up until we're all pretty familiar with them." "There's one other silent consonant pattern I'd like to tell you about. The letter pair **gh** is funny. At the beginning of a word, which only occurs in a few words, you just hear a /g/ sound, like **ghost** and **ghoul.** At the end of a word, **gh** is completely silent most of the time, like in **through** and **sigh.** Sometimes it spells the /f/ sound, like in **cough** and **rough.** There's even an old spelling of **hiccup,** where **gh** spells a /p/ sound (hiccough)! There's a word **slough** that you probably don't know that's really two words, with two meanings and pronunciations. A /sloo/ is like a swamp, and to /sluff/ off something is to shed it, like a snake's skin. So how in the world can you know if a word has **gh** in it?"	If you just guessed the word started with **kn,** you'd be wrong almost all the time, so you're probably better off just being familiar with the words that do. The **gh** spelling is a case where you really just have to know the word, and an example of how our spelling system isn't always very logical.

SILENT LETTERS: HOW DO I KNOW THEY'RE THERE?

 Some words have silent letters, letters you don't hear when you say the word. The only way to get them right is to know the word.

Who, When, and Why

Materials
▶ dictionaries
▶ copies of page 285

A good point to introduce this lesson is when kids have discovered silent letters and started including them when they're familiar with the word. The focus then is mainly on awareness and familiarity. Older students might want to explore if there's any way to make sure you never misspell a word with a silent letter in it. (Of course there isn't; discussion will help kids figure that out.) They may also want to research the origin of some of our silent letter patterns.

Background Knowledge

Silent letters are typically one of the first targets of spelling reformers, but for the foreseeable future they're here to stay. In this lesson, we're going to focus on silent consonants, since silent vowels are part of the larger patterns of vowel spellings that are covered in other lessons.

English has a number of silent letter patterns, and it's most useful to think of them as letter pairs in which (usually) the first letter is silent: primarily **wr, gn, kn,** and, less commonly, **pt** and **ps** at the beginnings of words and **mb** at the ends of words. (We've already dealt with the silent **h** in **wh** in Pattern 4.) Also, the letters **gh** are sometimes silent when preceded by a vowel. These patterns typically reflect historical change; a sound that used to be pronounced has become silent, but the spelling has stayed the same. **Knife** used to be pronounced kuh-NEEF-uh.

The only silent letter in Spanish is **h,** so that **hablar** sounds like it could be spelled ABLAR. Therefore, these letter pairs in which one is silent will be new to Spanish speakers. Interestingly, the **p** in **ps** is pronounced in Spanish, as in **psicología.**

The Lesson

1. **Get kids thinking about silent consonants:**

   Let's talk a little about silent consonants. What are they, and can you give some examples? Think especially about the ones at the beginnings of words. *(Focus on the obvious fact that some words have letters that you can't hear. As students name words, write them in groups. See Sample Words for a chart of silent letter patterns and examples of them. You can start with the words that occur to kids, and then suggest other groups.)*

2. **Bring out the idea that there aren't many of them and that they're often two-letter pairs.**

   So think about if you're going to write a word that starts with an **n** sound, like **nice** or **knife.** Some of the time, it's going to start with the letters **kn.** How do you know which words use **kn?** Somebody get two dictionaries, please. I'd like one person to find the **kn** words and, if you would, count how many of them there are. I'd like someone else to find the words that start with **n** and see how many pages of them there are. What does this tell us, and what strategy does it suggest? *(If you just guessed that the word started with kn, you'd be wrong almost all the time, so you're probably better off just being familiar with the words that do.)* And you know what? Some of the **kn** words you probably won't ever use, like **knickerbocker** and **knavishness** (though you might find it fun to read the definitions!), and others are related, so if you can spell **knee,** you can spell **kneel** and **kneecap.**

3. **You may want to offer copies of page 285 for kids to record kn, wr,** and **gn** words they think they might want to use in their writing.

   Would anybody like to make a list of the top ten **kn** words (or whatever number you think is best), maybe to add to our word wall? We could do the same for **wr** and **gn** words, and keep them up until we're all pretty familiar with them. *(Older kids might also want to add ps and pt words to the back of their chart, although there are very few of either.)*

4. **Briefly touch on the gh spelling:**

   There's one other silent consonant pattern I'd like to tell you about. The letter pair **gh** is funny. At the beginning of a word, which only occurs in a few words, you just hear a /g/ sound, like **ghost** and **ghoul.** At the end of a word, **gh** is completely silent most of the time, like in **through** and **sigh.** Sometimes it spells the /f/ sound, like in **cough** and **rough.** There's even an old spelling of **hiccup,** where **gh** spells a /p/ sound (hiccough)! There's a word **slough** that you probably don't know that's really two words, with two meanings and pronunciations. A /sloo/ is like a swamp, and to /sluff/ off something is to shed it, like a snake's skin. So how in the world can you know if a word has **gh** in it? This is a case where you really just have to know the word, and an example of how our spelling system isn't always very logical.

Spelling Strategies and Patterns

Next Steps

 Assessment

As a journal topic, suggest a question like:

📓 Would we be better off without silent letters? Is there anything good about them?

Sample Words

Words with silent letters:

kn	wr	gn	ps	pt
know	wrap	gnaw	psalm	ptarmigan
knee	wren	gnash	psychology	pterodactyl
knight	write	gnome	psychic	
knew	wrist	gnu		
knife	wrong	gnarl		
knock	wrestle	gnat		
knickknack	wrinkle	sign		
knit		align		
knot				
knob				
knuckle				

went back to be Molly
and Floppy looked for the
mouse. They found it!
But they didn't do anything
to it. It was crying. The
mouses name was Shorty.
Floppy and Molly asked
him what was rong and he
said "I felt sorry after
I bit you." The next day

Lesson at a Glance: TRICKY ENDINGS: -ABLE OR -IBLE?

What to Do	What to Say	What Kids Need to Know
INTRODUCE		
• Invite children to list words they know that end with **-able** or **-ible.** Write them in two columns as they do so. • Hand out copies of page 286 for kids to record their words.	"Let's list as many words as we can that end with either of the suffixes **-able** or **-ible.** You might want to record the words on this sheet and keep it in your spelling journal."	It's not always clear when to use **-able** and when to use **-ible.**
EXPLORE		
• Once you have a dozen or so words (see Sample Words), ask for hypotheses about when each suffix is used. • If there are exceptions in the list, mention that the pattern has exceptions and that there are indeed some listed.	"How do you think we know which one to use?"	With some exceptions, if a word contains a root that's a real word, the suffix is usually **-able;** if the root isn't a full word, or is a full word unrelated in meaning, the suffix is usually **-ible.**
SUMMARIZE		
• Summarize what you've talked about.	"This pattern works well enough to be worth using as a rule, but there are some exceptions, so spellchecking never hurts."	The rule is fairly reliable, but it's always a good idea to double-check.

TRICKY ENDINGS: -ABLE OR -IBLE?

 With some exceptions, if a word contains a root that's a real word, the suffix is usually -**able**; if the root isn't a full word, or is a full word unrelated in meaning, the suffix is usually -**ible**.

Who, When, and Why

Materials
▶ **copies of page 286**
▶ **spelling journals**

This is truly an advanced lesson, so I'd be prepared to drop it if you discover that kids aren't really using these suffixes in their writing. At the very least, they need to have a fair number of these words in their vocabulary.

Although it's a more advanced lesson, there's a pattern here that's actually fairly predictable and therefore worth learning. I've never met an adult who learned this pattern in school, even if she had years of traditional spelling curriculum.

Background Knowledge

If a word contains a root that's a real word, the suffix is usually -**able** (**laughable**); if the root isn't a full word, or is a full word unrelated in meaning, then the suffix is usually -**ible** (**visible, fallible: fall** is a word, but **fallible** doesn't mean "able to fall"). There are definitely exceptions (**capable, correctible**), but the pattern is still worth learning.

Spanish has these same two suffixes, but since every sound is fully pronounced, you can hear which one the word contains. In English, these suffixes are virtually always in unstressed syllables and therefore pronounced with a schwa, so you can't hear which vowel to use.

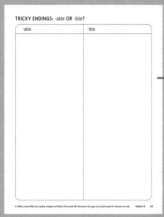

The Lesson

1. Invite children to list words they know that end with **-able** or **-ible.** Write them in two columns as they do so. You may want to distribute copies of page 286 so children can keep their own lists for future reference.

    > Let's list as many words as we can that end with either of the suffixes **-able** or **-ible.** You may want to record the words on this sheet and keep it in your spelling journal.

2. Once you have a dozen or so words (see Sample Words), ask for hypotheses about when each suffix is used.

    > How do you think we know which one to use? *(I've found that even when doing this with adults, people make hypotheses that focus on aspects such as what letter comes before the suffix. The lesson goes best if you treat all hypotheses in the same neutral way, bringing up exceptions—"Gee, **visible** has an **s** before the suffix, but so does **passable**"—but encouraging an open mind about which is likely to be right. Eventually, you can nudge the students toward recognizing the correct hypothesis, but it can be valuable to give them a day to think about it and look for more examples. If there are exceptions in the list, mention that the pattern has exceptions and that there are indeed some listed.)*

3. Finish up by mentioning that this pattern works well enough to be worth using as a rule, but that there are some exceptions, so spellchecking never hurts.

TRICKY ENDINGS: -able **OR** -ible**?**

-able	-ible
reasonable	terrible
table	horrible
stable	reversible
edable	possible
cable	
laughable	
disable	
fashionable	
comfortable	
suitable	

Spelling Strategies and Patterns

Next Steps

✓ Assessment

As a journal topic, suggest a question like:

 Since there are exceptions to this pattern, is it still worth using it to help you get these words right?

Sample Words

Words with -able and -ible:

	Easy	Medium	Harder
-able	burnable readable payable washable breakable	enjoyable lovable* usable* likable* sizable*	profitable manageable reliable admirable*
-ible	terrible possible horrible	visible edible	audible credible permissible

Exceptions: flexible, reversible
*Note that these words drop the final **e** before the suffix.

Lesson at a Glance: THOSE PESKY HOMOPHONES

What to Do	What to Say	What Kids Need to Know
WEEK 1		
• Introduce the spelling of **there** along with the words **here** and **where.** • You might want to leave this word family posted up for a while, perhaps in a "families" section of your word wall. The idea is to build a strong association between the three words. • If you think the kids would find it fun, you could also show them **hence, thence,** and **whence,** and **hither, thither,** and **whither.**	"Here's a tip that can help you with your spelling. Take a look at these three words: **here, there,** and **where.** What do you notice?" "So if you ever forget how to spell 'over **there**,' just think of this group of words."	You can remember the correct spelling of **there** by connecting it with **here** and **where**—all three words are related to location.
WEEK 2		
• Write **they** and **their** on the board or on chart paper and ask kids what they notice about them.	"Take a look at these two words. What do you notice?" "So if you get confused about how to spell '**their** house,' just think about starting with **they.**"	The meanings of **they** and **their** are related. **Their** sounds like **they** but with an /r/ sound at the end, so you follow the rule about changing **y** to **i.**

THOSE PESKY HOMOPHONES

 You need to edit for words that are the right spelling of the wrong word; the spellchecker won't catch these! You can also think of a trick to remember each word, but don't pair it with its homophone.

Who, When, and Why

Materials
► None

The misspelling of homophones often turns up in the spelling of older kids who are getting most other comparably easy words right. (Whoops; I originally typed **write!**) In these cases, it needs to be considered as a proofreading problem, too; I know I need to check for it in my own writing; it's not that I don't know the difference, but sometimes the wrong word comes out whether I'm writing by hand or typing.

This lesson is most appropriate for kids who are writing one homophone word in place of another. (I'd focus on the words that your kids are actually missing.) I'd wait until kids are beyond the point of inadvertently producing homophones because they're inventing spellings; look for the student who interchanges **road** and **rode,** not the one who comes up with ROAD or ROED while thinking about how the sounds in **rode** might be spelled.

This lesson is a two-part one, with the steps to be done on separate days. There's also a lesson on homophones in the strategy section of this program, which deals with catching homophones when you're proofreading (see page 107). The lesson here is an example using **there** and **their,** of how to get kids to remember the spellings of two words that get confused. I'd then create similar lessons for other specific homophones that children confuse; see Strategy 2.

Background Knowledge

*And why do I use the term **homophone** rather than **homonym?** Technically, homophones are words with the same sound (**homo** = same, **phone** = sound) but different spellings. Homonyms (**nym** = name) are words with the same sound and spelling but different meanings, like **bank** (of a river) and **bank** (for money), even though the term is rarely used this way. Homographs are words with the same spelling but different pronunciations, like **entrance** (noun) and **entrance** (verb).*

Okay, here's my theory: I think writers have trouble with homophones *because* we teach kids about them! Traditional spelling books were perhaps especially guilty of this. By the time you were through with a lesson on pairs of homophones such as **rode** and **road,** you would have seen each pair next to each other a number of times and been asked to proofread a passage where each was used incorrectly for the other. The problem then becomes, as Frank Smith (1982) has noted, not to remember the correct spelling but to forget the wrong one. The lesson has probably only strengthened the association between them. In fact, I think the homophones that kids are taught about are more likely to be misspelled than those that aren't; who's ever written **frays** for **phrase?**

I had an experience once I started teaching, which many of you may share, that I think supports this theory. I never used to confuse **their** and **there.** But once I started teaching, sometimes when I wrote I'd come out with the wrong one. I believe it came from seeing them misused in kids' writing; just the power of seeing **their** written down when it should have been **there** may have strengthened the unconscious link between them. So my approach to homophones will be a little different from what you've seen before.

Because of the way English spelling works, particularly the fact that every long vowel sound can be spelled in more than one way, we have a huge number of homophones. Those that are common words often persist in being misspelled, even when kids are no longer inventing most of their spellings. A second-grader may come up with the spelling MADE when writing **maid,** simply because of following the silent-e pattern; an older student is unlikely to, but may be interchanging **are** and **our.** (For most American speakers, it's these two that are homophones, not **our** and **hour.**)

Spanish has a few homophones: words with and without silent **h** (hasta/until, asta/flag pole), and potential homophones with **b** and **v** in the same position, though I couldn't find any in my dictionary.

The Lesson

1. You can use the following approach to help kids learn homophones they frequently confuse. Find a way to teach each individual spelling without relating the words to each other.

    Here's a tip that can help you with your spelling. Take a look at these three words: **here, there,** and **where.** What do you notice? *(Bring out that they all refer to places, and that they all include the letters of **here**.)* So if you ever forget how to spell "over **there**," just think of this group of words. *(You might want to leave this word family posted up for a while, perhaps in a "families" section of your word wall. The idea is to build a strong association between the three words. If you think the kids would find it fun, you could also show them **hence, thence,** and **whence,** and **hither, thither,** and **whither,** though I admit these are a little geeky!)*

2. Ideally, do this next step at least a week later.

    Take a look at these two words: **they, them,** and **their.** What do you notice? *(Bring out that their meaning is related, and that **their** sounds like **they** but with an /r/ sound at the end, so you follow the rule about changing **y** to **i**.)* So if you get confused about how to spell "**their** house," just think about starting with **they.**

    > Note that I've carried out these two lessons without ever linking **their** and **there** to each other. I'd deal with **they're,** if at all, in a lesson on apostrophes. If you find there are other homophones your students frequently miss, do similar lessons. For instance, **our** can be related to **your.**

3. As you find homophone confusions in kids' writing, help them think of a trick to remember the correct spelling. But don't let them connect the homophone pair in the trick.

Spelling Strategies and Patterns

Next Steps

» Follow-up

I might not even do any follow-up, since these are brief lessons dealing with just a few words. I would *not* ask kids to write about how not to confuse **their** and **there,** since we're trying to prevent rather than reinforce any relationship between them.

Sample Words

Homophones that may be confused include:

Easy	Medium	Harder
are/our	board/bored	cite/sight/site
there/their	past/passed	
of/'ve	break/brake	
hear/here	principle/principal	
to/too/two	which/witch	
by/bye/buy		

Also, look for what homophones kids misuse in their writing. Remember not to teach these pairs together, but focus on learning individual words at different times.

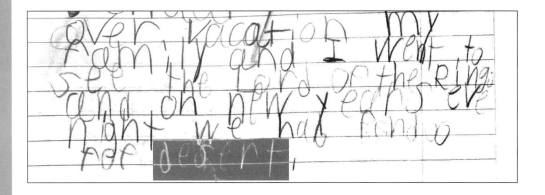

Lesson at a Glance: SPELLING LONG WORDS

What to Do	What to Say	What Kids Need to Know
INTRODUCE		
• Get kids thinking about the difference between spelling short words and spelling longer words.	"Let's talk about short words and long words. How good do you think you are at spelling short words, like ones that have four or five letters?" "How about long words? Are they harder for you to spell? Why do you think that is? Do you have any thoughts about what parts of long words are harder to get right? Let's try some out. Try writing **planetarium.** Next I'd like you to underline the letters you're pretty sure you got right."	It's hard to spell long words because there are so many letters to remember and get right.
EXPLORE		
• Invite students to share their spellings and record them on the board or on chart paper. • Write the correct spelling for children to see. • Give kids some more words to work with (tyrannosaurus, escalator, electronic, relationship).	"Now let's put some of your spellings up on the board. Here's the correct spelling. Were you pretty good at predicting which letters you got right? Why do you think those letters were easier?"	When spelling long words, some letters are easier to get right than others.
SUMMARIZE		
• Talk about strategies that can be used to spell long words. • Suggest that kids record in their spelling journals any long words they might want to use later.	"I'd like to suggest two strategies for when you're writing a long word; these are mainly strategies for when you're editing, since it makes sense to just write your best guess first and then keep going with your writing. One is pretty obvious: you can spell-check or look it up. But here's the other idea: underline or just think about the letters you're sure are right, then try changing one or more of the parts that you think might be wrong. You may be able to tell which one is right after you've done that. If not, spell-checking or looking up is what you'll have to do to get it right." "Here's one more thought: if there are long words you think you're going to use again in your writing, it might be worth either starting a list of them in your spelling journal, or just memorizing them as you come across them."	When spelling a long word, make your best guess, then try changing one or more of the parts that you think might be wrong. If that doesn't help, use a spell-checker or a dictionary.

SPELLING LONG WORDS

 When you write a longer word, it's harder to get it right. Make your best guess, then try changing one or more of the parts that you think might be wrong. If that doesn't help, use a spell-checker or a dictionary.

Who, When, and Why

Materials
▶ **paper**

This lesson is appropriate for students who have a pretty good handle on spelling one-syllable words and who are increasingly using longer words in their writing. With younger students, this would be more of an introduction to writing longer words, while you could help older children aim for getting them right as often as possible. Older children will also have more to say about what they've noticed about long words, and will be able to develop a more integrated sense of the features that make them challenging.

Background Knowledge

Even for one-syllable words, spelling is only predictable up to a point, and for words of two syllables or longer, writers mainly need to know the word itself, since there are so many possible spellings. This lesson won't produce a dramatic improvement in kids' ability to spell long words correctly; even adults struggle with it. The idea is primarily to increase their awareness and give them a few strategies.

Two features of longer words that most often make them harder to spell are addressed in other lessons: the schwa vowel (Pattern 17) and double consonants (Pattern 16). Schwa vowels by their nature only occur in longer words since they're found in unaccented syllables. (One exception: function words used in a sentence are often pronounced with a schwa; if we say "I bought a car," we almost always say the word **a** as a schwa rather than long **a**.) For a word like **arithmetic,** therefore, the two **i**'s are accented, but the writer can't hear how to spell the first and third vowel sounds. Typically half or more of the vowel sounds in longer words are schwas. And as we've already seen, beyond a few rules, double consonants are hard to predict. **Collect** has a double **l** and **select** doesn't; the same with **accommodate** and **homogenize** for **m.**

In Spanish, even long words are spelled predictably, so this is an aspect of English spelling that will be important for Spanish speakers to be aware of.

The Lesson

1. To get kids thinking about the difference between spelling short words and spelling longer words:

   Let's talk about short words and long words. How good do you think you are at spelling short words, like ones that have four or five letters? *(Even younger students are likely to be reasonably adept with shorter words.)*

   How about long words? Are they harder for you to spell? Why do you think that is? *(Children's answers are likely to focus on there just being so many letters to remember and get right.)* Do you have any thoughts about what parts of long words are harder to get right? Let's try some out. Try writing **planetarium** *(or another word that kids know the meaning of)*. Next I'd like you to underline the letters you're pretty sure you got right.

2. Invite students to share their spellings and record them on the board or on chart paper.

   Now let's put some of your spellings up on the board. *(They're likely to get all the consonants right, though some may stick in a double consonant or two. The first **a** is the vowel they're most likely to get right, all the others are harder.)* Here's the correct spelling. *(Write it on the board.)* Were you pretty good at predicting which letters you got right? Why do you think those letters were easier?
   (This discussion should focus on the kids talking about it in their own words. Their comments may include being able to just hear some letters, while for others they couldn't really tell. They also may say they weren't sure if there were double consonants or not.)

3. Give kids some more words to work with.

   > *Examples: tyrannosaurus, escalator, electronic, relationship. Also, see Sample Words.*

   Let's try this with a few more words. I'll say them, you write them, you underline the letters you think you got right, and we'll see how you did. *(Use words the kids have in their vocabulary, and if you like, ask them to contribute words, too.)*

4. Talk about strategies that can be used to spell long words.

   I'd like to suggest two strategies for when you're writing a long word; these are mainly strategies for when you're editing, since it makes sense to just write your best guess first and then keep going with your writing. One is pretty obvious: you can spell-check or look it up. But here's the other idea: underline or just think about the letters you're sure are right, then try changing one or more of the parts that you think might be wrong. You may be able to tell which one is right after you've done that. If not, spell-checking or looking up is what you'll have to do to get it right.

   > *Refer to Strategy 8 to help students learn to memorize words.*

   Here's one more thought: if there are long words you think you're going to use again in your writing, it might be worth either starting a list of them in your spelling journal, or just memorizing them as you come across them.

Next Steps

›› Follow-up

A few days later:

> Have you been paying more attention to how you spell long words? Can you see any improvement?

✓ Assessment

As a journal topic, suggest a question like:

> How do you think you can get better at spelling long words?

Sample Words

Longer words:

Easy	Medium	Harder
different	comfortable	demonstrate
basketball	forgotten	independence
important	recognize	restaurant
remember	collection	mischievous
cucumber	refrigerator	periscope
dinosaur	pediatrician	astronomy
environment	triceratops	velociraptor
underneath	electrify	zucchini

Lesson at a Glance: RELATED WORDS HAVE SIMILAR SPELLINGS

What to Do	What to Say	What Kids Need to Know
INTRODUCE		
• Introduce the idea that related words can have similar spellings by discussing the words **one, once,** and **only.**	"Did it ever strike you as weird that the word **one** is spelled the way it is? How do you think it should be spelled? And what about **once?** Any ideas as to why they might be spelled the way they are?" "Here's something to think about: the word **only.** Now that spelling makes sense, doesn't it? Can you make a connection? Know what? The words **one** and **once** used to be pronounced roughly "own-uh" and "ownce-uh" hundreds of years ago. The spelling would have been a better fit with the way people said them then, but the pronunciation changed and the spelling didn't."	Words with similar meanings are sometimes spelled in a similar way.
EXPLORE		
• Write the words **dinosaur, tyrannosaurus,** and **stegosaurus** on the board or on chart paper. • Talk about their spellings. • Write the words **medical** and **medicine,** and **critical** and **criticize** on the board or on chart paper. • Discuss the spelling of related words with sound changes.	"Let's think about some words we know that have similar meanings and similar spellings. For instance, have you ever thought about: **dinosaur, tyrannosaurus,** and **stegosaurus? Dinosaur** is the category that the others are part of, right? And what do you notice about how they're spelled? If somebody told you about a kind of dinosaur you hadn't heard of before, but it had the same ending, how do you think you'd do spelling it? My hunch is that even if you didn't get the first part of the word right, you'd get the **-saurus** part. And if you were reading and came across a word ending in **-saurus,** I think you'd be pretty likely to know it was related to all those other dinosaur words." "Sometimes the spelling stays the same even if the sound changes. What do you notice about **medical** and **medicine,** and **critical** and **criticize?** Yes, the **c**'s spell different sounds, sometimes /s/ and sometimes /k/, but if you know what the words mean, it helps you know they are spelled with the letter **c.**"	Knowing how to spell a word part can help you spell the whole word. Sometimes knowing the meaning of a word can help you spell it correctly.

RELATED WORDS HAVE SIMILAR SPELLINGS

 Sometimes if you know that two words have similar meanings, it can help you spell them correctly.

Who, When, and Why

Materials
▸ **none**

This should be useful for all students who have moved beyond phonetic spelling, though it'll be more meaningful for older students who are using more complex words, many of which have related roots or use common prefixes and suffixes.

Background Knowledge

*This principle works often but not always. A teacher once told me that her spelling-challenged husband had trouble remembering if **material** had one or two **t**'s. Then one day he told her that he'd found a way to always remember: since it's related to **matter,** it has two **t**'s. Whoops!*

Knowledge of meaning relationships between words is helpful in two cases: those where, due to historical change, a word's spelling no longer reflects its pronunciation; and those in which the pronunciation of a sound differs between two words but its spelling doesn't, as in **medical/medicine,** with their /k/ and /s/ sounds for **c.** Of course, it's also useful to realize that once you can spell **biology,** you can spell the last section of **ecology, geology,** and a bunch of other words. By the way, a spellchecker can help you find families of words that follow this principle. When I looked up **ology,* I found the names of dozens of sciences.

Because all Spanish words are spelled phonetically, and one doesn't need the extra boost from meaning, this is an important lesson for Spanish speakers who are learning to write in English.

The Lesson

1. By examining the related words **one, once,** and **only,** we can provide examples of words with similar meanings that have similar spellings:

   Did it ever strike you as weird that the word **one** is spelled the way it is? How do you think it should be spelled? *(Answers like **w-u-n** would be reasonable.)* And what about **once?** *(wunce or wunse)* Any ideas as to why they might be spelled the way they are? Here's something to think about: the word **only.** Now that spelling makes sense, doesn't it? Can you make a connection? *(The three words **one, once,** and **only** have a similar meaning. Saying it was the only apple means there was **one** apple, and **once** means "**one** time." And they're all spelled similarly, even though the spelling only makes sense for one of them.)* Know what? The words **one** and **once** used to be pronounced roughly "own-uh" and "ownce-uh" hundreds of years ago. The spelling would have been a better fit with the way people said them then, but the pronunciation changed and the spelling didn't.

2. Write the words **dinosaur, tyrannosaurus,** and **stegosaurus** on the board or on chart paper.

   Let's think about some words we know that have similar meanings and similar spellings. For instance have you ever thought about: **dinosaur, tyrannosaurus,** and **stegosaurus? Dinosaur** is the category that all the rest of them are part of, right? And what do you notice about how they're spelled? *(They all end with **-saur** or **-saurus.**)* If somebody told you about a kind of dinosaur you hadn't heard of before, but it had the same ending, how do you think you'd do spelling it? My hunch is that even if you didn't get the first part of the word right, you'd get the **-saurus** part. And if you were reading and came across a word ending in **-saurus,** I think you'd be pretty likely to know it was related to all those other dinosaur words.

   dinosaur
   tyrannosaurus
   stegosaurus

3. The words **medical** and **medicine,** and **critical** and **criticize** on the board or on chart paper extend the principle:

   Sometimes the spelling stays the same even if the sound changes. What do you notice about **medical** and **medicine,** and **critical** and **criticize?** Yes, the **c**'s spell different sounds, sometimes /s/ and sometimes /k/, but if you know what the words mean, it helps you know they are spelled with the letter **c.**

   medical
   medicine
   critical
   criticize

   > Other examples:
   > bicycle, cycle, cyclone, tricycle
   > please, pleasant, pleasure

» Follow-up

Ask students to be on the look-out for related words:

> Over the next few days, see if you notice or can find sets of words that have similar meaning and similar spelling. Also notice if this helps you at all in your writing.

A few days later, talk about what students have found.

✓ Assessment

As a journal topic, suggest a question like:

> How does looking for relationships between word meanings and spellings help you as a reader and writer?

+ Extension

You may want to introduce additional patterns, perhaps *-ology* (names of sciences or fields of study). See Sample Patterns.

Sample Patterns

Easy	Moderate	Difficult
-scope	bio-	audi-
-gram	tele-	chron-
port-	photo-	-phobia
micro-	meter	
	-phone	

Lesson at a Glance: WORDS WITH APOSTROPHES: POSSESSIVES

What to Do	What to Say	What Kids Need to Know
INTRODUCE		
For beginners: • Ask children if they are familiar with apostrophes. • If some don't know at all, show them what one looks like.	"How many of you know what an apostrophe is? Who'd like to describe it? By the way, here's how it's spelled; what a long word for such a little mark!"	Sometimes we use an apostrophe in our writing.
EXPLORE		
• To see whether kids use apostrophes when they write possessives, give them a few phrases to write. • Invite a student who used apostrophes to show where they placed them and explain why.	"Write quickly these three phrases: **the dog's bone; Linda's bike; my teacher's nose.** Who used apostrophes in these?" "I'd like someone who did use apostrophes to come up, write one of the phrases on the board, and tell us what you know about how and why to use the apostrophe."	Apostrophes help us know about ownership.
DISCOVER		
• Help kids generate a rule for using apostrophes in possessives. • Make a list of examples on the board or on chart paper. If appropriate, introduce the word **possessives** and write it on the board. • Help children understand how apostrophes are placed differently in plural possessives. • Explain that apostrophes are never used with possessive pronouns. If appropriate, introduce the word **pronouns.**	"Let's see if we can come up with a rule for this. It's sort of hard to put into words, but how does this sound: If you have a phrase like 'Someone's something,' where it's something belonging to someone, you use an apostrophe in the *someone's* part. Of course, the 'someone' doesn't have to be a person or even anything alive, it could be 'the chair's legs,' for instance." "I'd like to teach you a rule about an exception that sometimes happens for possessives. If the word's a plural that already ends in **s,** you add an apostrophe but not another **s.** So if you have more than one cat, it's the cats' tails. Anybody have a good way to remember this? It's not something you'll even use that often, but try to remember this rule when you do." "One other tip about apostrophes: you can put the words **my, your, his, her, its,** and **their** in the 'someone's something' phrase, like **my house, your pencil, its bowl, their happiness.** What do these all have in common, and how are they different from other words we'd use in these phrases? And you know what? You *never* use apostrophes with them! Even if you add an **s,** like if you say 'That baseball is theirs,' there's never an apostrophe. Easy, huh?"	You can use the phrase "someone's something" to help you remember where the apostrophe belongs. If the word's a plural that already ends in **s,** you add an apostrophe but not another **s.** You never use an apostrophe with words like **my, your, his, her, its,** and **their** (possessive pronouns).

WORDS WITH APOSTROPHES: POSSESSIVES

 Apostrophes are used for two main reasons. Here's the first: When you want to show ownership, use **'s** with the word that names the owner: the dog**'s** bed.

Who, When, and Why

Materials
▸ **none**

Parts of this lesson are suitable for younger students who are just starting to learn about the possessive apostrophe, and other parts are better suited for students who are older but could use some fine-tuning for any mistakes they still make. For younger students, use steps 1 through 3 of the lesson and maybe stop at that point. For older ones jump right in at step 3, perhaps preceded by a quick check on what their understanding is. You might say something like, "Tell your partner when you use apostrophe **s** and then we'll discuss it together."

Background Knowledge

Apostrophes are surprisingly challenging, even for some adults. Haven't we all seen signs selling "strawberry's"? I think they give spellers problems because we can't hear them and, although they're straightforward most of the time, there are a few tricky cases like **its/it's** and plural possessives.

To form a possessive, we add an apostrophe and an **s** to the word (John**'s** book). Since speakers already say and hear the **s,** it's only the apostrophe they need to learn. For plurals, only an apostrophe is added, not an extra **s** (the five dogs**'** owner). For proper names, some style guides say you do add the **s,** others not; therefore I wouldn't even bring it up, since either one is appropriate (Carlo**s's** homework, Carlo**s'** homework).

Possessive pronouns *never* have apostrophes. Some of them we wouldn't expect to since they don't end in **s: my, mine, your, her,** and so on. The ones that do end in **s** mostly don't cause any confusion because they don't occur in the possessive "slot" before a noun (the book is yours; your book). **His** does occur before nouns, but I've never seen anyone stick an apostrophe in it (except perhaps a very young writer). But we all know about how confusable **its** and **it's** are, so this will be addressed below.

When people misuse apostrophes, it's often by using them inappropriately in plurals, as in **my book's.** I've chosen not to even mention this in the lesson, to avoid introducing a point of possible confusion. I think a good way to work with students who misuse apostrophes in this way is just to say: "There's an apostrophe there because . . .?" They'll be unable to say that it's either a possessive or a contraction, so there's therefore no reason for the apostrophe.

Spanish doesn't use apostrophes, so this structure will be new to Spanish speakers. In Spanish, there are possessive pronouns (mi casa = my house), but possessive nouns are indicated by a phrase (la case de Juan = the house of Juan = Juan's house).

*French, similarly, doesn't have possessive apostrophes. In Canada, the possessive apostrophe once took on political overtones. In 1977, the province of Québec passed a French-only law affecting all public signage. The old-line English Canadian department store Eaton's was required to change all its signs to say merely **Eaton,** since the former was clearly not French.*

The Lesson

1. For beginners:

   How many of you know what an apostrophe is? Who'd like to describe it? *(If some don't know at all, show them what one looks like.)* By the way, here's how it's spelled; what a long word for such a little mark!

   If kids wonder where the word came from, it's from Greek roots meaning "to turn away," which doesn't have any obvious connection to its current meaning.

2. To see whether kids use apostrophes when they write possessives, give them a few phrases to write.

   Write quickly these three phrases: **the dog's bone; Linda's bike; my teacher's nose.** Who used apostrophes in these? *(With younger students, some will and some won't, so this gives you a sense of where they are in their knowledge of this feature.)* I'd like someone who did use apostrophes to come up, write one of the phrases on the board, and tell us what you know about how and why to use the apostrophe.

3. Help kids generate a rule for using apostrophes in possessives.

   Let's see if we can come up with a rule for this. It's sort of hard to put into words, but how does this sound: If you have a phrase like "Someone's something," where it's something belonging to someone, you use an apostrophe in the *someone's* part. Of course, the "someone" doesn't have to be a person or even anything alive, it could be "the chair's legs," for instance. *(You can make a list on the board.)*

someone's	something
Hillary's	book
the horse's	saddle
the razor's	edge

   If appropriate:

   These words with the "apostrophe **s**" are called **possessives** *(write on board)*; another way of saying to own something is to possess it, and it's like the someone owns the something. *(Note: I've intentionally played down technical terminology here; I think the "someone's something" phrasing I've used is one that kids can operationalize as they write, but you may want to teach them the term possessive to have another way to refer to it.)*

   By the way, do you know where this whole thing came from? Back in the day, hundreds of years ago, people would say "John his book" and it eventually got shortened to "John's book."

4. Help children understand how apostrophes are placed differently in plural possessives.

   I'd like to teach you a rule about an exception that sometimes happens for possessives. If the word's a plural that already ends in **s,** you add an apostrophe but not another **s.** So if you have more than one cat, it's the cats' tails. Anybody have a good way to remember this? *(There's no good way to explain it, but kids may come up with something that works for them. There's no real logic to it; it's just a convention.)* It's not something you'll even use that often, but try to remember this rule when you do.

5. Explain that apostrophes are never used with possessive pronouns.

One other tip about apostrophes: you can put the words **my, your, his, her, its,** and **their** *(write on board)* in "someone's something" phrases, like **my house, your pencil, its bowl, their happiness.** What do these all have in common, and how are they different from other words we'd use in these phrases? *(They're all words that can be used for a lot of different people or things, usually one we've referred to before, like we might say Maria dropped her math book.)* They're called **pronouns,** because they're used in place of a noun. And you know what? You *never* use apostrophes with them! Even if you add an **s,** like if you say "That baseball is theirs," there's never an apostrophe. Easy, huh?

Next Steps

» Follow-up

Keep an eye out for any errors in possessive apostrophes in kids' writing, and do some reteaching or conferencing if it seems necessary.

✓ Assessment

As a journal topic, suggest a question like:

What apostrophe rules do you know and why are they so easy?

hole and it bit Molly! By
the time Laura got there
Molly's paw was out of
the hole. So Laura yelled
at Molly and she went
back to bed. When Laura
went back to be Molly
and Floppy looked for the
mouse. They found it!
But they didn't do anything
to it. It was crying. The
mouses name was Shorty.

Lesson at a Glance: WORDS WITH APOSTROPHES: CONTRACTIONS

What to Do	What to Say	What Kids Need to Know
EXPLORE		
• Hand out copies of page 287. • Help students develop a rule for using apostrophes in contractions. • Repeat for the second group of words on page 287.	"Take a look at these pairs of words in the first group. What do you notice? Can you come up with a rule?" "Take a look at these pairs of words in the second group. What do you notice?"	When you have a word like **isn't** that comes from a word plus **not,** you put the words together and use an apostrophe to show what's been left out. The contracted words are all forms of **is, have,** and **will,** but we still add the apostrophe where the letters are missing.
SUMMARIZE		
• Suggest that students keep the handout in their spelling journals for future reference.	"Keep this piece of paper in your spelling journal so you can refer to it later."	Having a handy list of common contractions can help get spelling right.

WORDS WITH APOSTROPHES: CONTRACTIONS

 There are a lot of words in our language that are really two words run together, and we use an apostrophe to show where the missing letters were.

Who, When, and Why

Materials
▶ copies of page 287
▶ spelling journals

A good point to do this lesson is when students have started writing some contractions with apostrophes, but not always consistently. (I even once saw a student overgeneralize the apostrophe to write BU'T. When asked, he said, "It's like **don't,** sort of like bad news.") Older students may not need this lesson, since contraction apostrophes are a little easier than possessive ones. Don't bother doing it if students don't need it.

Background Knowledge

The major occasions where contraction apostrophes occur in English is when **not** is attached to the preceding word, usually an auxiliary verb; and when an auxiliary like **will** or a form of **is** or **has** is attached to the preceding noun or, even more often, a pronoun.

*One other thought: Some people think that contractions aren't appropriate for writing, but this is true only for the most formal writing. For instance, did you flinch when you saw **aren't** in the previous sentence? Probably not. Contractions actually make writing more natural. I experienced this when I wrote my first book,* You Kan Red This! *(Wilde, 1992). A chapter or two grew out of the dissertation I'd written a few years before (Wilde, 1987). One of the changes I made in adapting that work to make it more reader-friendly for teachers was to go through and create contractions from the more formal, uncontracted academic language.*

For more advanced students, you could mention the two other usages of apostrophes— but they don't come up often: in the plurals of single letters, such as **p's and q's,** and in omissions that aren't contractions, like **rock 'n' roll** and **back in the '90s.**

As with possessive apostrophes, contraction apostrophes don't exist in Spanish, so they may need to be taught.

1. Hand out copies of page 287.

Take a look at these pairs of words in the first group. What do you notice? Can you come up with a rule? *(Encourage them to develop a rule, in their own words, along the lines of, "When you have a word like isn't that comes from a word plus not, you put the words together and use an apostrophe to show what's been left out." Really, any phrasing is fine. Note that can't is a little different since cannot is conventionally written as a single word and two letters are omitted, but this doesn't make it any harder.)*

If you like, you could write **ain't** and ask students where they think it comes from. It was originally a contraction for **are not,** but is also used for **is not** and is the only way to contract **am not** (although we can contract by saying **I'm not** rather than **I ain't**). If this leads into a discussion of the "acceptability" of **ain't,** make it clear that it *is* a word, it's in the dictionary, but society has decided it just sounds too slangy or informal for many situations.

2. Repeat for the second group of words on page 287.

Take a look at these pairs of words in the second group. What do you notice? *(The difference here is that a lot more combining words are involved, but they're all forms of is, have, and will. These auxiliary verbs get contracted because they're less strongly pronounced than full verbs. It's hard to describe this pattern very understandably, so accept and build on whatever students say.)*

3. Then you might suggest:

Keep this piece of paper in your spelling journal so you can refer to it later.

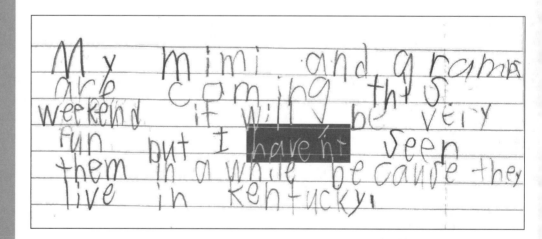

Next Steps

✓ Assessment

As a journal topic, suggest a question like:

 What would you tell a younger kid if you wanted to teach her about contractions?

Sample Words

Contractions with...

not	am/is/are	have/has	will	would
is not/isn't	I am/I'm	I have/I've	I will/I'll	I would/I'd
have not/haven't	you are/you're	you have/you've	you will/you'll	you would/you'd
had not/hadn't	he is/he's	he has/he's	he will/he'll	he would/he'd
has not/hasn't	she is/she's	she has/she's	she will/she'll	she would/she'd
did not/didn't	it is/it's	it has/it's	it will/it'll	they would/they'd
cannot/can't	Jack is/Jack's	Jack has/Jack's	Jack will/Jack'll	we would/we'd
was not/wasn't	we are/we're	we have/we've	we will/we'll	
are not/aren't	they are/they're	they have/they've	they will/they'll	
will not/won't				
does not/don't				

Lesson at a Glance: WHAT I WONDER ABOUT SPELLING

What to Do	What to Say	What Kids Need to Know
INTRODUCE		
• Start off the conversation by talking about why we have 26 letters in our alphabet. • Allow time for kids to come up with their own theories, however fanciful.	"Here's something I wonder about spelling: Why do we have 26 letters, anyway? What do you think? How could we find out?"	Thinking about spelling can be fun and interesting.
EXPLORE		
• Give children an opportunity to pose questions they have about spelling. • List questions on chart paper as kids pose them. • Choose a few of the questions and discuss the possible answers as a class.	"I thought it would be fun today to see what your questions are about spelling. These could be factual questions like the one about why we have 26 letters, or they could be just things that you wonder about." "Let's pick a couple of your questions to discuss. Let's keep this list up here for a while; you can add more questions as you think of them, and if you find out or think of answers to any of them, we'll make time for that, too."	There are lots of things about spelling that can be explored.

WHAT I WONDER ABOUT SPELLING

 It's interesting to think about spelling and wonder about why it works the way it does.

Who, When, and Why

This is an open-ended lesson meant to give all students an opportunity to think about spelling as an object of inquiry. Some students will be more interested in spelling than others are and may decide to do some exploring on their own. Students who are literate in languages other than English may have additional questions or insights.

Background Knowledge

You may feel like you don't have enough background knowledge yourself to answer kids' questions about spelling. That's okay; they can be pursued with a "let's see what we can discover together" approach. However, do take a look at my annotated bibliography of children's and adult books about spelling; your school's library may have some of them or could order them. By the way, not all kids' questions about spelling will have answers, other than "That's just the way it is." You'll end up with three kinds of questions:

- those that have factual answers and that you have resources for investigating (some questions about spelling can be answered with just a dictionary);

- those that have factual answers that you don't have resources for (which might include some obscure questions); and

- those that are more philosophical.

A good stance would be, "Let's research some of these that we can, let's think about others, and if there's some that we can't find the answers to, let's decide if we want to pursue them further by seeing if a librarian can help us." You can decide if you want to have this be a short session that's mainly about wondering about spelling, or the prelude to a stretch of research. It also serves as an introduction for the following enrichment lessons on word origins.

The Lesson

1. **Start off the conversation by talking about why we have 26 letters in our alphabet.**

    Here's something I wonder about spelling: Why do we have 26 letters, anyway? What do you think? *(Allow time for kids to come up with their own theories, however fanciful.)* How could we find out? *[Reference books on this topic include* Do you Speak American? *(MacNeil and Cran, 2005);* Alphabetical Order *(Samoyault, 1998) for adults and kids.]*

2. **Give children an opportunity to pose questions they have about spelling.**

    I thought it would be fun today to see what your questions are about spelling. These could be factual questions like the one about why we have 26 letters, or they could be just things that you wonder about. *(List questions on chart paper as kids pose them.)*

3. **Choose a few of the questions and discuss the possible answers as a class.**

    Let's pick a couple of your questions to discuss. *(Spend several minutes discussing questions of students' choice.)* Let's keep this list up here for a while; you can add more questions as you think of them, and if you find out or think of answers to any of them, we'll make time for that, too.

If kids need help getting started:

- *Why aren't words just spelled the way they sound?*
- *Why don't we have enough vowel letters for all the vowel sounds?*
- *Why do letters have the shapes that they do?*

Next Steps

» Follow-up

If students seem interested, revisit the questions periodically, particularly if any of them are doing research on them.

✓ Assessment

As a journal topic, suggest a question like:

📓 What are your thoughts on a possible answer to one of our questions about spelling?

⊕ Extension

We've got some books in our classroom and in the school library about our language. Would any of you like to volunteer to research any of these questions and report back to us?

Lesson at a Glance: HOW PEOPLE USED TO SPELL

What to Do	What to Say	What Kids Need to Know
INTRODUCE		
• Hand out copies of page 288, and point out the texts at the top of the page • Make a list of the words that still exist today.	"Take a look at these two pieces of writing. They don't even look like English, do they? But they are. Beowulf is before the year 1000, and Gawain is late 14th century. Let's look at them, along with the modern translation. Let's make a list of the words that still exist today, with how they're spelled now and how they were spelled then."	Some English words used to look very different.
EXPLORE		
• Get kids thinking about why spellings might change over time. • Turn kids' attention to the bottom of page 288.	"Why do you think people used to spell a lot of words differently than they do now? You know what? There isn't any one reason. Language just changes. But let me show you one example of why and how it changes." "Take a look at these words. Any thoughts about why they changed?" "Here's another one: **whale** and **white** used to be spelled **hwæl** and **hwit.** Any idea why? The old spellings actually fit with the way they used to be pronounced, with an /h/ sound before the /w/ sound: /hwal/ and /hwit/ (say with long vowels). We don't know why the spelling changed, though."	Language changes by nature, so spellings will change.
DISCOVER		
• Hand out copies of page 289.	"One more thought on this. Take a look at these spellings. The ones in the left-hand column are from different years in the history of English. The ones in the right-hand column are from kids of different ages. As you know, when you were younger you just used sounds to spell words, but now you know a lot more. Isn't it interesting that back in the day, hundreds of years ago, everybody spelled like young kids do today?"	Early English spellings looked much like those of early learners now.

HOW PEOPLE USED TO SPELL

English spelling hasn't always looked the way it does now; in fact, some of it we couldn't even read today.

Who, When, and Why

This is purely an enrichment topic. The idea of language changes will be more understandable to older students, but even younger ones can appreciate the ideas. Some students may be interested enough to explore further on their own.

Background Knowledge

English spelling has changed a lot over the years, and what is likely to be interesting for students is that English spelling has gone through stages that look a lot like the way kids spell over their years of development (Invernizzi et al., 1994).

There are many histories of the English language (see the bibliography). I won't try to give an entire history here, but will mention a few major points. First, our spelling system has become less phonetic over time, in part because pronunciations have changed faster than spellings. One example is the Great Vowel Shift (linguists always capitalize it!) in the 1400's, when five vowels shifted in how they were pronounced. (Chomsky and Halle, 1968.)Back before the shift, the spellings of vowels with similar sounds had similar pronunciations; this is no longer true. Second, over the centuries English has taken in more and more words from other languages; English has Germanic roots with a strong French overlay, but it also has many words taken from other languages. So our spelling system used to be simpler. Third, standard spelling has become the expectation; there used to be more latitude for variation.

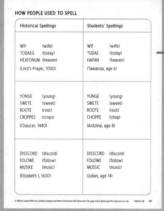

1. Hand out copies of page 288, and point out the texts at the top of the page.

   Take a look at these two pieces of writing. They don't even look like English, do they? But they are. Beowulf is before the year 1000, and Gawain is late 14th century. Let's look at them, along with the modern translation. Let's make a list of the words that still exist today, with how they're spelled now and how they were spelled then.

2. Get kids thinking about why spellings might change over time.

   Why do you think people used to spell a lot of words differently than they do now? *(Give kids time to explore their theories.)* You know what? There isn't any one reason. Language just changes. But let me show you one example of why and how it changes.

   Turn kids' attention to the bottom of page 288.

   Take a look at these words. Any thoughts about why they changed? *(Linguists think it was to make the spellings more alike, since we use them the same way in sentences.)*

   Here's another one: **whale** and **white** used to be spelled **hwæl** and **hwit.** Any idea why? The old spellings actually fit with the way they used to be pronounced, with an /h/ sound before the /w/ sound: /hwal/ and /hwit/ (say with long vowels). We don't know why the spelling changed, though. Maybe so it would look like the other digraphs **sh, ch,** and **th** (Cummings, 1988).

3. Hand out copies of page 289.

   One more thought on this. Take a look at these spellings (Invernizzi, et al., 1994). The ones in the left-hand column are from different years in the history of English. The ones in the right-hand column are from kids of different ages. As you know, when you were younger you just used sounds to spell words, but now you know a lot more. Isn't it interesting that hundreds of years ago, everybody spelled like young kids do today?

Next Steps

» Follow-up

You can make resources available to students for seeing examples of English spelling from earlier eras. (See bibliography.)

✓ Assessment

As a journal topic, suggest a question like:

📓 Do you think spelling will continue to change in the future? Why or why not?

Lesson at a Glance: WHY ENGLISH SPELLING IS SO WEIRD

What to Do	What to Say	What Kids Need to Know
INTRODUCE		
• Write the words **tough, cough, though, through, plough** (also spelled **plow**), and **hiccough** (also spelled **hiccup**) on the board or on chart paper. • Discuss the **ough** spelling and talk about how it would be spelled phonetically. Invite kids to spell orally or come to the board.	"Take a look at these words. Does anything seem weird about the way they're spelled to you? They all have the letters **ough** in them, but every one of them pronounces those letters differently." "Let's try writing them the way they'd be spelled if they were spelled phonetically, which means spelled the way it sounds."	Sometimes words are spelled very differently from the way they sound.
EXPLORE		
• Get kids thinking of the benefits and drawbacks of phonetic spelling. • Hand out copies of page 290. Have kids try to read the bottom paragraph	"Do you think we'd be better off if words were just spelled like they sound? What would be good about it? Is there anything that would be bad about it?" "Try reading the paragraph at the bottom. It would be harder to read, wouldn't it, at least for a while until we got used to it?"	If we had phonetic spellings, it would be a lot easier to learn to spell, and you wouldn't have to do so much proofreading. But it would be hard to change from what we have now.
DISCOVER		
• Write the words **knot, Don, Dawn, pizza, sign,** and **signal** on the board. • Talk about why those words are spelled the way they are. • Have kids work in pairs to discuss why they think English spelling is so wierd. Then share as a class.	"Did you ever wonder how our spelling got so weird? The word **knot** used to be pronounced something like **kuh-not.** We don't say the /k/ anymore, but we still write it. Some people say the names **Don** and **Dawn** the same and some say them differently (which do you do?), but they have different spellings." "You'd think **pizza** should be spelled something like PEETSA but it comes from Italian, so it's spelled the way they'd spell it in Italy. And **sIgn** has a silent letter, but if we just spelled it SINE, we wouldn't be able to see that it's related to **signal.**"	English spelling doesn't always fit the way it sounds because: 1) words might be spelled the way they used to be pronounced; 2) words might be spelled the way some people say them but not others; 3) words might be spelled the way they would be in the language they came from; and 4) words might be spelled like other words they're related to.
SUMMARIZE		
• Lead a discussion about the value of changing the English spelling system to a phonetic one. • Point out the fact that language is always changing.	"There have been people over the years who have said we should change English spelling to be phonetic, so that it fits the way it sounds. Do you think this would ever happen? None of them have ever gotten very far. Why do you think that is?" "Remember, English spelling used to be pretty phonetic, but it didn't stay that way."	It would be really hard to change the spelling system to a phonetic one—whose pronunciation would you use? Also, it would change again anyway.

WHY ENGLISH SPELLING IS SO WEIRD

 The way words are pronounced changes over time, but the spelling of the words may not change, so sometimes words just seem to be spelled strangely.

Who, When, and Why

Materials
▶ copies of page 290

This lesson is of interest to everyone, but students will benefit from it most if they can understand the abstractions of how spelling systems work and if they know a little about the history of the United States. Students who are literate in other languages will be especially able to contribute to the discussion.

Background Knowledge

A lot of people believe that the best spelling system is a phonetic one, but it's just not what we've got, and it's not going to happen, either. Alphabetic spelling systems tend to start out phonetic but become less so over the years, as pronunciation changes and spellings reflect meaning and history as well as sound. For instance **knife** used to be a phonetic spelling, but it isn't anymore.

Some alphabetic languages are pretty regular in their spelling; Spanish, for instance, has a single letter to represent every sound, and does so consistently. Hawaiian is really simple; it has only twelve sounds (five vowels plus **h, k, l, m, n,** and **w**), and the written form is new enough (the Hawaiian alphabet was developed in the 1820's) that it's stayed pretty consistent. (In the 2006 National Spelling Bee, some of the words in the championship round were from Hawaiian and were quite obscure, but once the contestants knew the words were Hawaiian, they were extremely easy to spell!)

English spelling, however, has about 40 sounds but only 26 letters. English also has a long history, with many pronunciation changes, plus additions from many other languages, reflecting the histories of England and the United States as world powers and the United States as a country of immigrants. Also, English is a world language with a lot of variation in pronunciation even within North America, yet a single spelling system for everyone (except for a few very minor variations between British and American spelling, with Canada using some of each).

The Lesson

tough
cough
though
through
plough   (plow)
hiccough (hiccup)

1. Write the following words on the board or on chart paper: **tough, cough, though, through, plough** (also spelled **plow**), and **hiccough** (also spelled **hiccup**).

    Take a look at these words. Does anything seem weird about the way they're spelled to you? They all have the letters **ough** in them, but every one of them pronounces those letters differently. *(Read the pronunciation of **ough** in each word aloud if you like.)* Let's try writing them the way they'd be spelled if they were spelled phonetically, which means spelled the way it sounds. *(Invite kids to spell orally or come to the board; likely spellings are TUFF, COFF, THO, THRU, PLOW, and HIKUP, but any phonetic ones will do.)*

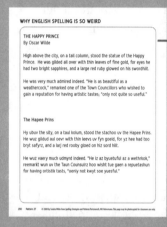

2. To get kids thinking of the benefits and drawbacks of phonetic spelling, hand out copies of page 290.

    Do you think we'd be better off if words were just spelled like they sound? What would be good about it? *(It would be a lot easier to learn to spell, and you wouldn't have to do so much proofreading.)* Is there anything that would be bad about it? Try reading the paragraph at the bottom. *(Allow time for kids to read.)* Easier to read? Certainly not for those of us who now read standard spelling. *(And, of course, if the phonetically spelled version had been written by Oscar Wilde himself, with his Irish accent of a century ago, it would be even harder for us to read.)* It would be harder to read, wouldn't it, at least for a while until we got used to it? And there are all those millions of books out there written in the spelling we use now.

> It's harder than you might think to translate writing into phonetic spelling without using phonetic symbols. I've used a system called "New Spelling 90," which I found on the website of the Simplified Spelling Society (www.spelling society.org/aboutsss/leaflets/ns90.php).
>
> I've chosen to translate the beginning of The Happy Prince, by Oscar Wilde, since we share a last name (no relation, though!). The system doesn't say what symbol to use for the unaccented schwa vowel, so I've used u since the short u sound is closest to it, as seen in the first vowel of **above.**

knot
Don
Dawn
pizza
sign
signal

3. Write the words **knot, Don, Dawn, pizza, sign,** and **signal** on the board.

    Did you ever wonder how our spelling got so weird? The word **knot** used to be pronounced something like KUH-NOT. We don't say the /k/ anymore, but we still write it. Some people say the names **Don** and **Dawn** the same and some say them differently (which do you do?), but they have different spellings. *[If you, the teacher, don't distinguish them, the latter, and other **aw** words, are pronounced by many Americans (but usually not Canadians) with a strong /aw/ sound that's different from short **o**.]* You'd think **pizza** should be spelled something like PEETSA but it comes from Italian, so it's spelled the way they'd spell it in Italy. And **sign** has a silent letter, but if we just spelled it SINE, we wouldn't be able to see that it's related to **signal.**

4.   Have kids work in pairs to discuss.

   👥 Talk to your partner and see if, based on these words we've just looked at, you can explain some reasons why English spelling is weird.

   What did you come up with? (*Build on their ideas, and bring out the following principles: English spelling doesn't always fit the way it sounds because: 1) words might be spelled the way they used to be pronounced; 2) words might be spelled the way some people say them but not others; 3) words might be spelled the way they would be in the language they came from; and 4) words might be spelled like other words they're related to.*)

5.   Lead a discussion about the value of changing the English spelling system to a phonetic one.

   There have been people over the years who have said we should change English spelling to be phonetic, so that it fits the way it sounds. Do you think this would ever happen? (*Discuss.*) None of them have ever gotten very far. Why do you think that is? (*I think there are two reasons: first, it would be really hard to do! For one, whose pronunciation would you use? Second, it would change again anyway.*) Remember, English spelling used to be pretty phonetic, but it didn't stay that way. And one of the fun aspects of our spelling system is that it shows us something about the history of our words (how they used to be pronounced) and the geography (all the different places they came from).

Next Steps

✓ Assessment

As a journal topic, suggest a question like:

   📓 Do you like our spelling system the way it is, or do you wish it were more phonetic? Why do you feel that way?

⊕ Extension

For interested students:

   You might like to read about where some of our more interesting words came from. (*See the annotated bibliography.*) Look in a book or a dictionary that has word histories. (Merriam-Webster's Primary *and* Elementary Dictionaries, *highlight histories that are particularly interesting to kids.*) Then we'll discuss what you've found.

Lesson at a Glance: WORDS FROM SPANISH

What to Do	What to Say	What Kids Need to Know
INTRODUCE		
• Write the following words on the board or on chart paper: **buckaroo, rodeo, alligator, mustang, mosquito, tornado.** • Ask students what they think the words have in common and give them time to speculate. • Explain that they all come from Spanish. • If you like, have some students look up the words in an adult dictionary to find out the original Spanish meaning; if you'd rather just tell them yourself, refer to page 242.	"Take a look at these words: Any idea of what they all have in common?" "Guess what; they all come from Spanish. Do you have any idea why these words might have come from Spanish?" "Who'd like to look them up in a dictionary to find the original meanings?"	Some words come from different languages.
EXPLORE		
• Write the following words on the board or on chart paper: **avocado, chocolate, and tomato.** • Ask students to speculate on the origin of the words. • Explain that the words have a Nahuatl origin.	"There are three other words I'd like to tell you about, that come from Mexico, but not originally from Spanish: **avocado, chocolate,** and **tomato.** Why do you think these words came from Mexico?" "All three words come from the language Nahuatl, spoken by the Aztecs. The Nahuatl words were **ahuacatl, chocolatl,** and **tomatl** (**tomate** in Spanish)."	Many words of the words we know that came from Spanish are things that we learned about from Spanish.

WORDS FROM SPANISH

 We have a lot of words in English that came from Spanish.

Who, When, and Why

The focus of Patterns 28-31 is on words in English that have come to us from other languages, but, particularly if you have students who speak those other languages, it would also be fun to learn some words in that language. Since today's classrooms are particularly likely to have Spanish-speakers, I'll include examples in this lesson of how you might include them.

This is an enrichment lesson that will be especially interesting to students in communities with a lot of Latinos, but valuable for all students in the United States, where Spanish is increasingly prevalent. For Latino students, it will be worthwhile to see how many words from their language have made it into English. Older students might want to read about word origins beyond what you cover in the lesson. Spanish-speaking students will of course be able to contribute a huge amount.

Background Knowledge

We have a lot of words in English that came from Spanish, since there were Spanish settlers here hundreds of years ago, plus we have a close relationship with Mexico and lots of immigrants from Latin America.

The most common Spanish words in English are place names (especially in California and the Southwest) and food names (Mexican and other Latin American food have of course become a huge part of our menu in the last few decades). But plenty of other words have become incorporated into English from Spanish, to the point where we often don't realize their origin.

The Lesson

buckaroo
rodeo
alligator
mustang
mosquito
tornado

1. Write the following words on the board or on chart paper: **buckaroo, rodeo, alligator, mustang, mosquito, tornado.**

   Take a look at these words. Any idea of what they all have in common? *(Looking at the list, I can imagine someone saying "They're all violent"! They may not know **buckaroo,** so define it if necessary, since its origin is interesting.)* Guess what; they all come from Spanish. Do you have any idea why these words might have come from Spanish? *(Some of them are cowboy kinds of words, and the Southwest, much of which used to be part of Mexico, is where cowboys often worked. Alligators, mosquitoes, and tornadoes might all have been discovered by Spanish settlers when they first came to America.)*

2. If you like, have some students look up the words in an adult dictionary to find out the original Spanish meaning; if you'd rather just tell them yourself, here they are:

   • **buckaroo:** probably taken from **vaquero,** which means "cowboy," from **vaca** (cow), and changed to align with **buck** as in "bucking bronco"

   • **rodeo:** from **rodear,** "to surround"

   • **alligator: el ligarto,** "the lizard"

   • **mustang:** from **mestengo,** "stray"

   • **mosquito:** the same in Spanish, meaning "little fly." In Spanish, most words can add an **-ito** ending to become a diminutive, and it's often used affectionately, so that *Juan* becomes *Juanito*

   • **tornado:** from **tronada,** "thunderstorm"

3. Write the following words on the board or on chart paper: **avocado, chocolate,** and **tomato.**

   There are three other words I'd like to tell you about, that come from Mexico, but not originally from Spanish: **avocado, chocolate,** and **tomato.** Why do you think these words came from Mexico? *(Because the foods came from Mexico, so the Spanish explorers who came over here from Europe hundreds of years ago, who'd never seen the foods before, learned the names from the Indians who lived in Mexico.)* All three words come from the language Nahuatl, spoken by the Aztecs. The Nahuatl words were **ahuacatl, chocolatl,** and **tomatl** (**tomate** in Spanish).

avocado
chocolate
tomato

Next Steps

✓ Assessment

As a journal topic, suggest a question like:

📝 How do you think Spanish has contributed to the English language?

➕ Extension

Here are two project ideas for anyone who might be interested: make a list of Mexican foods or other foods with Spanish names. You can find out from the adult dictionary or someone in the class who speaks Spanish what a lot of these words mean originally. For instance, did you know that **enchilada** means "flavored with chiles," and **burrito** means "little donkey"?

Another idea is to get the atlas and see how many town names you can find in California and the Southwest that come from Spanish and what they mean (use a Spanish/English dictionary or ask a Spanish-speaking friend). Any town that starts with *San* or *Santa* is the name of a saint, like San Bernardino and Santa Barbara. See if you figure out some ways to tell which other place names come from Spanish.

Either of these could make a good informational writing project, a piece, or a short book.

Sample Words

More words from Spanish:

Easy	Medium	Harder
cargo	armada	barracuda
Colorado	fiesta	aficionado
hurricane	guitar	anchovy
lasso	coyote	barbeque
nacho	flamingo	papaya
Nevada	hammock	
poncho	iguana	
potato	jaguar	
pronto	stampede	
ranch	tuna	
tango	Alamo	
cabana		
canyon		

Lesson at a Glance: WORDS FROM ALL OVER THE WORLD

What to Do	What to Say	What Kids Need to Know
INTRODUCE		
• Write the following words on the board: **moccasin, igloo, llama, chimpanzee, rabbi, polka,** and **samurai.** • Ask children to share what they know about the word **igloo.**	"Do you know these words? What they all have in common is that they came from another language before they were part of English. And their meanings give you a hint as to what language they might come from." "Let's take an easy one: **igloo.** What's your guess as to what language it comes from and why?"	**Igloo** comes from the people and language that you may know as Eskimo but today are called Inuit. In Inuit, **igloo** just means "house."
EXPLORE		
• Have pairs discuss their thoughts on the rest of the words. • After they've discussed, share as a class. See page 246 for word origins and meanings.	"Talk with a partner and come up with your best guesses for the rest of them."	Some words that we use in English come from other languages.
DISCOVER		
• Get kids thinking about why the English language has so many "borrowed words."	"What does this tell you about our language? Why do you think we have words that come from other languages?" "Do these words seem any harder to spell to you than other words? Sometimes they might be, if they keep the spelling they have in the other language. For instance, we don't usually see two **l**'s at the beginning of words, but **llama** went from Quechua into Spanish, which does use **ll** this way. But the cool thing about these different spellings is that it sometimes gives us a hint that the word is from another language."	It's interesting to think about what language a word might have come from.

WORDS FROM ALL OVER THE WORLD

Because so much of the world has influenced American culture, our language is made up of words from all over the world. These are often words that are a little trickier to spell since they may keep the spelling of the home language.

Who, When, and Why

Materials
▶ copies of page 291

At this age, looking at Greek and Latin roots isn't very useful since so many of the words they'd help kids make connections between are beyond a reasonable level of vocabulary for elementary school. As adults, we can (maybe) appreciate the common root meaning "run" in the words **concur, cursive, currency,** and **occur,** but it's a pretty dry topic and not really all that interesting for kids. However, it can be a lot of fun to explore all the different countries and cultures that our words come from, particularly because the geographic information is interesting and partly because the words themselves are often enjoyable and interesting.

This lesson is of interest to everyone. It would be an especially good fit at a time when you're studying cultures in other parts of the world, or the diverse groups that make up American culture, in social studies. The focus of the lesson should be on exploration and celebration of the richness of our language.

Older students will be able to look up etymologies themselves, where with younger ones you can adapt the lesson so that you provide the information and the class merely discusses it. Students from other countries will be able to contribute words from their language that have become part of English.

Background Knowledge

I've used an adult reference book on the English language as a source of words for this lesson (MacArthur, 1992; see his "Borrowing" entry. There are also a lot of both children's and adult books on where our words came from. See annotated bibliography.)

moccasin
igloo
llama
chimpanzee
rabbi
polka
samurai

1. Write the following words on the board: **moccasin, igloo, llama, chimpanzee, rabbi, polka**, and **samurai.**

   Do you know these words? What they all have in common is that they came from another language before they were part of English. And their meanings give you a hint as to what language they might come from. Let's take an easy one: **igloo.** What's your guess as to what language it comes from and why? *(From the people and language that you may know as Eskimo but today are called Inuit. In Inuit, **igloo** just means "house.")*

   Talk with a partner and come up with your best guesses for the rest of them.

2. After they've discussed, share their ideas and provide the following answers (if I don't list the meaning, it's identical to the English meaning):

   - **moccasin:** Algonquian (northeastern Woodlands tribes), "shoe"

   - **llama:** Quechua (spoken in Peru)

   - **chimpanzee:** Kongo (Africa)

   - **rabbi:** Hebrew, "my master"

   - **polka:** Czech, "Polish woman"

   - **samurai:** Japanese, "member of the warrior aristocracy"

3. Get kids thinking about why the English language has so many "borrowed words."

   What does this tell you about our language? Why do you think we have words that come from other languages? Do these words seem any harder to spell to you than other words? Sometimes they might be, if they keep the spelling they have in the other language. For instance, we don't usually see two **l**'s at the beginning of words, but **llama** went from Quechua into Spanish, which does use **ll** this way. But the cool thing about these different spellings is that it sometimes gives us a hint that the word is from another language.

Next Steps

 ## Follow-up

A world map would be a great place to display what you've found out about word origins. Throughout the year, as you study different cultures and countries, you can make a point of learning a few words that came into English from their language.

 ## Assessment

As a journal topic, suggest a question like:

> Do you think it's a good idea that English has so many words from other languages? Why or why not?

Extension

Given the difficulty of the task, I'd recommend this activity more for older students. Hand out copies of page 291.

> Here's a list of words from other languages *(I've included mostly non-European examples)*, and it's not as obvious what part of the world they might have come from. I'd like everyone to sign up for one to look up over the next few days, and then we'll report back. You should look both for what language it came from and if it had a meaning different from the current one in English.

You're likely to need an adult dictionary—a dictionary of etymologies would also be great—to find these word origins. I'd also suggest a little instruction to point out that they look for the earliest origin listed; **llama,** for instance, is described as "Sp, from Quechua." Understanding this involves knowing that the language listed last is the original source of the word; also, common languages like Spanish are typically abbreviated, but the dictionary will have a list of these.

WORDS FROM ALL OVER THE WORLD

aardvark	giraffe	sauna
apricot	gnu	shampoo
barbecue	hammock	skunk
bug	hurricane	sofa
camel	jaguar	spinach
canoe	kangaroo	tattoo
cashew	kayak	tea
cheetah	leprechaun	turquoise
chipmunk	mongoose	ukulele
chopsticks	moose	yak
cinnamon	orangutan	yeti
coffee	pajamas	yoga
condo	parka	yogurt
coyote	peach	zero
genie	pecan	zombie
geyser	potato	
ghoul	robot	

Lesson at a Glance: SPELLING IN OTHER LANGUAGES

What to Do	What to Say	What Kids Need to Know
INTRODUCE		
• Get kids thinking about the Spanish language by leading a discussion. • You might find it valuable to make and post a Spanish alphabet chart.	"How many of you can read in Spanish? Does Spanish use the same alphabet as English? You know what? You may not be aware of this, but even though it looks the same, it's not exactly the same. Spanish didn't originally have two letters that English does, **k** and **w**, though every once in a while you'll see a word with one of those letters in Spanish because it's been taken from another language. Spanish does have the sound that **k** spells in English, but uses other letters for it. You can see the two spellings of /k/ in **taco** and **taquería.** It sounds like there's a /w/ sound spelled with **u** in words like **guapo** and **sueño,** but that's really an /oo/ sound." "And here's something else: if you see the Spanish alphabet, it'll include the four letters that English does not have **ch, ll, rr,** and **ñ;** they're considered separate letters because they have their own sounds."	Different languages can even use different letters.
EXPLORE		
If you feel that students are ready to explore other languages, proceed with the following. • Introduce Hawaiian into the conversation. • If the kids have any familiarity with Hawaii, ask them to list Hawaiian words they know. Or you can just list some words for them: **aloha, ukulele, Maui, Mauna Loa, lei, hula, kahuna, Oahu.** • Discuss the words and the language. • Write the following words on the board: **cwm, eglwys, llwyn, fford, fynydd, dydd Sadwrn,** and **Croeso i Gymru.** • Discuss the words and their origin.	"Let's take another language, Hawaiian. They use the same alphabet as English, but do they seem different at all? Hawaiian only uses 12 letters, 5 vowels and the consonants **h, k, l, m, n, p,** and **w.** Why do you think that is? It's because there are only that many sounds in the whole Hawaiian language." "Now take a look at these words. These words use our alphabet but *really* look strange, don't they? Any idea what language they're from? They're from Welsh, a language spoken in the country of Wales, which is next to England. Some of these words look like you could barely pronounce them, don't they? I'm not going to try (!), but the letters **w** and **y** are always vowels in Welsh, so that helps to explain how you could say these words. If you're interested, they mean 'valley,' 'church,' 'bush,' 'road,' 'mountain,' 'Saturday,' and 'Welcome to Wales.'"	It can be interesting to learn about different alphabets and languages.

SPELLING IN OTHER LANGUAGES

 A lot of languages use the same alphabet we do, but not always exactly the same letters. Also, other languages have spellings that don't look at all like ours.

Who, When, and Why

Materials
▶ none

This lesson will be of interest to everyone, especially older students who can grasp the abstractions involved. Students who are literate in other languages using the Roman alphabet can contribute their knowledge to the discussion. I've given extra attention to Spanish since you're most likely to have Spanish-speaking students.

Background Knowledge

This lesson is meant to help students learn, really just for fun and enrichment, that other languages, even those using the same letters as we do, may do things differently.

Our alphabet, known as the Roman alphabet, is used for many other languages, including many that have only recently been written down. (There's a group called the Summer Institute of Linguistics that has worked for decades developing transcription methods for previously unwritten languages, often with a motive of creating Bibles in those languages.)

However, since other languages have other sound systems, they don't always use the same number of letters as English does. They also sometimes have different sound/letter relationships than English, so that their words' spellings won't always give us reliable clues to their pronunciation.

The Lesson

1. Get kids thinking about the Spanish language:

   How many of you can read in Spanish? Does Spanish use the same alphabet as English? You know what? You may not be aware of this, but even though it looks the same, it's not exactly the same. Spanish didn't originally have two letters that English does, **k** and **w,** though every once in a while you'll see a word with one of those letters in Spanish because it's been taken from another language. Spanish does have the sound that **k** spells in English, but uses other letters for it. You can see the two spellings of /k/ in **taco** and **taquería.** It sounds like there's a /w/ sound spelled with **u** in words like **guapo** and **sueño,** but that's really an /oo/ sound. And here's something else: if you see the Spanish alphabet, it'll include the four letters that English doesn't have **ch, ll, rr,** and **ñ;** they're considered separate letters because they have their own sounds.

2. Now introduce Hawaiian into the conversation:

   Let's take another language, Hawaiian. *(If the kids have any familiarity with Hawaii you can say the following.)* Let's try to list as many words as we can that are Hawaiian place names or things. *(Or you can just list some words for the students:* **aloha, ukulele, Maui, Mauna Loa, lei, hula, kahuna, Oahu.***)* They use the same alphabet as English, but do they seem different at all? Hawaiian only uses 12 letters, 5 vowels and the consonants **h, k, l, m, n, p,** and **w.** Why do you think that is? It's because there are only that many sounds in the whole Hawaiian language.

3. Optional:

   Have you ever noticed Hawai'i written this way, with an apostrophe? Any ideas as to what that's for? It's not like the apostrophes in English, it shows that there's sort of a sound there. *(Say the word with the glottal stop in it at the apostrophe, which is like the catch in the throat in the middle of "uh-oh"; it ends up sounding and feeling like there's a break between the last two syllables rather than gliding between them.)* So if you ever see an apostrophe in a Hawaiian word, it's sort of like a letter because it shows you something about the sound.

   cwm
   eglwys
   llwyn
   fford
   fynydd
   dydd Sadwrn
   Croeso i Gymru

4. Write the following words on the board: **cwm, eglwys, llwyn, fford, fynydd, dydd Sadwrn,** and **Croeso i Gymru.**

   Now take a look at these words. These words use our alphabet but *really* look strange, don't they? Any idea what language they're from? They're from Welsh, a language spoken in the country of Wales, which is next to England. Some of these words look like you could barely pronounce them, don't they? I'm not going to try (!), but the letters **w** and **y** are always vowels in Welsh, so that helps to explain how you could say these words. If you're interested, they mean "valley," "church," "bush," "road," "mountain," "Saturday," and "Welcome to Wales."

Spelling Strategies and Patterns

>> **Follow-up**

If the children seem interested in this topic, you could look for books or pages on the Internet written in other languages using the Roman alphabet. They could also research the origins of the Roman alphabet. (See bibliography.)

✓ **Assessment**

As a journal topic, suggest a question like:

📓 What languages would be easier or harder to learn to spell in? Or, Hawaiian or Welsh: easier or harder to learn to spell than English, and why?

Lesson at a Glance: WRITING IN OTHER ALPHABETS AND WITHOUT ALPHABETS

What to Do	What to Say	What Kids Need to Know
INTRODUCE		
• Hand out copies of page 292. • Talk about languages with different systems of writing. If you like, point out on a map the countries where they're used. • Give kids time to talk about these alphabets in any way they like.	"Take a look at numbers one through three. What do you think? They really look different from our writing, don't they? They're written in Arabic, Chinese, Korean, and Russian. The Russian alphabet has some of the same letters we do, but they don't always represent the same sounds. Wouldn't it be interesting to visit one of those countries? You couldn't even try to pronounce the words on signs in the street because you wouldn't even know the alphabet. And of course people from those countries would feel the same way if they came here."	Some systems of writing have different letters.
EXPLORE		
• Show some examples of writing in Chinese and hieroglyphics. • Allow time for open-ended discussion.	"Now take a look at number 4. These characters are different from letters; does anybody know how?" "The very first writing systems were like this, before alphabets were developed (**?**). Can you think of any advantages to this kind of writing system? Here's one: There are several different languages spoken in China, and they can sound very different, but most people can read the same written language regardless of the language they speak, since it represents the meanings of words."	Other systems have pictures or characters to represent words or ideas.

WRITING IN OTHER ALPHABETS AND WITHOUT ALPHABETS

 Some languages use different alphabets than ours, and some don't even use alphabets at all. They use written symbols to represent whole words or ideas, not sounds.

Who, When, and Why

Materials
▶ copies of page 292
▶ any other samples of writing in languages with other alphabets that you'd like to share

This lesson should be of interest to anyone, particularly if your class has students who speak any of the languages involved. Take advantage of any relevant contributions from students fluent in these other languages. Some students may want to do further research on the topic. Like the previous lesson, this one is for the purposes of enrichment and interest.

Background Knowledge

The world's languages are written in a number of different alphabets (you can see samples, some current and some extinct, at omniglot.com). There are also syllabic systems, where symbols represent either entire syllables or consonants with attached markings to show the vowels. There are also a few writing systems that are non-alphabetic, such as Chinese and a few other Asian languages, as well as ancient hieroglyphics. In these systems, known as logographic writing, characters represent whole meanings or words rather than sounds. The variety and history of world writing systems are fascinating, and have been written about in books for both adults and children (see annotated bibliography), but in this lesson we'll just do a brief overview.

1. Hand out copies of page 292.

Take a look at the second through fifth examples. What do you think? They all say the same thing, but they really look different from our writing, don't they? They're written in Arabic, Chinese, Korean, and Russian. *(If you like, point out on a map the countries where they're used.)* The Russian alphabet has some of the same letters we do, but they don't always represent the same sounds. Wouldn't it be interesting to visit one of those countries? You couldn't even try to pronounce the words on signs in the street, because you wouldn't even know the symbols. And of course people from those countries would feel the same way if they came here.

Give kids time to talk about these writing systems in any way they like.

2. Focus on the writing in Chinese.

Now take a look at the third example. These characters are different from letters; does anybody know how? *(Each symbol represents an idea, not the sounds of the word the way an alphabet does.)* Some early writing systems were like this, before alphabets were developed. Can you think of any advantages to this kind of writing system? Here's one: There are several different languages spoken in China, and they can sound very different, but most people can read the same written language regardless of the language they speak, since it represents the meanings of words.

Again, allow time for open-ended discussion.

➤➤ Follow-up

If students are taken by the topic, they may want to read more on it. (See bibliography.) You might want to encourage kids to research a variety of other systems of writing. A terrific book I'd recommend for a read-aloud is **Sequoyah** (Rumford, 2004; the book is written bilingually in both English and the Cherokee script that Sequoyah developed), the story of a Cherokee leader who developed an alphabet (actually a syllabic writing system) for his language around 1809. The book gives a lot of information about, and examples of, the writing system itself. Children might also find it fun to develop their own alphabets or logographic systems.

✓ Assessment

As a journal topic, suggest a question like:

📓 Do you think that kids with other writing systems find it harder to learn to read and write? Why would you or wouldn't you like a system like Chinese, where each word has its own character?

Lesson at a Glance: CRAZY SPELLING OUT IN THE WORLD

What to Do	What to Say	What Kids Need to Know
INTRODUCE		
• Get kids thinking about reasons people might misspell words on purpose. • Talk about the spelling of Froot Loops, Krispy Kreme, and Kwik Kopy.	"Who knows how to spell **Froot Loops?** Go ahead and write it on the board. **Krispy Kreme?** Why do you think **froot** is spelled this way instead of **fruit?** No, it's not that someone didn't proofread; it's on purpose! With **Froot Loops,** the cereal is in the shape of **o**'s, so they probably thought it would look cute spelled that way. Do you think **Krispy Kreme** draws more customers than **Crispy Cream** would? Do you think it's a good idea for companies to do this, since it might help them sell more, or a bad idea, because it might confuse people? Here's an interesting one. There are places where you can photocopy called **Kwik Kopy;** this name has three /k/ sounds, and every one is spelled wrong!"	Some misspellings might be intentional—to get attention.
EXPLORE		
• Point out that misspellings can hide product flaws. • Discuss the spellings of **Krab Salad** and **Nilla Wafers.**	"Here's something else to think about. Sometimes in the fish section of the supermarket, you can find a package with a name like 'krab salad' on it. Any ideas why it's spelled that way? When you look at the list of ingredients, it doesn't have real crabmeat in it, just imitation crabmeat made from fish." "There are some cookies that used to be called **Vanilla Wafers,** but now they're called **Nilla Wafers** because they don't have real vanilla in them. So do you think **Froot Loops** have real fruit in them? You can check the next time you're in a supermarket."	A misspelling could be a hint that something is being covered up.
DISCOVER		
• Ask kids to work with a partner to think about the value of misspellings. • Have kids share their ideas.	"So when would it make sense for you to spell something wrong on purpose? These could be thoughts about your writing now or about when you are grown up. Brainstorm with a partner and we'll share your ideas."	Intentional misspelling can have a place.

CRAZY SPELLING OUT IN THE WORLD

 Some business and product names are spelled incorrectly for a purpose, to draw attention and look cute.

Who, When, and Why

This lesson is of interest to all students, particularly those who are old enough to notice when words are misspelled out in the world.

Background Knowledge

Kozy Korner, Kwik Kopy, and of course Krispy Kreme. Some people are annoyed by commercial intentional invented spellings, but hey, they're here, so let's talk about them and maybe have some fun with them. Usually when we see words spelled wrong out in public, it's just a mistake, but when it's the name of a business or a product, it's almost certainly on purpose, to look cute and attract attention. (Though I know that the several restaurants I've seen with **Pizzaria** *[sic]* as part of their names didn't spell it that way on purpose, it was just a mistake!) However, in some product names, it's for what appears to be legal reasons related to the naming of ingredients—as we'll see.

1. **Get kids thinking about reasons people might misspell words on purpose.**

   Who knows how to spell **Froot Loops?** Go ahead and write it on the board. **Krispy Kreme?** Why do you think **froot** is spelled this way instead of **fruit?** *(Write both product names on the board if kids haven't done so.)* No, it's not that someone didn't proofread; it's on purpose! With **Froot Loops,** the cereal is in the shape of **o**'s, so they probably thought it would look cute spelled that way. Do you think **Krispy Kreme** draws more customers than **Crispy Cream** *(write on board)* would? Do you think it's a good idea for companies to do this, since it might help them sell more, or a bad idea, because it might confuse people? Here's an interesting one. There are places where you can photocopy called **Kwik Kopy;** this name has three /k/ sounds, and every one is spelled wrong!

2. **Point out that misspellings can hide product flaws.**

   Here's something else to think about. Sometimes in the fish section of the supermarket, you can find a package with a name like **krab salad** on it. Any ideas why it's spelled that way? When you look at the list of ingredients, it doesn't have real crabmeat in it, just imitation crabmeat made from fish. There are some cookies that used to be called **Vanilla Wafers,** but now they're called **Nilla Wafers** because they don't have real vanilla in them. So do you think **Froot Loops** have real fruit in them? You can check the next time you're in a supermarket *(or alternatively, bring in a box).*

3. **Ask kids to think about the value of misspellings.**

   So when would it make sense for you to spell something wrong on purpose? These could be thoughts about your writing now or about when you are grown up. Brainstorm with a partner and we'll share your ideas. *(Bring out: intentional misspelling can have a place; any answers are fine.)*

Next Steps

» Follow-up

You know that a supermarket has thousands of products; the next time you're in one, see how many you can spot that use invented spellings.

✓ Assessment

As a journal topic, suggest a question like:

If you were inventing a product or starting a company, would you use invented spelling in the name? What are some that you might try and why?

Lesson at a Glance: THE NATIONAL SPELLING BEE

What to Do	What to Say	What Kids Need to Know
INTRODUCE		
• Modify this lesson as necessary if your school participates in the National Spelling Bee. • Get the kids thinking about spelling bees.	"How many of you have heard of the National Spelling Bee? What do you know about it? It's a fun idea, isn't it, that you can compete in spelling just like people compete in sports. It's like an Olympics of language."	Competing in the National Spelling Bee can be a fun idea to consider.
EXPLORE		
• Ask kids to think about what it would be like to participate in a spelling bee. • Consider showing one of the two recommended movies.	"What do you think it takes for a kid to rise to the top in the National Spelling Bee? It helps to be a naturally good speller, of course, just like you probably need to be a naturally good runner if you want to make it to the 100-meter in the Olympics. But how much work and study do you think it involves? Here's a hint: the people who run the National Spelling Bee have a list of more than 20,000 words that they give kids to study, but they also use words that aren't even on that list. To even get to the national competition, kids have to study huge amounts."	Winning the National Spelling Bee takes a lot of time and commitment.
DISCOVER		
• See if kids would be interested in participating in a spelling bee. • Point out that the first step to participating in the National Spelling Bee is to take part in a simple classroom bee.	"So what do you think? Is the National Spelling Bee worthwhile? What do you think of the kids who choose to enter it and try to win?"	It might be fun to participate in a spelling bee.

THE NATIONAL SPELLING BEE

 For kids who are really into words, language, and spelling, there's a big national contest every year where the best spellers in the country spell on national television.

Who, When, and Why

Of interest to everyone; the National Spelling Bee is held in May or June, so the lesson can be timed to lead up to it.

Background Knowledge

The National Spelling Bee, which has been in existence since 1925, has come into new prominence, with movies, a book, and national broadcasting on ESPN (hey, it's a sport!), and, most recently, a spot on ABC in primetime. Whether or not your school participates in the bee, it's fun to learn about.

The National Spelling Bee has a website (spellingbee.com) where you can find information about its history, winners, and so on, and download word lists and other study material. I'd also recommend two movies: the documentary *Spellbound* and the fictional film *Akeelah and the Bee,* both suitable for classroom use, and the (adult) book *American Bee* (Maguire, 2006), which provides a history of the Bee, scenes from one year's competition, and portraits of a number of previous winners and contestants.

One of the interesting aspects of the National Spelling Bee is that it has begun to use more and more words that are often only obscurely used in English; the 2006 competition included a number of unfamiliar Hawaiian words and was won by Katherine Close on the German word **ursprache,** meaning "an early or precursor language." This reflects how competitive the bee has become; in earlier years, contestants were eliminated on much easier words. I'm a strong speller with a large vocabulary, but was only able to correctly spell about half of the words in 2006's championship round.

By the way, I *don't* think that regular classroom spelling bees are a good idea. I love the national bee as an extracurricular activity, like a sport, for those who are interested, but so many adults have bad memories of humiliation in mandatory classroom spelling bees. Those bees perhaps seem unnecessarily cruel, and, at least as importantly, have little relationship to spelling in writing.

The Lesson

1. Modify this lesson as necessary if your school participates in the National Spelling Bee.

How many of you have heard of the National Spelling Bee? What do you know about it? It's a fun idea, isn't it, that you can compete in spelling just like people compete in sports. It's like an Olympics of language.

2. Get kids thinking about what it would be like to participate in a spelling bee.

What do you think it takes for a kid to rise to the top in the National Spelling Bee? It helps to be a naturally good speller, of course, just like you probably need to be a naturally good runner if you want to make it to the 100-meter in the Olympics. But how much work and study do you think it involves? Here's a hint: the people who run the National Spelling Bee have a list of more than 20,000 words that they give kids to study, but they also use words that aren't even on that list. To even get to the national competition, kids have to study huge amounts.

3. I'd recommend showing one of the two movies I mentioned earlier. Both are terrific stories and provide a strong feel of both the determination involved to be in the national bee and what the finals look and feel like.

4. See if kids would be interested in participating in a spelling bee.

So what do you think? Is the National Spelling Bee worthwhile? What do you think of the kids who choose to enter it and try to win?

Point out that the first step to participating in the National Spelling Bee is to take part in a simple classroom bee.

Next Steps

✓ Assessment

As a journal topic, suggest a question like:

 Is entering the National Spelling Bee something you'd like to do? Why or why not?

Sample Words

Refer to spellingbee.com for information on word lists.

Appendix

SPELLING QUESTIONNAIRE

1. _____ It's fun for me to notice odd spellings.

      OR

   _____ Odd spellings just make life hard for me.

2. _____ Spelling bores me. I'd rather focus on my ideas.

      OR

   _____ I'd enjoy being in a big spelling bee.

3. _____ I really have to work at getting words spelled right.

      OR

   _____ Spelling's usually not that hard for me.

4. _____ I'm not afraid to use big words in my writing, because I can do my best at figuring out how to spell them.

      OR

   _____ I'm a little nervous about using big words in my writing, because I'm afraid I won't get them right.

5. _____ It bugs me if I've written something and then discover words that are still misspelled in the final draft.

      OR

   _____ I care mostly about my ideas when I write, and I don't mind so much if the words are spelled right.

6. _____ I'd rather come up with my own spelling, because it makes me think.

      OR

   _____ I like asking an adult how to spell a word so I can get it right.

SPELLING INTERVIEW

Why is spelling important to you?	When is spelling important to you?	Name:

DOLCH WORD LIST

about	came	gave	keep	open	so	use
after	can	get	kind	or	some	very
again	carry	give	know	our	soon	walk
all	clean	go	laugh	out	start	want
always	cold	goes	let	over	stop	warm
am	come	going	light	own	take	was
an	could	good	like	pick	tell	wash
and	cut	got	little	play	ten	we
any	did	green	live	please	thank	well
are	do	grow	long	pretty	that	went
around	does	had	look	pull	the	were
as	done	has	made	put	their	what
ask	don't	have	make	ran	them	when
at	down	he	many	read	then	where
ate	draw	help	may	red	there	which
away	drink	her	me	ride	these	white
be	eat	here	much	right	they	who
because	eight	him	must	round	think	why
been	every	his	my	run	this	will
before	fall	hold	myself	said	those	wish
best	far	hot	never	saw	three	with
better	fast	how	new	say	to	work
big	find	hurt	no	see	today	would
black	first	I	not	seven	togeth-	write
blue	five	if	now	shall	er	yellow
both	fly	in	of	she	too	yes
bring	for	into	off	show	try	you
brown	found	is	old	sing	two	your
but	four	it	on	sit	under	
buy	from	its	once	six	up	
by	full	jump	one	sleep	upon	
call	funny	just	only	small	us	

HOW TO MEMORIZE WORDS

How to Memorize a Word

1. Write it.

2. Check and think.

3. Try again.

4. Check again tomorrow; repeat if you need to.

TRYING IT TWO WAYS

First Try	Second Try	My Notes

USING A SPELL-CHECKER

Your Spelling	Describe Your Results (Check one.)	What Did You Learn? (Include the correct spelling.)
1.	____ 1. I got a list of words. ____ 2. I had it right. ____ 3. I got just one word. ____ 4. No words listed.	
2.	____ 1. I got a list of words. ____ 2. I had it right. ____ 3. I got just one word. ____ 4. No words listed.	
3.	____ 1. I got a list of words. ____ 2. I had it right. ____ 3. I got just one word. ____ 4. No words listed.	

BLANK CHECKLIST

Checklist for _____

☐ _____

☐ _____

☐ _____

☐ _____

☐ _____

☐ _____

☐ _____

☐ _____

HOW TO ACHIEVE 100% CORRECT SPELLING

1. Try to get words right in your first draft.

2. Mark your invented spellings when you write them.

3. Read through your piece, focusing just on spelling.

4. Have an adult look over your piece.

/S/ SOUND WORDS

sa	ca
se	ce
si	ci
so	co
su	cu
sy	cy
s + any other letter	c + any other letter

/J/ SOUND WORDS

gyroscope	jelly	jump	gypsy	joy	geography
jog	jeep	giant	jail	gentleman	jab
Jim	juggle	genius	jeans	John	judge
job	gem	juice	jack	gel	jig
jam	giraffe	jittery	gym	junior	jet

TRICKY CONSONANT SOUNDS

chicken	scissors	phone	pickle
phoenix	jacket	cough	enough
hockey	science	black	graph
laugh	scene	tough	photo

LONG A PATTERNS

-aid (maid)	-ade (made)	-ay (may)

PAPER WORD WALL

E	J	O	U	Z
D	I	N	T	Y
C	H	M	S	X
B	G	L	R	W
A	F	K	P/Q	V

LONG E PATTERNS

beet	chief	me	weak	receive
freak	cheap	tree	key	kitty
bean	cheese	need	peace	steal
seize	heat	bee	sleet	believe
keep	funny		freeze	

BLANK WORD CARDS

LONG I PATTERNS

ide	ime
bride	time

ine	ipe
pine	wipe

ite	ie
white	pie

y	igh
fly	high

LONG U AND THE TWO OO'S

_ube	_ude	_ule	_ume

_une	_use	_ute	other

VOWELS AND THE LETTER R

cord	word	door	carry	tire
Harry	more	heart	steer	dairy
car	fire	poor	stir	sour
our	fear	flour	pair	wire

I BEFORE E

ie (long e)	cei (long e)	ei (long a)	Doesn't Fit
piece	receive	neighbor	weird

WORDS WITH SILENT LETTERS

kn	wr	gn

others

TRICKY ENDINGS: -able OR -ible?

-able	-ible

WORDS WITH APOSTROPHES: CONTRACTIONS

he is	he's
we are	we're
Jack will	Jack'll
it has	it's
we have	we've

did not	didn't
had not	hadn't
cannot	can't
was not	wasn't
is not	isn't

HOW PEOPLE USED TO SPELL (IN ENGLISH!)

Old English:	Translation:
BĒOWULF Hwät! we Gâr-Dena in geâr-dagum þeód-cyninga þrym gefrunon, hû þâ äðelingas ellen fremedon. Oft Scyld Scêfing sceaðena þreátum, monegum mægðum meodo-setla ofteáh. Egsode eorl, syððan ærest wearð feá-sceaft funden: he þäs frôfre gebâd, weôx under wolcnum, weorð-myndum âh, ôð þät him æghwylc þâra ymb-sittendra ofer hron-râde hŷran scolde,	LO, praise of the prowess of people-kings of spear-armed Danes, in days long sped, we have heard, and what honor the athelings won! Oft Scyld the Scefing from squadroned foes, from many a tribe, the mead-bench tore, awing the earls. Since erst he lay friendless, a foundling, fate repaid him: for he waxed under welkin, in wealth he throve, till before him the folk, both far and near, who house by the whale-path, heard his mandate,

Middle English:	Translation:
SYR GAWAYN AND THE GRENE KNYƷT Sien þe sege & þe assaut watƷ sesed at Troye, þe borƷ brittened & brent to brondeƷ & askeƷ, þe tulk þat þe trammes of tresoun þer wroƷt, WatƷ tried for his tricherie, þe trewest on erthe; Hit watƷ Ennias þe athel, & his highe kynde, þat siþen depreced prouinces, & patrounes bicome WelneƷe of al þe wele in þe west iles, Fro riche Romulus to Rome ricchis hym swyþe, With gret bobbaunce þat burƷe he biges vpon fyrst, & neuenes hit his aune nome, as hit now hat;	The siege and assault having ceased at Troy as its blazing battlements blackened to ash, the man who had planned and plotted that treason had trial enough for the truest traitor! Then Aeneas the prince and his honored line plundered provinces and held in their power nearly all the wealth of the western isles. Thus Romulus swiftly arriving at Rome sets up that city and in swelling pride gives it his name, the name it now bears;

Old English	Middle English	Modern American English
cuthe	couthe, coude	could
sceolde	scholde	should
wolde	wolde	would

from Cummings, 1988

HOW PEOPLE USED TO SPELL

Historical Spellings	Students' Spellings
WIF (wife) TODAEG (today) HEAFONUM (heaven) (Lord's Prayer, 1000)	WIF (wife) TUDAE (today) HAFAN (heaven) (Tawanda, age 6)
YONGE (young) SWETE (sweet) ROOTE (root) CROPPES (crops) (Chaucer, 1440)	YUNGE (young) SWETE (sweet) ROOTE (root) CHOPPE (chop) (Antoine, age 8)
DISSCORD (discord) FOLOWE (follow) MUSIKE (music) (Elizabeth I, 1600)	DISSCORD (discord) FOLOWE (follow) MUSSIC (music) (Julian, age 14)

WHY ENGLISH SPELLING IS SO WEIRD

THE HAPPY PRINCE
By Oscar Wilde

High above the city, on a tall column, stood the statue of the Happy Prince. He was gilded all over with thin leaves of fine gold, for eyes he had two bright sapphires, and a large red ruby glowed on his swordhilt.

He was very much admired indeed. "He is as beautiful as a weathercock," remarked one of the Town Councillors who wished to gain a reputation for having artistic tastes; "only not quite so useful."

The Hapee Prins

Hy ubuv the sity, on a taul kolum, stood the stachoo uv the Hapee Prins. He wuz gildud aul oevr with thin leevs uv fyn goeld, for yz hee had too bryt safyrz, and a larj red rooby gloed on hiz sord hilt.

He wuz vaery much udmyrd indeed. "He iz az byuetuful az a wethrkok," reemarkt wun uv the Taun Counsulrz hoo wisht tue gaen a repuetashun for having ortistik tasts, "oenly not kwyt soe yuesful."

WORDS FROM ALL OVER THE WORLD

aardvark	giraffe	sauna
apricot	gnu	shampoo
barbecue	hammock	skunk
bug	hurricane	sofa
camel	jaguar	spinach
canoe	kangaroo	tattoo
cashew	kayak	tea
cheetah	leprechaun	turquoise
chipmunk	mongoose	ukulele
chopsticks	moose	yak
cinnamon	orangutan	yeti
coffee	pajamas	yoga
condo	parka	yogurt
coyote	peach	zero
genie	pecan	zombie
geyser	potato	
ghoul	robot	

OTHER ALPHABETS

English:
Good morning. I hope you have a nice day.

Arabic:

صباح الخير. أتمنى لكم يوما طيبا.

Chinese:

早上好。希望您有愉快的一天。

Korean:

좋은 아침입니다. 좋은 하루되세요.

Russian:

Хорошего всем дня, и доброго утра.

ASSESSMENT TOOLS AND PROCEDURES

We all want to know how kids are doing with their spelling, so I've provided this set of tools to help you look at children's spelling from a variety of perspectives. There are a number of dimensions to look at: knowledge, strategies, attitudes, and what we might call achievement: how well students spell in their writing. I've provided tools for each of these, as follows: (Students' spelling journal entries also provide assessment information in a less formal way.)

Knowledge: diagnostic dictation tests, with optional explanations; how to look at kids' invented spellings

- High-Frequency Words Dictation
- Pattern Quiz
- Invented Spelling Analysis

Strategies and attitudes: observation protocol; questionnaire/interview

- Strategy Observation
- Strategy/Attitude Questionnaire

Achievement: quantity and quality evaluation of spelling in writing

- Quantitative Spelling Record
- Qualitative Evaluation Record

Special cases: this kid's spelling makes no sense to me

SPELLING KNOWLEDGE

We can think about children's knowledge of spelling as made up of two components: the words they know how to spell correctly, and the developmental level, or sophistication, of their invented spellings. I've provided evaluation tools for both of these, and they serve somewhat different purposes.

High-Frequency Words Dictation:

Assessing Knowledge of High-Frequency Words

What does a quick diagnostic test of high-frequency words tell you about your students? It's one measure of how much they've grown as spellers. Even young writers will soon begin to spell *the* and *of* correctly, even though these letters aren't predictable from their sounds. I've provided a list of the 500 most frequently used words in English. There wasn't an obvious list for us to use, so we compiled our own using a variety of sources. I suggest using your intuition as to where to start a dictation test using the list. Let's talk first about how to carry out the test and use the results, and then return to which words to test.

A screening of kids' spelling of high-frequency words is meant to do three things: get a general measure of the strength and development of their spelling, identify words that they might want to work on during the school year, and give the students themselves a sense of what words they know "cold." A little more about knowing words cold: these are the words you don't even have to think about, that you never get wrong other than an occasional slip of the pen (or keyboard: I occasionally type *hte* for *the*). Therefore, you'll carry out this assessment in a very particular way.

Tool

List of 500 high-frequency words, pages 301–305

Carry Out the Assessment

First, decide how many words you'd like to assess. Fifty is a good number, and I've broken the 500 words into groups of fifty. You can either start from the beginning (giving kids a sense of success at seeing that they spell the most common words correctly) or pick the group of fifty that seems most likely to identify varied results for your class. Although you're checking on fifty words, I'd only do ten to twenty at a sitting.

Here's how you do it: Tell the students that you're going to read them a list of words to find out which ones they really, really know. For instance, *how many of you can spell the word* he *really fast? Everybody, right? Because you just know it. Today, I'm not going to give you time to think about how the word might be spelled, because I want to find out if you know it cold. If you aren't sure or know you don't know, just leave it blank. I'm not going to repeat any words, so if you can't write a word fast, just go on to the next one. It's not a test, it's a check-up, like when the eye doctor wants to know if you can read the letters on the chart.* Then read the words at a steady pace, slow enough for the kids to write the words but fast enough that they don't have time to think about them. If anyone asks for repeats, tell them to just leave it blank and go on to the next word.

Interpret Your Results

Once the test is done, give the kids a copy of the list and have them correct their own papers. Each group of fifty words is available on the CD-ROM as a sticker template which can be printed on Easy Peel white mailing labels (Avery product #5267) so students can be given stickers to put in their spelling notebooks and check off the words they know. (Use the blanks on each sheet to record and print kids' personal or one-second words.) Collect the data for yourself—perhaps have the student write her name and the words she missed on a slip of paper. What to do with the information? First, it gives you a sense of how your students compare on one dimension of their spelling growth. Second, it can provide information to students about what words they might like to work on individually. (See Strategy 7: One-Second Words.) Third, if there are some words that many or most of your students miss, you can work on helping everyone find easy ways to remember them (probably one word at a time). Fourth, if students haven't missed too many words, you can set them the challenge of seeing if the whole class can get 100% on the same list in a couple of weeks. (If they missed a lot of words, I'd drop back and assess the previous fifty words on the list.)

Pattern Quiz:

Assessing Knowledge of Spelling Patterns

As a support for the lessons about spelling patterns in this curriculum, I've created a two-part assessment tool, one part word dictation and the other part open-ended questions. Each one is keyed to a pattern lesson. You can use these quizzes in two ways. First, at the beginning and end of the school year you can use them in their entirety as pre- and post-assessments; second, you can pick out a single item and ask the kids to answer it before the relevant lesson and perhaps afterwards (maybe even a week later) as well. Each dictated word focuses on a spelling feature and is meant to assess the child's understanding of that feature. For instance, in spelling *cackle*, we're looking to see if a student knows that the /k/ sound can be spelled with a *c* before the letter *a*; the mistake if she spelled it *cakkle* would be irrelevant to this question, though it does give us information about her sense of double letters. For each word, I've provided information about what pattern it relates to and a follow-up question that you can ask the student to respond to in writing.

Please note that the tool isn't meant to assess individual children's knowledge of spelling patterns; it's meant merely to give a sense of the class and of the range of knowledge its members have.

Tool

Pattern Quiz, pages 306–307

Carry Out the Assessment

First, go through and test the words as a dictated list. (This can be done as a whole class.) Second, for any pattern and children that you wish, ask the questions either in interview format or in writing. When you're done with the dictation, give kids the list of words and have them correct their own spellings.

Interpret Your Results

Used at the beginning of the year, these words and questions can help you decide whether you need to do all of the pattern lessons, and which ones kids might need a little more time with. The pattern quiz chart shows the lessons that address each of the assessed patterns; I've included most of the patterns except for a few that don't work well with this format. The dictated words themselves are a good quick overview of children's internalized sense of spelling patterns; their answers to the accompanying questions will tell you even more. They should answer the questions before they've seen the correct spelling of the word, so that they won't answer defensively if they've misspelled it; you just want to know what their thinking was.

If I used the dictated words and lists of questions at the beginning of the school year, I'd also use them at the end. I've provided a second form of the quiz for this purpose. Some of the students' growth will be due to a year's reading and writing, but it should also give you a sense of the impact of your lessons. Single words and questions can also be used as a quick pre-check before a lesson, letting you know both where kids are starting from and what their thinking is about the topic.

Invented Spelling Analysis:

How to Look at Invented Spellings

Here I'll provide some general principles about how to look at children's invented spellings in their writing; on the accompanying CD-ROM I walk through some writing samples orally to show how I think about a piece as I look at it.

Tool

Invented Spelling Analysis, page 308

Carry Out the Assessment

When and how should you look at kids' writing to get a sense of what their invented spellings tell you? I'd start by sitting down with a writing sample from every student in the class at the beginning of the year. I've provided a form on which you can take list the words they are exploring and note the kinds of patterns their spellings explore. For instance, are many of them unsure whether words start with *w* or *wh*? Do you see a lot of different, yet reasonable, spellings of long vowels?

You can also take a look at several writing samples over time from a single child, particularly one you're concerned about, perhaps focusing on a single feature before and after a lesson on that pattern. A point to remember is that what's most important about a thoughtful look at kids' invented spellings is the awareness it gives you. Researchers have come up with schemes for assigning spellings to stages, but I believe it's always more complex than that; do you think that looking at and thinking intelligently about a child's invented spellings might in some ways be like appreciating a work of art?

Interpret Your Results

First, it's important to switch your stance from "This spelling is wrong" to "This spelling gives me interesting information." For instance (all the examples I use here are real ones), a child who writes MAMEL for *mammal* has failed to double the *m* and misspelled the second (schwa) vowel, but getting either of those features right involves knowing the spelling of this specific word, so her spelling involves a lack of particular word knowledge, not the failure to understand a pattern. Now you may think that the short first vowel requires that the consonant be doubled, but this rule is far from universal; in fact, if she'd followed the same spelling pattern for the rhyming word *camel*, she would have gotten it right!

By contrast, YELLOE for *yellow* tells you something about the writer's understanding of a spelling pattern, in this case long *o*. She knows that you need more than one letter to spell a long vowel, but hasn't yet internalized the idea that *ow* is more common than *oe* at the ends of words, at least in longer words. I'd therefore say she's at a transitional stage in her understanding of this pattern, and further development is likely to come not so much from learning about the rule as from more experience with reading so that she'd realize that YELLOE just *looks* weird.

The second important principle in looking at invented spelling is that of recognizing what kinds of spellings are common and expected as opposed to unusual. One good rule of thumb for the purposes of this curriculum is that if I've included a spelling pattern, it's because it's one that students in upper elementary school are typically still sorting out and could use some work on. This will be reflected in their spellings. You'll also see spellings that just seem to be the result of writing too quickly, for instance leaving out a letter or two. I've added a column where you can note if the word is close to the correct spelling or not.

The more you start looking at and thinking about your students' invented spellings, the more you'll realize that most kids have very similar kinds of invented spellings. Others don't, however. For instance, fourth-grader Elaine wrote AREY BOTAE and POLYEAN for *everybody* and *pumpkin*. Most kids' invented spellings make sense, but these just don't, a signal that Elaine needed some extra attention to her spelling from the teacher. The most useful next step with these kids is to watch and ask. Sit down with her as she writes, and when you see one of these unusual spellings, say something like, "Tell me how you knew what letters to put in that word" and take it from there. Elaine used these fairly random spellings when she was in a hurry to get her ideas out and didn't want to take the time to do a good invented spelling. Other children possibly haven't yet developed a stable set of associations between sounds and letters.

One further note: some of your students who are less developed may have spellings that look like those of early primary-grade children. If you see a child omitting *n*'s before other consonants, and using *ch* to spell *t* before an *r* (CHRUCK for *truck)*, it doesn't mean there's anything wrong with his hearing; it's just a sign of a less mature speller. (See Wilde, 1992, for further examples and explanations.)

The third principle for looking at invented spelling is that not every spelling can be analyzed and explained. It's most useful to look at consistent patterns that can be connected to teaching; everything else eventually comes down to proofreading. For example, one piece of student writing spelled *visited* as VISATID and *except* as EXEPT. The two misspelled vowels in *visited* are schwas, which are hard to hear, and this curriculum has a lesson that can at least help make kids more aware of schwas and give them strategies to get them right (although there are no quick tricks or shortcuts). But leaving out the *c* in *except*? Some words start with *exce* but others start with *exe* (*exempt*). But there's nothing to teach there; you just have to know the words.

The Invented Spelling Analysis can be repeated throughout the school year.

 # SPELLING STRATEGIES AND ATTITUDES

Every strategy lesson in this curriculum gives the teacher a chance to assess how children are coming up with spellings and getting them right. What I'd like to do here is provide a couple of slightly more formal measures that can give you a profile of individual students. One gives you ideas for observing and interacting with kids as they write, the other is a series of questions that can be used for interviews or written responses, and that also assesses kids' beliefs and attitudes about spelling.

Strategy Observation:

Noting How Students Come Up With a Spelling

The year I started graduate school, I worked on a research project in which we watched kids writing in the classroom (Goodman & Wilde, 1992). My interest in invented spelling developed through watching the spellings of words unfold in front of me as kids thought out loud about what letters to use in a word, erased and tried again, asked friends, used dictionaries. Since we were taking detailed field notes, we had a record of all of this, and I ended up writing later about what I'd seen (Wilde, 1986, 1990). I've created a simpler version of taking field notes for classroom use.

It's obviously time-consuming to sit with a child for several minutes as she writes and take detailed notes about her spelling. This isn't something you can do every day. But I think it's valuable to do it a few times just to see what it tells you, and to do occasionally with students you're more concerned about—or, alternatively, with students whose spelling strategies are so good that you think others might be able to learn from them.

Tool

Strategy Observation, page 309

Carry Out the Assessment and Discuss Your Results

I've created a simple form for note taking. As you sit with a student, every time he uses a strategy of some kind to come up with a spelling (that is, whenever a word isn't just written automatically), make a note of the word and what he does to create or perhaps also edit its spelling. Do you see him just pause and think a little, or does he try it two ways? Does he go outside his own head by looking at the word wall or consulting with a friend? Are some of the invented spellings written as quickly as correct spellings, with no visible conscious strategy? I've also included a third column in case you discuss the child's strategies with her, often best done at the end of the writing time rather than interrupting the process. Simple, common-sense, open-ended questions are all you need: *Tell me how you came up with that spelling. How did you decide which dictionary to pick? When do you ask a friend instead of figuring out the spelling yourself? How often do you try to get a spelling right in the first draft?* It's all about trying to get inside the child's head to see what she does as a speller when she writes.

Strategy/Attitude Questionnaire:

Discovering What Students Feel and Believe About Spelling

A good way to ask kids about their strategies and what they feel and believe about spelling is through interviews and questionnaires.

Tool

Strategy/Attitude Questionnaire, page 310

Carry Out the Assessment and Discuss Your Results

I've included a list of questions—some that incorporate strategy ideas included in the lessons and some that don't—that can be used in a number of ways. First, you can turn them into a written questionnaire, particularly for the beginning and end of the school year. (They're in a file on the CD-ROM so that you can pick and choose and make up your own list of whatever length you like from them.) Second, you can use them to interview kids. You can sit down with a single student and talk about several of the questions, or you could pick one question and incorporate it into that week's writing conferences with all your students. It might even be useful to look at the list of questions occasionally as conversation starters for when you're circulating around the room during writers' workshop.

SPELLING ACHIEVEMENT

How well should kids be spelling? I think that for many teachers, this is really a two-part question. First, what's a reasonable expectation for my students for spelling in their writing? Second, how do my kids stack up as spellers? Are they where they should be for their age compared to other kids? What we're asking here is a little different from the previous section on spelling knowledge. There we were trying to <u>understand</u>; here we're trying to <u>quantify</u>.

I'll answer the second question first. The National Assessment of Educational Progress (Applebee et al, 1987) found that nine-year-olds spelled 92% of words correctly on writing done to a prompt. The kids at the tenth percentile spelled 80% correctly and those at the 75th percentile spelled 98.1% correctly, so everybody did pretty well. (Scores for black and white students were virtually identical; English language learners weren't considered.) If you consider this to be fourth-grade student writing, you can use it as a very rough benchmark for what a reasonable level of spelling accuracy is in grades 3-5, particularly at a point in the writing process where kids are trying to get the words spelled right.

This is a slightly different question from what reasonable expectations are for *your* students, since each of them is an individual. I'd like to suggest some ways of looking at their spelling achievement in terms of both quantity and quality, in ways that can help you better work with them to increase that achievement.

Quantitative Spelling Record:

Quantitative Assessment of Spelling Achievement

The simplest and most consistent measure of spelling achievement is purely quantitative: what percentage of words in a piece of writing is spelled correctly? (Realize, though, that this may change from one piece of writing to another, so is only an approximation of the student's underlying ability.) I think it's most relevant to measure it on a piece of writing that the child has already edited for spelling, since it's the ability to get spelling right when it matters that's most important, not how you do in a first draft.

Tool

Quantitative Spelling Record, page 311

Carry Out the Assessment

It's a little tedious to figure out percentages, but you can simplify it by asking the student to count the number of words in his piece and then mark the words he thinks might be wrong. Then you can check through and mark any other misspellings. The formula, then, for finding the percentage of correct spellings is as follows: 1. Subtract the number of misspellings from the total number of words to find the number of correct spellings; 2. Multiply by 100; 3. Divide by the total number of words to get the percentage of spellings that are correct. For instance, if a 150-word piece has 8 misspelled words, 142 correct words x 100 = 14200, divided by 150 words = 94.6 = 95% correct.

I'd definitely do this once at the beginning of the year for each child and then perhaps periodically throughout the year and again at the end, to see what growth there's been. If you're required to give a grade for spelling, one way to do so is to ask students to pick a piece of writing (final draft) that they'd like to have assessed for spelling. You can assign grades by establishing that 90% or more correct spelling equals an A, and so on.

Interpret Your Results

How else can you use this information? First, you're likely to discover that some of your students are already spelling at close to an adult proficiency level in their writing. (I'd define that as 95% correct or above.) Those are the kids whose spelling you won't have to worry much about, since they probably read a lot and have good natural spelling ability. They just need to continue to read and pick up new words. Second, you'll find out which of your kids have a hard time getting words spelled right even when they're trying to for a final draft. You can't predict how many there will be, but you might well see a clear distinction between them and the kids who are doing reasonably well. This can be an important part of a beginning-of-the-year assessment of kids' literacy in general. These students are likely to be the ones to keep an eye on to see if your spelling instruction is clicking with them.

One other use of this information is to help kids set spelling goals for themselves. If you talk about spelling words correctly in final-draft writing as being an important goal for the whole class to work on this year, they can use their starting percentages to decide for themselves how much better they'd like to get. One caution: you don't want kids competing with each other and feeling superior or inferior to other kids based on their spelling, heaven forbid! Therefore any talk of goal setting should be prefaced by talking about how we're all at different places in our spelling, just like we are with how fast we run, and that what matters is advancing from where we are now.

Qualitative Evaluation Record:

How Good are Students' Invented Spellings?

In looking at kids' spelling achievement, we want to look not just at how many words are spelled right but at how good the invented spellings are. ELAPHENT is a better spelling than ELFENT. In previous writing, I've suggested a fairly elaborate way of categorizing invented spellings (Wilde, 1989), but here I'd like to suggest a simpler version. You can do this informally, just by thinking about spellings as you look at them, but you can also do it more formally and keep a written record.

Tool

Qualitative Evaluation Record, page 312

Carry Out the Assessment

Use the Qualitative Evaluation form to categorize the invented spellings you find in your students' writing. You can think of invented spellings as falling into three groups. The first is those that are so close, they're off by just one letter. One letter is missing (KANGARO), added (ZEBRAH), or changed (GERBAL). (I'm using kids' real spellings of mammal names for all the examples.) Once you've identified these words, next look for spellings where all the sounds are there and spelled in reasonable ways (DALFIN, POLERBARE, JERAF). These are pretty good, just not quite as good as the first group. For your third group, the invented spellings left over are those that just aren't quite as good (ORDVRK, SQUORLE, SEOTRA; aardvark, squirrel, and sea otter, respectively).

Interpret Your Results

This is meant to be a quick screen to give you a sense of how well kids spell a word when they don't get it right and can also be used to track change over time. You can keep a quantitative record of these through the school year by recording or graphing the totals at different points in time.

These assessments should give you and your students useful insight into their spelling knowledge, strategies, attitudes, and achievement. What young writers need most, both in school and in their future adult lives, is strategies that will enable them to function— whether they are excellent spellers or not—and a healthy self-accepting attitude about their ability at what is clearly only a very small part of writing and life.

1 to 50

1	the	14	for	27	said	39	as
2	and	15	on	28	can	40	my
3	to	16	his	29	all	41	then
4	a	17	but	30	so	42	me
5	in	18	we	31	an	43	see
6	it	19	she	32	him	44	from
7	I	20	had	33	are	45	if
8	he	21	they	34	with	46	there
9	you	22	be	35	one	47	go
10	of	23	have	36	no	48	this
11	is	24	do	37	like	49	were
12	at	25	up	38	out	50	what
13	that	26	her				

51 to 100

51	when	64	who	77	where	89	much
52	get	65	two	78	down	90	work
53	will	66	after	79	us	91	because
54	them	67	could	80	any	92	away
55	did	68	little	81	too	93	again
56	come	69	make	82	know	94	got
57	by	70	before	83	now	95	right
58	their	71	here	84	came	96	not
59	just	72	into	85	good	97	first
60	or	73	put	86	take	98	give
61	very	74	over	87	new	99	saw
62	been	75	our	88	am	100	want
63	how	76	look				

101 to 150

101	some	114	find	127	may	139	call
102	would	115	which	128	think	140	around
103	big	116	long	129	many	141	found
104	must	117	does	130	only	142	start
105	four	118	every	131	made	143	those
106	about	119	play	132	never	144	better
107	say	120	old	133	these	145	gave
108	use	121	tell	134	yes	146	try
109	both	122	ask	135	today	147	best
110	five	123	help	136	own	148	ten
111	under	124	three	137	run	149	small
112	has	125	always	138	off	150	far
113	why	126	let				

151 to 200

151	black	164	don't	177	open	189	write
152	round	165	should	178	until	190	gave
153	keep	166	way	179	live	191	white
154	kind	167	year	180	sleep	192	part
155	once	168	ran	181	other	193	funny
156	full	169	last	182	walk	194	fast
157	upon	170	home	183	school	195	sit
158	read	171	house	184	night	196	carry
159	day	172	each	185	stop	197	second
160	man	173	end	186	same	198	more
161	than	174	mother	187	well	199	grow
162	back	175	thing	188	six	200	also
163	eat	176	jump				

Spelling Strategies and Patterns

201 to 250

201	red	214	soon	227	hand	239	head
202	name	215	light	228	myself	240	money
203	people	216	ride	229	might	241	water
204	most	217	left	230	hold	242	though
205	pretty	218	next	231	buy	243	early
206	book	219	door	232	ate	244	sure
207	together	220	green	233	close	245	show
208	such	221	high	234	cut	246	morning
209	another	222	done	235	set	247	leave
210	anything	223	men	236	third	248	turn
211	while	224	wish	237	clean	249	hard
212	bring	225	love	238	took	250	along
213	car	226	cold				

251 to 300

251	time	264	seven	277	hot	289	happy
252	boy	265	eight	278	sing	290	sat
253	between	266	pick	279	enough	291	seem
254	through	267	great	280	week	292	feel
255	even	268	fly	281	change	293	eyes
256	world	269	during	282	almost	294	above
257	something	270	ball	283	room	295	woman
258	please	271	friend	284	able	296	across
259	thank	272	party	285	become	297	being
260	brown	273	seen	286	face	298	present
261	yellow	274	warm	287	dog	299	father
262	place	275	fall	288	food	300	still
263	children	276	wash				

301 to 350

301	top	314	hurt	327	fact	339	whole
302	behind	315	mean (v)	328	street	340	half
303	city	316	outside	329	gone	341	problem
304	view	317	box	330	less	342	bed
305	thought	318	girl	331	form	343	clothes
306	life	319	near	332	family	344	fine
307	against	320	stand	333	already	345	fire
308	need	321	tree	334	nothing	346	hear
309	since	322	group	335	large	347	hope
310	number	323	draw	336	side	348	mind
311	different	324	important	337	country	349	sister
312	really	325	state	338	yesterday	350	either
313	without	326	often				

351 to 400

351	probably	364	land	377	oh	389	you're
352	follow	365	believe	378	drink	390	young
353	body	366	else	379	Mr.	391	power
354	person	367	free	380	within	392	letter
355	main	368	move	381	pull	393	town
356	care	369	brought	382	color	394	paper
357	began	370	lost	383	dear	395	police
358	themselves	371	few	384	women	396	interest
359	real	372	air	385	says	397	question
360	job	373	I'm	386	information	398	ago
361	line	374	yours	387	laugh	399	ever
362	special	375	blue	388	can't	400	wrong
363	idea	376	yeah				

Spelling Strategies and Patterns

401 to 450

401	month	414	church	427	remember	439	front
402	million	415	death	428	hundred	440	I'd
403	child	416	sometimes	429	didn't	441	easy
404	itself	417	matter	430	someone	442	wasn't
405	word	418	story	431	everything	443	fish
406	south	419	heard	432	short	444	sound
407	study	420	table	433	reason	445	wall
408	age	421	trade	434	class	446	answer
409	north	422	Mrs.	435	stay	447	below
410	west	423	Ms.	436	talk	448	kept
411	inside	424	century	437	couldn't	449	simple
412	late	425	dark	438	field	450	wouldn't
413	cost	426	usually				

451 to 500

451	heart	464	page	477	caught	489	catch
452	everyone	465	brother	478	beautiful	490	sky
453	stood	466	maybe	479	learn	491	boat
454	finally	467	ready	480	plant	492	lunch
455	list	468	lady	481	rain	493	dream
456	size	469	earth	482	instead	494	lots
457	space	470	heavy	483	build	495	store
458	wrote	471	river	484	stuff	496	snow
459	watch	472	trouble	485	fight	497	throw
460	summer	473	begin	486	animal	498	teach
461	hour	474	baby	487	dry	499	grade
462	wait	475	winter	488	dinner	500	scared
463	picture	476	teacher				

	Word	Pattern	Question to Ask	Lesson
1.	ceiling	/s/ sound	How did you know what to put for the first letter?	Pattern 1
2.	cackle	/k/ sound	How did you know whether to start the word with a **c**, **k**, or **q(u)**?	Pattern 2
3.	gingerbread	/j/ sound	How did you know whether to start the word with a **j** or a **g**?	Pattern 3
4.	whisker	w or wh	How did you know whether to start the word with **w** or **wh**?	Pattern 4
5.	braid	long a	How did you know how to spell the long **a** sound in this word?	Pattern 6
6.	creep	long e	How did you know how to spell the long **e** sound in this word?	Pattern 7
7.	wipe	long i	How did you know how to spell the long **i** sound in this word?	Pattern 8
8.	float	long o	How did you know how to spell the long **o** sound in this word?	Pattern 9
9.	flute	long u	How did you know how to spell the vowel sound in this word?	Pattern 10
10.	brief	i before e	How did you know whether to use **ie** or **ei** in this word?	Pattern 12
11.	worried	Adding suffixes: y to i	Did you have to do anything when you added the ending?	Pattern 13
12.	hiding	Adding suffixes: dropping final **e**	Did you have to do anything when you added the ending?	Pattern 14
13.	running	Adding suffixes: doubling the final consonant	Did you have to do anything when you added the ending?	Pattern 15
14.	hammer	double consonants	How did you know whether to write one **m** or two?	Pattern 16
15.	compliment	schwa	How did you know what vowel to put in the middle syllable?	Pattern 17
16.	knife	silent letters	How did you know how to spell the beginning of this word?	Pattern 18
17.	Massachusetts* *If you live in this state, pick another long word.*	long words	What strategies do you use to spell long words?	Pattern 21
18.	didn't	apostrophes: contractions	How did you know where to put the apostrophe in this word?	Pattern 24

	Word	Pattern	Question to Ask	Lesson
1.	<u>c</u>ell phone	/s/ sound	How did you know what to put for the first letter?	Pattern 1
2.	<u>c</u>uckoo	/k/ sound	How did you know whether to start the word with a **c**, **k**, or **q(u)**?	Pattern 2
3.	geography	/j/ sound	How did you know whether to start the word with a **j** or a **g**?	Pattern 3
4.	<u>wh</u>ip	w or wh	How did you know whether to start the word with **w** or **wh**?	Pattern 4
5.	j<u>a</u>d<u>e</u>	long **a**	How did you know how to spell the long **a** vowel sound in this word?	Pattern 6
6.	cl<u>ea</u>ned	long **e**	How did you know how to spell the long **e** sound in this word?	Pattern 7
7.	m<u>i</u>c<u>e</u>	long **i**	How did you know how to spell the long **i** sound in this word?	Pattern 8
8.	c<u>o</u>n<u>e</u>	long **o**	How did you know how to spell the long **o** sound in this word?	Pattern 9
9.	s<u>oo</u>n	long **u**	How did you know how to spell the vowel sound in this word?	Pattern 10
10.	n<u>ie</u>ce	i before e	How did you know whether to use **ie** or **ei** in this word?	Pattern 12
11.	bab<u>ies</u>	Adding suffixes: y to i	Did you have to do anything when you added the ending?	Pattern 13
12.	bak<u>ing</u>	Adding suffixes: dropping final **e**	Did you have to do anything when you added the ending?	Pattern 14
13.	hop<u>ping</u>	Adding suffixes: doubling the final consonant	Did you have to do anything when you added the ending?	Pattern 15
14.	su<u>mm</u>er	double consonants	How did you know whether to write one **m** or two?	Pattern 16
15.	med<u>i</u>cal	schwa	How did you know what vowel to put in the middle syllable?	Pattern 17
16.	<u>w</u>rong	silent letters	How did you know how to spell the beginning of this word?	Pattern 18
17.	Connecticut* *If you live in this state, pick another long word.*	long words	What strategies do you use to spell long words?	Pattern 21
18.	doesn<u>'</u>t	apostrophes: contractions	How did you know where to put the apostrophe in this word?	Pattern 24

Spelling	Analysis				
Invented Spelling	Close to correct?	Consonants	Vowels	Word Structures (suffixes, 's, etc.)	Other

Teaching Notes

Student Name_____ Date_____

Spelling	How student came up with it	Discussion?

Strategy/Attitude Questionnaire

1. What do you do when you don't know how to spell a word?

2. When would you ask a friend to help you spell a word?

3. Where do you look for words in our classroom?

4. What do you do when you can't find the spelling of a word anywhere?

5. When do you try most to get words right, in your first draft or when editing?

6. How good are you at getting all the words right in the final draft?

7. What words especially give you trouble? What do you do about them?

8. Do you notice how words are spelled when you read?

9. Tell me about the dictionary you like best.

10. Do you enjoy trying to figure out how words are spelled, or is it sort of boring to you?

11. Do you think spelling will be important to you when you get older? Why or why not?

12. Do you think being a good speller is something you're born with, or something you work at? Why?

13. What advice would you give a kid who wanted to be a good speller?

Quantitative Spelling Record

Name	Date %	%	%	%	%	%	%	%	%	%
1.										
2.										
3.										
4.										
5.										
6.										
7.										
8.										
9.										
10.										
11.										
12.										
13.										
14.										
15.										
16.										
17.										
18.										
19.										
20.										
21.										
22.										
23.										
24.										
25.										
26.										
27.										
28.										

Student Name_____ Date_____

Evaluation	Invented Spellings	Number of Invented Spellings
Off by one letter		
All the sounds, reasonably spelled		
Not as good		

Total Invented Spellings: _____

If you read the newspapers, you'd think that invented spelling was a creation of the latter decades of the twentieth century, when teachers stopped caring about correctness and let kids write any way they want. But if we cast our vision back almost two centuries, we'll discover that invented spelling was alive and well in the journals of Meriwether Lewis and (especially) William Clark.

How are we using the term "invented spelling?" In its most general sense, an invented spelling is what we come up with when we want to write a word and don't know how to spell it. In today's elementary schools, invented spelling is what enables even young children to say anything they want in writing without teacher support. In doing so, they actively think about sounds and letters and how they go together; as they mature, and read more, their spellings get more sophisticated as they move toward correctness. In the early 1800s, invented spelling enabled Lewis and Clark to write whatever they wanted to say in their extensive, richly informative journals, without having to lug a dictionary or the not-yet-invented spellchecker.

Of the two explorers, William Clark is the more renowned for his spelling, Landon Y. Jones, the editor of *The Essential Lewis and Clark* (2000), comments that "[Clark's] journal entries are peppered with a delightful array of misspellings and grammatical errors, many of them rendered imaginatively and fearlessly" (xvi-xvii). Lewis's journals, however, weren't immune from invented spellings either, although they were less frequent.

What we've learned from some thirty years of recent research on invented spelling (see Wilde, 1992, 1999 for overviews) is that children's spellings aren't random but reflect their underlying and developing knowledge of how written English (or another language) works. A younger child might spell *laugh* as LAF (one letter per sound), but a few years later spell it LAUHG (moving beyond the phonetic, showing she's seen it in print). Even when older and adult writers spell most words correctly, invented spelling is the best way to ensure that your writing includes even more challenging words that you don't know how to spell (at least until you can get to the dictionary). These more mature invented spellings often show predictable patterns, as we shall see in the spellings of Lewis and Clark.

In order to examine the explorers' spellings, I've chosen, fairly randomly, an excerpt of a few pages from each and compiled the invented spellings. Taken from *The Essential Lewis and Clark* (Jones, 2000), in which Jones has chosen to retain "the original spellings, in all their rococo glory" (p. x), these are Clark's entry of September 26, 1804, dealing with a visit to the village of a Sioux chief (pp.18-21), and Lewis's entry of a June 13, 1805 (pp. 59-62), describing his impressions of a waterfall.

Although Lewis has fewer invented spellings than Clark, they don't differ much in quality, so I'll discuss both together. I've followed the usual convention in which invented spellings are rendered in upper case, followed by a slash and the standard spelling. I've also used a parenthetical *L* or *C* to show which man's spelling it was. For instance, when Lewis spells *dozen* as DOUZEN, I write it as DOUZEN/dozen (L). It should also be noted that both Lewis and Clark spelled most words correctly, including many challenging ones. Also, the same word may be spelled wrong in one spot and correctly in another, even in the same entry.

What did I find? These two passages contained a total of 91 invented spellings (59 from Clark, 32 from Lewis, in passages of roughly equal length). When I analyzed them, I discovered that they reflected a surprisingly small number of what might be called error types. The vast majority involved problems with spelling various vowels (including the schwa, which I'll define in a bit) and double consonants.

In 29 of their 91 invented spellings, Lewis and Clark spelled a vowel wrong, usually the main or only vowel in the word. (I give the full list of words and how I categorized them at the end of this article.) Why did they do so? Often, there's more than one way a vowel sound can be spelled, and one has to know the word in question to know which is right. Both HIGHT/height (L) and CHEARFULL/cheerful (C) are reasonable spellings, they just happen not to be the right ones. Sometimes when the writer gets the vowel wrong, it produces the correct spelling of the word's homophone, as in BEET/beat (C) AND BRAKES/breaks (L). In writing CHEIFS/chiefs (C), the *I* before *e* rule would have helped Clark, but in writing FIEST/feast (C), there's no way it would have told him that he needed another vowel combination altogether.

In addition to these 29 words, there were 16 cases where the schwa vowel was spelled wrong. The schwa sound is the unstressed vowel found in the first syllable of about, and it's the hardest vowel sound to spell because one can't really hear what letter should be used. (Technically, it's a reduced vowel, meaning it's pronounced very weakly.) Words like DEVERSIFIED/diversified (L) are spelled wrong only because of this single sound; without a dictionary, Lewis and Clark could not have corrected them.

Twenty of the invented spellings involved double consonants, most frequently doubling when they shouldn't have (ARRISE/arise (L), COLLUMN/column (L), UNTILL/until (C)), but also failing to double (ROLING/rolling (L); DISERTATION/dissertation (C)) or making the wrong choice about how to double a particular consonant (ASCERT/assert (L). There *are* rules for when to double consonants, but they aren't always obvious. For instance, how does one explain why *roll* and *dissertation* double the *l* and *s*, respectively?

Lewis and Clark also spelled words in ways that reflected how challenging some other features of our language are. When does a word have a silent *e* at the end (BUFFALOE/buffalo (L), FOLDES/folds (C), and POTATOE/potato (C))? What are the rules for changing the root word when one adds a suffix (COMEING/coming (C); HURRYED/hurried (L))? How does one know if a word has a silent letter (SENERY/scenery (L))? Do I use a *g* or a *j* (GINGLING/jingling (C))?

Only a few of these 91 spellings do not fall into straightforward categories such as these. Lewis's and Clark's spellings are far from random; they represent, rather, the attempts of intelligent, adventurous men, writing by hand in the wild, to represent the full range of their extensive vocabularies as best they could while grappling with the multiple inconsistencies and idiosyncrasies of written English. Their invented spellings are largely reasonable, logical, and not very far off from correct. A spellchecker would have fixed most of them.

What does this mean for today's English language arts teachers? First of all, recognize that our students today are dealing with the same spelling issues as Lewis and Clark when they write. A good knowledge of phonics takes one only so far as a speller; beyond that one needs a sense of how spellings patterns work and, most importantly, of how to spell a lot of individual words. Spelling comes harder to some students than others, but these William Clarks of our classrooms need not feel inferior as a result; Clark was a powerful writer. Students might even find it interesting to look at Lewis's and Clark's spellings themselves. Why did they spell these words the way they did? Are there spelling rules that would have helped, or did they just live some 200 years early for spellcheckers?

Students could follow a process similar to what I did in writing this article: pick a passage or two by each explorer, list the invented spellings, and try to come up with logical reasons why they spelled each word the way they did. It could also be interesting for the teacher to pick a passage, dictate the words with invented spellings to her students, and see how their spellings compare to those of Lewis and Clark. I suspect that many of today's high school students (and younger) would compare favorably to Lewis and Clark (who were adults) in their spelling. Not only has the spelling of English become more standardized, our whole world is far more literate.

Categorizations for Lewis's and Clark's invented spellings *(Some words appear in more than one category.)*

Reasonable spellings of vowels (other than schwa)

AGIN/again (L)
BEATIFULL/beautiful (L)
BEET/beat (C)
BRAKES/breaks (L)
CHEARFULL/cheerful (C)
CHEARFULLNESS/cheerfulness (C)
CHEIFS/chiefs (C)
CONCILL/council (C)
CORSE/course (C)
COURANT/current (L)
DOUZEN/dozen (L)
FIEST/feast (C)
FIEW/few (C)
FROATH/froth (L)
GRESE/grease (C)
HIGHT/height (L)
INDEAVOURED/endeavored (L)
LOOSE/lose (L)
NEETLY/neatly (C)
NOUMEROUS/numerous (C)
PROCEDED/proceeded (L)
ROAB/robe (C)
SHOLDER/shoulder (C)
SMOTH/smooth (L)
SOWN/sewn (C)
SPREV/spray (L)
TAMBEREENS/tambourines (C)
TAMBOREN/tambourine (C)
TAMBORIN/tambourine (C)

Double consonant problems

APROVEING/approving (C)
ARRISE/arise (L)
ASCERT/assert (L)
BEATIFULL/beautiful (L)
CHEARFULL/cheerful (C)
CHEARFULLNESS/cheerfulness (C)
COLLUMN/column (L)
CONCILL/council (C)
COURANT/current (L)

DECKERATED/decorated (C)
DISERTATION/dissertation (C)
MAGNIFFICENT/magnificent (L)
PENING/penning (L)
PERMITED/permitted (C)
PETICOAT/petticoat (C)
PRISSNERS/prisoners (C)
REGRETED/regretted (L)
ROLING/rolling (L)
UNTILL/until (C)

Problems spelling schwa

ACCURRUNCES/occurrences (C)
DECKERATED/decorated (C)
DETURMINED/determined (C)
DEVERSIFIED/diversified (L)
ELEGENT/elegant (C)
HEAVINS/heavens (C)
MINITS/minutes (C)
SACREFISE/sacrifice (C)
SELICITIATIONS/solicitations
SEPERATED/separated (L)
SIMILER/similar (C)
TAMBEREENS/tambourines (C)
TAMBOREN/tambourine (C)
TAMBORIN/tambourine (C)
TREMEDIOUS/tremendous (L)
WOMIN/women (C)

Silent *e* problems

BUFFALOE/buffalo (L)
FOLDES/folds (C)
HANDSOM/handsome (C)
HARANGE/harangue (C)
LEDG/ledge (L)
MINITS/minutes (C)
NINTY/ninety (L)
PLAC/place (C)
POTATOE/potato (C)
PREPAREING/preparing (C)
PROMIS/promise (C)
SOM/some (C)

Suffix problems

APPROACHD/approached (C)
APROVEING/approving (C)
COMEING/coming (C)
DESTROYD/destroyed (C)
HURRYED/hurried (L)
MUSITIONS/musicians (C)
PERMITED/permitted (C)
PREPAREING/preparing (C)

Other consonant problems

GINGLING/jingling (C)
PRODUZED/produced (L)
SACREFISE/sacrifice (C)
SERJEANT/sergeant (C)
TROPIES/trophies (C)

Words from other languages

BAUREILY/Bois brulé
BAWE ROLEY/bois roule
BOUS RULIE/Bois brulé
PEMITIGON/pemmican

Other silent letters

PRISSNERS/prisoners (C)
RETCHED/wretched (C)
SENERY/scenery (L)

Punctuation problems

IT'S/its (L)
MY SELF/myself (C)

Not otherwise categorizable

ADECRATED/decorated (C)
CLIFT/cliff (L)
CRIMEE/camera (L)
DISPEAR/disappear (L)
PRARRALLEL/parallel (L)
SHEW/show (C)
SPREV/spray (the *v* may be a poorly written *y*)
SQUARS/squaws (C)
TURROW/terror (C)

References

Jones, Landon Y. (Ed.). (2000). *The essential Lewis and Clark.* New York: Harper Collins

Wilde, Sandra. (1992). *You kan red this! Spelling and punctuation for whole language classrooms, K-6.* Portsmouth, NH: Heinemann.

Wilde, Sandra. (1999). "How children learn to spell: Evidence from decades of research." In Gay Su Pinnell & Irene Fountas (Eds.), *Voices on word matters: Learning about phonics and spelling in the literacy classroom* (pp. 173-187). Portsmouth, NH: Heinemann.

Sandra Wilde, *Professor in the Graduate School of Education at Portland State University, is widely recognized for her expertise in developmental spelling and her advocacy of holistic approaches to the teaching of the language arts.*

Applebee, Arthur N., Judith A. Langer, and Ina V. Mullis. 1987. *Grammar, Punctuation, and Spelling: Controlling the Conventions of English at Ages 9, 13, and 17*. Princeton, NJ: Educational Testing Service.

Barbe, Walter B., and Azalia S. Francis. 1983. *Spelling: Basic Skills and Application*. Columbus, OH: Zaner-Bloser.

Chomsky, Carol. 1971. "Invented Spelling in the Open Classroom." *Word* (27) 499-51.

Chomsky, Noam, and Morris Halle. 1968. *The Sound Pattern of English*. New York: Harper and Row.

Clarke, Linda K. 1988. "Invented Versus Traditional Spelling in First Graders' Writings: Effects on Learning to Spell and Read." *Research in the Teaching of English*, 22 (3) 281-309.

Culham, Ruth. 2003. *6 + 1 Traits of Writing: The Complete Guide (Grades 3 and Up)*. New York: Scholastic.

Cummings, D. W. 1988. *American English Spelling: An Informal Description*. Baltimore, MD: Johns Hopkins University Press.

Cunningham, Patricia M. 1995. *Phonics They Use: Words for Reading and Writing*. Boston: Allyn & Bacon.

Fitzsimmons, Robert J., and Bradley M. Loomer. 1978. *Spelling: Learning and Instruction*. Des Moines: Iowa State Department of Public Instruction.

Frith, Uta. 1980. *Cognitive Processes in Spelling*. London: Academic Press.

Goodman, Yetta M., and Sandra Wilde, eds. 1992. *Literacy Events in a Community of Young Writers*. New York: Teachers College Press.

Graves, Donald H. 1983. *Writing: Teachers and Children at Work*. Exeter, NH: Heinemann.

Hanna, Paul R., Jean S. Hanna, Richard E. Hodges, and Erwin H. Rudorf, Jr. 1966. *Phoneme-Grapheme Correspondences as Cues to Spelling Improvement*. Washington: U.S. Office of Education.

Harste, Jerome C., Virginia A. Woodward, and Carolyn Burke. 1984. *Language Stories and Literacy Lessons*. Portsmouth, NH: Heinemann.

Invernizzi, Marcia, Mary P. Abouzeid, and J. Thomas Gill. 1994. "Using Students' Invented Spellings as a Guide for Spelling Instruction that Emphasizes Word Study." *The Elementary School Journal* 95 (2) 155-67.

Krashen, Stephen D. 2004. *The Power of Reading: Insights from the Research, 2nd edition*. Portsmouth, NH: Heinemann.

MacArthur, Tom. 1992. *The Oxford Companion to the English Language*. New York: Oxford.

Maguire, James. 2006. *American Bee: The National Spelling Bee and the Culture of Word Nerds*. Emmaus, PA: Rodale Books.

Morris, Darrell. 1982. "'Word Sort': A Categorization Strategy for Improving Word Recognition Ability." *Reading Psychology* 3 (3) 247-59.

Spelling Strategies and Patterns

Nagy, William E., Patricia A. Herman, and Richard C. Anderson. 1985. "Learning Words from Context." *Reading Research Quarterly* 20 (2) 233-53.

National Reading Panel. 2000. *Teaching Children to Read: An Evidence-Based Assessment of the Scientific Research Literature on Reading and Its Implications for Reading Instruction. Reports of the Subgroups*. Bethesda, MD: National Reading Panel. www.nationalreadingpanel.org..

Pinker, Steven. 1994. *The Language Instinct: How the Mind Creates Language*. New York: HarperCollins Publishers.

Read, Charles. 1971. "Pre-school Children's Knowledge of English Phonology." *Harvard Educational Review* (41) 1-34.

Root, Betty. 1993. *My First Dictionary*. New York: Dorling Kindersley.

Routman, Regie. 1999. *Conversations: Strategies for Teaching, Learning, and Evaluating*. Portsmouth, NH: Heinemann.

Rumford, James. 2004. *Sequoyah: The Cherokee Man Who Gave His People Writing*. New York: Houghton Mifflin Company.

Shusterman, Neal. 2004. *The Schwa was Here*. New York: Dutton Children's Books.

Smith, Frank. 1982. *Writing and the Writer*. New York: Holt, Rinehart, and Winston.

Snow, Catherine E., M. Susan Burns, and Peg Griffin, eds. 1998. *Preventing Reading Difficulties in Young Children*. Washington: National Academy Press.

Snowball, Diane, and Faye Bolton. 1993. *Teaching Spelling: A Practical Resource*. Portsmouth, NH: Heinemann.

Vygotsky, L. S. 1978. *Mind in Society: The Development of Higher Psychological Processes*. Cambridge: Harvard University Press.

Vygotsky, L. S. 1962. *Thought and Language*. Cambridge: The MIT Press.

Wheat, Leonard B. 1932. "Four Spelling Rules." *Elementary School Journal* (32) 697-706.

Wilde, Sandra. 1986. *An Analysis of the Development of Spelling and Punctuation in Selected Third and Fourth Grade Children*. Doctoral dissertation. University of Arizona.

Wilde, Sandra. 1990. "Spelling Textbooks: A Critical Review." *Linguistics and Education*, (2) 259-80.

Wilde, Sandra. 1992. *You Kan Red This! Spelling and Punctuation for Whole Language Classrooms, K-6*. Portsmouth, NH: Heinemann.

Wilde, Sandra. 2003. "The Spelling of Lewis and Clark." *Oregon English Journal*, XXV (1) 52-55.

Books for Teachers and Kids about Spelling and Related Matters

This list is meant to suggest some books you might like to read yourself and some that you might like to have available in your classroom. Although not all the books are still in print, used copies of almost any book can be found on online, often at prices starting at a penny. The list of kids' books ends with a discussion of the two dictionary series I find best.

For Teachers

This list isn't meant to be comprehensive, just a list of some books about spelling, words, and language that you might find fun and informative.

Comrie, Bernard, Stephen Matthews, and Maria Polinsky, eds. 1997. *The Atlas of Languages*. New York: Bloomsbury Publishing.

> A beautifully illustrated book that includes, along with much else, samples of different writing systems from around the world. Although it's not written for children, they might enjoy the maps, photos, and alphabets.

Crystal, David. 1998. *Language Play*. Chicago, IL: University of Chicago Press.

> Linguist David Crystal has discovered a surprising amount to say about language play of all kinds, some involving spelling ("Please ptell me, pterodactyl") and including a whole chapter on children's language play.

Cummings, D. W. 1988. *American English Spelling: An Informal Description*. Baltimore, MD: Johns Hopkins University Press.

> For spelling geeks only, but if you are one, this is the masterwork. In this 500+ page compendium, Cummings gives a brief history of English spelling and then describes all the ways that every sound might be spelled, with plenty of examples and history.

Dunn, Mark. 2001. *Ella Minnow Pea: A Progressively Lipogrammatic Epistolary Fable*. New York: MacAdam/Cage Publishing.

> The only novel on this list, it's unique. If you say the title aloud, you'll have a hint as to the theme. This is an epistolary novel; that is, one in which the whole story is told in letters written between its characters. In a very convoluted plot, the residents of a small island are required to gradually eliminate more and more letters of the alphabet from their speech and writing. Very clever, and more fun than it sounds.

Grambs, David. 1989. *Death by Spelling: A Compendium of Tests, Super Tests, and Killer Bees*. New York: HarperCollins Publishers.

> With introductory sections on the history and principles of English spelling, the heart of this book is its collection of more than 100 spelling tests, including tough words, commonly misspelled words and patterns, and dozens of subject matter spelling tests.

MacNeil, Robert, and William Cran. 2004. *Do You Speak American?* New York: Nan A. Talese.

> This companion to the PBS televised series (available on DVD) explores the varieties of American regional English, where they come from, and our attitudes about them. The companion Web site (www.pbs.org/speak) includes a variety of informational and educational links.

Maguire, James. 2006. *American Bee: The National Spelling Bee and the Culture of Word Nerds*. Emmaus, PA: Rodale Books.

A history of The National Spelling Bee, coverage of it as an event, and profiles of contestants over the years. A terrific read.

Merriam-Webster's Collegiate Dictionary (new editions come out regularly, but a used slightly older one is fine). Springfield, MA: Merriam-Webster.

Many dictionaries have the name *Webster's* in the title, but the ones published by Merriam-Webster are consistently the best. I'd recommend that every classroom have one of the *Collegiate,* which is their standard adult dictionary. It's especially good for etymology (word origins). Also, check out their Web site, www.m-w.com, for everything dictionary.

Proctor, William. 1993. *The Terrible Speller: A Quick-And-Easy Guide to Enhancing Your Spelling Ability*. New York: William Morrow & Company.

A pocket-sized guide to becoming a better speller, with tips on commonly misspelled words and patterns. Any bookstore will have a variety of similar books.

Vos Savant, Marilyn. 2000. *The Art of Spellin: The Madness and the Method*. New York: W. W. Norton & Company.

A good book, by the well-known *Parade Magazine* columnist, for the general adult reader about how we learn to spell and how to be a better speller.

For Kids

Books for Learning More About Language

Rumford, James. 2004. *Sequoyah: The Cherokee Man Who Gave His People Writing*. New York: Houghton Mifflin Company.

Not only is this the terrific story of a Native American man who invented an alphabet and writing system for the Cherokee language, the book is bilingual, with the text in both English and Cherokee. Sequoyah's alphabet is provided in an appendix to the book.

Samoyault, Tiphaine. 1997. *Give Me a Sign!: What Pictograms Tell Us Without Words*. New York: Viking Juvenile.
Samoyault, Tiphaine. 1998. *Alphabetical Order: How the Alphabet Began*. New York: Viking Juvenile.

These companion books provide terrific introductions to, respectively, how pictograms use conventionalized symbols to communicate meaning without language, and an illustrated history of the alphabet.

Trinkle, Barrie, Carolyn Andrews, and Paige Kimble. 2006. *How to Spell Like a Champ*. New York: Workman Publishing.

This terrific book, written by people from the National Spelling Bee, introduces kids to the Bee, as well as providing lots of tips about language and strategies for competing. This is my favorite book on this list.

Wordplay Books

(Note: These are all picture books and may therefore seem intended for younger audiences, but students in grades 3-5 can enjoy them at a more sophisticated level for what they show us about how words work.)

Clements, Andrew. 1997. *Double Trouble in Walla Walla*. Brookfield, CT: Millbrook Press.

Not really spelling as such, but a lot of fun wordplay in a picture-book format. Everything's topsy-turvy and hippity-hoppity.

Gwynne, Fred. 1976. *A Chocolate Moose for Dinner* New York: Simon & Schuster Children's Publishing.
Gwynne, Fred. 1980. *The King Who Rained*. New York: Simon & Schuster Children's Publishing.
Gwynne, Fred. 1988. *A Little Pigeon Toad*. New York: Simon & Schuster Children's Publishing.

> The classic books about how homophones and idioms can be misunderstood. They're especially fun to read aloud and guess what the picture is before seeing it.

Scieszka, Jon, and Lane Smith. 2001. *Baloney (Henry P.)*. New York: Viking Juvenile.

> An intergalactic adventure where every page includes real words from different languages, including Swahili, Inuktitut, and Latvian.

Shulman, Mark, and Adam McCauley. 2006. *Mom and Dad are Palindromes*. San Francisco: Chronicle Books.

> This playful picture book includes 101 palindromes ("I drank some POP for PEP. It made me GAG. I DID a good DEED for a NUN.")

Turner, Priscilla. 1996. *The War Between the Vowels and the Consonants*. New York: Farrar, Straus and Giroux.

> A playful picture book about two tribes that mistrust each other until they learn to work together.

Reference Book

Terban, Marvin. 1994. *Time to Rhyme: A Rhyming Dictionary*. Honesdale, PA: Boyds Mills Press.

> Just what the title says. An inexpensive and useful reference.

Dictionaries

The four dictionaries listed here are my top picks for classroom use. I'd recommend getting at least a few of each. The elementary ones are the obvious choices for grades 3-5, but the ones for younger kids are useful to have around too. With a good adult dictionary in the classroom as well, kids should be able to develop good strategies for finding any word they want to. All these dictionaries periodically come out in new editions.

Merriam-Webster's Primary Dictionary. 2005. Springfield, MA: Merriam-Webster.

> This publisher's dictionaries are always of the highest quality, and this one features illustrations by noted picture-book artist Ruth Heller. Some special features are word histories, bonus words (typically synonyms), and head-scratchers (interesting facts about words).

Merriam-Webster's Elementary Dictionary. 2005. Springfield, MA: Merriam-Webster.

> Appreciably more sophisticated than the primary dictionary, this book includes an excellent introduction to how the dictionary works. It's the best single reference for the upper elementary classroom.

Scholastic First Dictionary. 2006. New York: Scholastic Reference.

> Illustrated with photographs. Both primary dictionaries use words in sentences rather than providing traditional definitions. Unlike Merriam-Webster, Scholastic provides pronunciation guides at this level.

Scholastic Children's Dictionary. 2007. New York: Scholastic Reference.

> Very similar to the *Merriam-Webster Elementary Dictionary*, this one uses a bigger font and may be slightly easier to use.

Spellcheckers

My recommendation for choosing a spellchecker is to go to the Web site of Franklin Electronic Publishers (www.franklin.com) and look at their selection. They have children and adult versions at a range of prices.